FDNY
Crisis
Counseling

FDNY Crisis Counseling

Innovative Responses to 9/11 Firefighters, Families, and Communities

PAUL GREENE, DIANNE KANE, GRACE CHRIST,
SALLIE LYNCH, AND MALACHY CORRIGAN

WILEY

John Wiley & Sons, Inc.

This book is dedicated to those who lost their lives attempting to save others and to the families who have endured so much as a result of their sacrifice.

In Memoriam

Peter J. Ganci, Jr., Chief of Department
Chief William Feehan, First Deputy
  Commissioner
Gerard Barbara, Assistant Chief, Citywide
  Tour Commander
Donald Burns, Assistant Chief, Citywide
  Tour Commander
Dennis Cross, Battalion Chief*, Battalion 57
Thomas DeAngelis (1), Battalion Chief,
  Battalion 8
Dennis Devlin, Battalion Chief, Battalion 9
Raymond Downey, Battalion Chief*,
  Special Operations
John Fanning (2), Battalion Chief, Haz-Mat
  Operations
Edward Geraghty, Battalion Chief*,
  Battalion 9
Joseph Grzelak, Battalion Chief, Battalion 48
Thomas Haskell, Jr., Battalion Chief,
  Division 15
Charles Kasper, Battalion Chief*, SOC
  Battalion
Joseph Marchbanks, Jr., Battalion Chief*,
  Battalion 57
William McGovern, Battalion Chief,
  Battalion 2
John Moran, Battalion Chief, Battalion 49
Orio Palmer*, Battalion Chief, Battalion 7
John Paolillo*, Battalion Chief, Battalion 11
Richard Prunty, Battalion Chief, Battalion 2
Matthew Ryan, Battalion Chief, Battalion 1
Fred Scheffold, Battalion Chief, Battalion 12
Lawrence Stack, Battalion Chief, Battalion 50
John Williamson, Battalion Chief, Battalion 6
Mychal Judge, Chaplain
James Amato, Captain*, Squad 1
Daniel Brethel, Captain, Ladder 24
Patrick Brown, Captain, Ladder 3
Vincent Brunton, Captain, Ladder 105
William Burke, Jr., Captain, Engine 21
Frank Callahan, Captain, Ladder 35
James J. Corrigan, Captain, Retired—
  Engine 320
Martin Egan, Jr., Captain, Division 15
Thomas Farino, Captain, Engine 26
Joseph Farrelly, Captain*, Division 1
John Fischer, Captain—Formerly,
  Lieutenant Ladder 20
Terence Hatton, Captain*, Rescue 1
Brian Hickey, Captain*, Rescue 4
Walter Hynes, Captain, Ladder 13
Frederick Ill, Jr., Captain, Ladder 2
Louis Modafferi, Captain*, Rescue 5
Thomas Moody, Captain, Division 1
William O'Keefe, Captain, Division 15
Vernon Richard, Captain, Ladder 7
Timothy Stackpole, Captain, Division 11
Patrick Waters (2), Captain, Special
  Operations
David Wooley, Captain, Ladder 4
Brian Ahearn, Lieutenant, Engine 230
Gregg Atlas, Lieutenant, Engine 10
Steven Bates, Lieutenant, Engine 235
Carl Bedigian, Lieutenant, Engine 214
John Crisci, Lieutenant, Haz-Mat Co. 1

Edward Datri, Lieutenant, Squad 1
Andrew Desperito, Lieutenant, Engine 1
Kevin Donnelly, Lieutenant, Ladder 3
Kevin Dowdell, Lieutenant, Rescue 4
Michael Esposito, Lieutenant*, Squad 1
Michael Fodor, Lieutenant, Squad 1
Gary Box, Firefighter, Squad 1
Michael Boyle, Firefighter, Engine 33
Kevin Bracken, Firefighter, Engine 40
Michael Brennan, Firefighter, Ladder 4
Peter Brennan, Firefighter, Rescue 4
Andrew Brunn, Firefighter, Ladder 5
Greg Buck, Firefighter, Engine 201
John Burnside, Firefighter, Ladder 20
Thomas Butler, Firefighter, Squad 1
Patrick Byrne, Firefighter, Ladder 101
George Cain, Firefighter, Ladder 7
Salvatore Calabro, Firefighter, Ladder 101
Michael Cammarata, Firefighter, Ladder 11
Brian Cannizzaro, Firefighter, Ladder 101
Dennis Carey, Firefighter, Haz-Mat
  Company 1
Michael Carlo, Firefighter, Engine 230
Michael Carroll, Firefighter, Ladder 3
Peter Carroll, Firefighter, Squad 1
Thomas Casoria, Firefighter, Engine 22
Michael Cawley, Firefighter, Ladder 136
Vernon Cherry, Firefighter, Ladder 118
Nicholas Chiofalo, Firefighter, Engine 235
John Chipura, Firefighter, Engine 219
Michael Clarke, Firefighter, Ladder 2
Steven Coakley, Firefighter, Engine 217
Tarel Coleman, Firefighter, Squad 252
John Collins, Firefighter, Ladder 25
Robert Cordice, Firefighter, Squad 1
Ruben Correa, Firefighter, Engine 74
James Coyle, Firefighter, Ladder 3
Robert Crawford, Firefighter, Safety
  Battalion 1
Thomas Cullen III, Firefighter, Squad 41
Robert Curatolo, Firefighter, Ladder 16
Michael D'Auria, Firefighter, Engine 40
Scott Davidson, Firefighter, Ladder 118
Edward Day, Firefighter, Ladder 11
Manuel Delvalle, Firefighter*, Engine 5
Martin Demeo, Firefighter, Haz-Mat Co. 1
David DeRubbio, Firefighter, Engine 226
Gerard Dewan, Firefighter, Ladder 3
George DiPasquale, Firefighter, Ladder 2
Gerard Duffy, Firefighter, Ladder 21
Michael Elferis, Firefighter, Engine 22
Francis Esposito, Firefighter, Engine 235
Robert Evans, Firefighter, Engine 33
Terrence Farrell, Firefighter, Rescue 4
Lee Fehling, Firefighter, Engine 235
Alan Feinberg, Firefighter, Battalion 9
Michael Fiore, Firefighter, Rescue 5
Andre Fletcher, Firefighter*, Rescue 5
John Florio, Firefighter, Engine 214
Thomas Foley, Firefighter, Rescue 3
David Fontana, Firefighter*, Squad 1
Robert Foti, Firefighter, Ladder 7
Andrew Fredericks, Firefighter*, Squad 18
Thomas Gambino, Jr., Firefighter, Rescue 3
Thomas Gardner, Firefighter, Haz-Mat Co. 1

Joseph Maffeo, Firefighter, Ladder 101
William Mahoney, Firefighter, Rescue 4
Joseph Maloney, Firefighter, Ladder 3
Kenneth Marino, Firefighter, Rescue 1
John Marshall, Firefighter, Ladder 27
Joseph Mascali, Firefighter, Tactical
  Support 2
Keithroy Maynard, Firefighter, Engine 33
Brian McAleese, Firefighter, Engine 226
John McAvoy, Firefighter, Ladder 3
Thomas McCann, Firefighter, Battalion 8
Dennis McHugh, Firefighter, Ladder 13
Robert McMahon, Firefighter, Ladder 20
Robert McPadden, Firefighter, Engine 23
Terence McShane, Firefighter, Ladder 101
Timothy McSweeney, Firefighter, Ladder 3
Martin McWilliams, Firefighter, Engine 22
Raymond Meisenheimer, Firefighter,
  Rescue 3
Charles Mendez, Firefighter, Ladder 7
Steve Mercado, Firefighter, Engine 40
Douglas Miller, Firefighter, Rescue 5
Henry Miller, Jr., Firefighter, Ladder 105
Robert Minara, Firefighter, Ladder 25
Thomas Mingione, Firefighter, Ladder 132
Manuel Mojica, Firefighter, Squad 18
Carl Molinaro, Firefighter, Ladder 2
Michael Montesi, Firefighter, Rescue 1
Vincent Morello, Firefighter, Ladder 35
Christopher Mozzillo, Firefighter, Engine 55
Richard Muldowney, Jr., Firefighter,
  Ladder 7
Michael Mullan, Firefighter, Ladder 12
Dennis Mulligan, Firefighter, Ladder 2
John Napolitano, Firefighter*, Rescue 2
Peter Nelson, Firefighter, Rescue 4
Gerard Nevins, Firefighter, Rescue 1
Dennis Oberg, Firefighter, Ladder 105
Douglas Oelschlager, Firefighter, Ladder 15
Joseph Ogren, Firefighter, Ladder 3
Samuel Oitice, Firefighter, Ladder 4
Patrick O'Keefe (1), Firefighter, Rescue 1
Eric Olsen, Firefighter, Ladder 15
Jeffrey Olsen, Firefighter, Engine 10
Steven Olson, Firefighter, Ladder 3
Kevin O'Rourke, Firefighter, Rescue 2
Michael Otten, Firefighter, Ladder 35
Jeffrey Palazzo, Firefighter, Rescue 5
Frank Palombo, Firefighter, Ladder 105
Paul Pansini, Firefighter*, Engine 10
James Pappageorge, Firefighter, Engine 23
Robert Parro, Firefighter, Engine 8
Durrell Pearsall, Firefighter, Rescue 4
Christopher Pickford, Firefighter, Engine
  201
Shawn Powell, Firefighter, Engine 207
Vincent Princiotta, Firefighter, Ladder 7
Kevin Prior, Firefighter, Squad 252
Lincoln Quappe, Firefighter, Rescue 2
Leonard Ragaglia, Firefighter, Engine 54
Michael Ragusa, Firefighter, Engine 250
Peter Freund, Lieutenant, Engine 55
Charles Garbarini, Lieutenant, Battalion 9
Vincent Giammona, Lieutenant*, Ladder 5
John Ginley, Lieutenant, Engine 40

Geoffrey Guja, Lieutenant, Battalion 43
Joseph Gullickson, Lieutenant, Ladder 101
Vincent Halloran, Lieutenant, Ladder 8
Harvey Harrell, Lieutenant, Rescue 5
Stephen Harrell, Lieutenant, Battalion 7
Michael Healey, Lieutenant, Squad 41
Timothy Higgins, Lieutenant, Special Operations
Anthony Jovic, Lieutenant, Battalion 47
Ronald Kerwin, Lieutenant, Squad 288
Joseph Leavey, Lieutenant, Ladder 15
Charles Margiotta, Lieutenant, Battalion 22
Peter Martin, Lieutenant, Rescue 2
Paul Martini, Lieutenant, Engine 201
William McGinn, Lieutenant*, Squad 18
Paul Mitchell, Lieutenant, Battalion 1
Dennis Mojica, Lieutenant, Rescue 1
Raymond Murphy, Lieutenant, Ladder 16
Robert Nagel, Lieutenant, Engine 58
Daniel O'Callaghan, Lieutenant, Ladder 4
Thomas O'Hagan, Lieutenant, Battalion 4
Glenn Perry, Lieutenant, Ladder 25
Philip Petti, Lieutenant, Battalion 7
Kevin Pfeifer, Lieutenant, Engine 33
Kenneth Phelan, Lieutenant, Engine 217
Michael Quilty, Lieutenant, Ladder 11
Robert Regan, Lieutenant, Ladder 118
Michael Russo, Lieutenant, Special Operations
Christopher Sullivan, Lieutenant, Ladder 111
Robert Wallace, Lieutenant, Engine 205
Michael Warchola, Lieutenant, Ladder 5
Glenn Wilkinson, Lieutenant, Engine 238
Ronald Bucca, Fire Marshal
Joseph Agnello, Firefighter*, Ladder 118
Eric Allen, Firefighter, Squad 18
Richard Allen, Firefighter, Ladder 15
Calixto Anaya Jr., Firefighter, Engine 4
Joseph Angelini, Firefighter, Rescue 1
Joseph Angelini Jr., Firefighter, Ladder 4
Faustino Apostol Jr., Firefighter, Battalion 2
David Arce, Firefighter, Engine 33
Louis Arena, Firefighter, Ladder 5
Carl Asaro, Firefighter, Battalion 9
Gerald Atwood, Firefighter, Ladder 21
Gerald Baptiste, Firefighter, Ladder 9
Matthew Barnes, Firefighter, Ladder 25
Arthur Barry, Firefighter, Ladder 15
Stephen Belson, Firefighter, Ladder 24
John Bergin, Firefighter, Rescue 5
Paul Beyer, Firefighter, Engine 6
Peter Bielfield, Firefighter, Ladder 42
Brian Bilcher, Firefighter, Squad 1
Carl Bini, Firefighter, Rescue 5
Christopher Blackwell, Firefighter, Rescue 3
Michael Bocchino, Firefighter, Battalion 48
Matthew Garvey, Firefighter, Squad 1
Bruce Gary, Firefighter, Engine 40
Gary Geidel, Firefighter, Rescue 1

Denis Germain, Firefighter, Ladder 2
James Giberson, Firefighter, Ladder 35
Ronnie Gies, Firefighter*, Squad 288
Paul Gill, Firefighter, Engine 54
Jeffrey Giordano, Firefighter, Ladder 3
John Giordano (1), Firefighter, Engine 37
Keith Glascoe, Firefighter, Ladder 21
James Gray, Firefighter, Ladder 20
Jose Guadalupe, Firefighter, Engine 54
David Halderman, Firefighter*, Squad 18
Robert Hamilton, Firefighter, Squad 41
Sean Hanley, Firefighter, Ladder 20
Thomas Hannafin, Firefighter, Ladder 5
Dana Hannon, Firefighter, Engine 26
Daniel Harlin, Firefighter, Ladder 2
Timothy Haskell, Firefighter, Squad 18
Michael Haub, Firefighter, Ladder 4
Philip T. Hayes, Firefighter, Retired—Engine 217
John Heffernan, Firefighter, Ladder 11
Ronnie Henderson, Firefighter, Engine 279
Joseph Henry, Firefighter, Ladder 21
William Henry, Firefighter, Rescue 1
Thomas Hetzel, Firefighter, Ladder 13
Jonathon Hohmann, Firefighter, Haz-Mat Co. 1
Thomas Holohan, Firefighter, Engine 6
Joseph Hunter, Firefighter, Squad 288
Jonathan Ielpi, Firefighter, Squad 288
William Johnston, Firefighter, Engine 6
Andrew Jordan, Firefighter, Ladder 132
Karl Joseph, Firefighter, Engine 207
Angel Juarbe, Jr., Firefighter, Ladder 12
Vincent Kane, Firefighter*, Engine 22
Paul Keating, Firefighter, Ladder 5
Thomas Kelly, Firefighter, Ladder 15
Thomas Kelly, Firefighter*, Ladder 105
Richard Kelly, Jr., Firefighter, Ladder 11
Thomas Kennedy, Firefighter, Ladder 101
Michael Kiefer, Firefighter, Ladder 132
Robert King, Jr., Firefighter, Engine 33
Scott Kopytko, Firefighter, Ladder 15
William Krukowski, Firefighter, Ladder 21
Kenneth Kumpel, Firefighter*, Ladder 25
Thomas Kuveikis, Firefighter, Squad 252
David LaForge, Firefighter, Ladder 20
William Lake, Firefighter, Rescue 2
Robert Lane, Firefighter, Engine 55
Peter Langone, Firefighter, Squad 252
Scott Larsen, Firefighter, Ladder 15
Neil Leavy, Firefighter, Engine 217
Daniel Libretti, Firefighter, Rescue 2
Robert Linnane, Firefighter, Ladder 20
Michael Lynch, Firefighter, Engine 40
Michael Lynch, Firefighter*, Ladder 4
Michael Lyons, Firefighter, Squad 41
Patrick Lyons, Firefighter*, Squad 252
Edward Rall, Firefighter, Rescue 2
Adam Rand, Firefighter, Squad 288

Donald Regan, Firefighter, Rescue 3
Christian Regenhard, Firefighter, Ladder 131
Kevin Reilly, Firefighter, Engine 207
James Riches, Firefighter, Engine 4
Joseph Rivelli, Jr., Firefighter, Ladder 25
Michael Roberts, Firefighter, Engine 214
Michael Roberts, Firefighter, Ladder 35
Anthony Rodriguez, Firefighter, Engine 27
Matthew Rogan, Firefighter, Ladder 11
Nicholas Rossomando, Firefighter, Rescue
Paul Ruback, Firefighter, Ladder 25
Stephen Russell, Firefighter, Engine 55
Thomas Sabella, Firefighter, Ladder 13
Christopher Santora, Firefighter, Engine 5
John Santore, Firefighter, Ladder 5
Gregory Saucedo, Firefighter, Ladder 5
Dennis Scauso, Firefighter, Haz-Mat Co. 1
John Schardt, Firefighter, Engine 201
Thomas Schoales, Firefighter, Engine 4
Gerard Schrang, Firefighter, Rescue 3
Gregory Sikorsky, Firefighter, Squad 41
Stephen Siller, Firefighter, Squad 1
Stanley Smagala, Jr., Firefighter, Engine 22
Kevin Smith, Firefighter, Haz-Mat Co. 1
Leon Smith, Jr., Firefighter, Ladder 118
Robert Spear, Jr., Firefighter, Engine 50
Joseph Spor, Firefighter, Ladder 38
Gregory Stajk, Firefighter, Ladder 13
Jeffrey Stark, Firefighter, Engine 230
Benjamin Suarez, Firefighter, Ladder 21
Daniel Suhr, Firefighter, Engine 216
Brian Sweeney, Firefighter, Rescue 1
Sean Tallon, Firefighter, Ladder 10
Allan Tarasiewicz, Firefighter, Rescue 5
Paul Tegtmeier, Firefighter, Engine 4
John Tierney, Firefighter, Ladder 9
John Tipping II, Firefighter, Ladder 4
Hector Tirado, Jr., Firefighter, Engine 23
Richard VanHine, Firefighter, Squad 41
Peter Vega, Firefighter, Ladder 118
Lawrence Veling, Firefighter, Engine 235
John Vigiano II, Firefighter, Ladder 132
Sergio Villanueva, Firefighter, Ladder 132
Lawrence Virgilio, Firefighter, Squad 18
Jeffrey Walz, Firefighter*, Ladder 9
Kenneth Watson, Firefighter, Engine 214
Michael Weinberg, Firefighter, Engine 1
David Weiss, Firefighter, Rescue 1
Timothy Welty, Firefighter, Squad 288
Eugene Whelan, Firefighter, Engine 230
Edward White, Firefighter, Engine 230
Mark Whitford, Firefighter, Engine 23
William X. Wren, Firefighter, Retired—Ladder 166
Raymond York, Firefighter, Engine 285
Carlos Lillo, Paramedic, Battalion 49
Ricardo Quinn, Paramedic, Battalion 57
Frank Bonomo, Firefighter, Engine 230

---

* indicates posthumous promotions. Three of the names on this list were retired firefighters.

Contents

Preface

D ISASTERS TAKE people away and bring others together. We came together first as helpers and later as authors, each of us bringing our individual professional training and experiences to this work. All the
stories are true.

The authors of this text have discussed, reflected, and given feedback on all
that is included. This process has been consistent with the type of collaboration we have come to value throughout our work together and have included
as one of the principles underlying our work. While the Introduction and
Conclusion were written by all, each of the other chapters has a primary author and we felt it important to offer that to the reader. *Paul Greene wrote Chapters 5 and 6; Dianne Kane, Chapters 4, 7, 9, and 10; Grace Christ, Chapter 8; Sallie
Lynch, Chapter 3; and Malachy Corrigan, Chapter 2.*

PAUL GREENE, PhD

As my work with the New York City Fire Department (FDNY) began to wind
down in 2003, I approached Dianne Kane, the person I reported to at the
FDNY Counseling Service Unit (CSU), about obtaining CSU consent to do
some writing for the professional community on my experiences. FDNY CSU
was the entity I worked for, and psychologists' ethics would require permission before writing about them. Usually, when writing a case study, the
people can be so disguised that even they could not recognize themselves. In
this case, it would not be possible to disguise the subject. She seemed appreciative and maybe surprised that someone would actually follow that ethical guide, probably because a number of professionals were already writing
about the FDNY without consent. Dianne suggested meeting with Grace,
Sallie, and Mal.

It had been my impression that CSU was doing an excellent job. They, like most of the FDNY, are modest about their accomplishments. They certainly take pride in their work and believe in not only what they do but how they do it. Often, they think about who might have been helped or helped more, not necessarily whom they helped successfully. Lost opportunities and the suffering of others are primary concerns for them. From my perspective as a relative outsider, I felt CSU accomplishments matched the firefighters whose strength helped clear the World Trade Center site in record time, with few injuries, and with special sensitivity to the losses they and the country suffered on 9/11.

I asked them to tell their story and share their insights. Together we began the process of creating this book. The innovations in crisis intervention and counseling belong to CSU leaders and staff, both professional and peer, and the organizations they chose to partner with for delivering services.

When the first plane struck, I was at my desk at Iona College in New Rochelle, a suburb north of New York City. I was absorbed in preparations to deliver a lecture on personality psychology and the great theorists who were influenced by the horrors of World War II. My clinical exposure to treating traumatized people began in the mid-1970s while in training with the Veterans Administration and working with the psychological casualties of World War II through Vietnam. That was before the *Diagnostic and Statistical Manual* recognized posttraumatic stress disorder as a distinct mental illness. Through the 1980s part of my practice included working with victims of assault and/or rape, accident victims left with chronic, intractable pain, and grieving families and mental health clinicians suffering losses from murders and suicides. These experiences prepared me to volunteer when the New York State Psychological Association started a Disaster Response Network in 1991.

I have heard estimates that as many as two thirds of the population will suffer a traumatic event in their lifetime. The implications are that we all know at least one traumatized person, if we ourselves have not been. I would argue that traumatic events also have a generational influence. My father's earliest memory was witnessing mass executions. The experience certainly influenced his life and mine, so it is to his memory that I dedicate my work on this book. I do not know how people can be involved in trauma response without loving family, friends, and community. Surely, my well-being has been sustained by my wife, Barbara, and children, David and Julie. Iona College and my colleagues have been generously supportive.

My deepest gratitude belongs to the firefighters who let me into their homes and families, and their other home, the firehouse. The FDNY Brotherhood is strong because these people hold fast to the traditions that honor their community and encourage them to do the right thing. If we are going to reduce the harmful effects of trauma and improve the response for this generation and the next, we all have to learn much more from them.

DIANNE KANE, DSW, CGP

When Paul first approached me about his desire to do *some writing* he connected with a part of me that I had put on hold. When others recommended that we write about our work at CSU for publication I agreed but could not yet imagine finding a way to make that happen. As with many projects reflected in this book and throughout my post-9/11 experience, it is through collaboration with dedicated and talented colleagues that many things that seem impossible are brought to fruition.

My work with first responders began just after the first attack on the World Trade Center (WTC) in 1993. I was drawn to the position—working with emergency medical services (EMS)—heading up a trauma intervention program; still, I questioned my decision, having at that point never once had the instinct to rush to the scene of either WTC or any other national disaster. Later I would learn that this instinct was not necessarily unhelpful and that my background in training and staff development would be valuable and well utilized along with my clinical skills.

At the time of the event I was in my office at CSU seeing a client I had known for a while: I recall feeling annoyed that for some reason my phone kept ringing. Eventually colleagues knocked on the door, and Joe and I rushed out to watch the towers already in flames, eventually crumble to the ground. He along with the other firefighters at the office had left by then; it would be hours before I knew he was safe. For years he has called me on September 11, no matter how far from New York he has been. The connection we have to those we were with in the earliest moments of the disaster are etched forever in our minds.

Almost from that moment on my responsibilities at CSU began to extend into the external community. With ambivalence I increasingly stepped back from the daily clinical operations within CSU to attend to the business of developing programs and the partnerships and collaborations necessary to implement them. This shift has rewarded me with connections to many wonderful, generous, and capable individuals and organizations that I have had the privilege of working with during the last 4 years. It is no accident that this volume represents the work of people who came together as relative strangers but represent the mix of internal and external resources who contributed to CSU's response in the aftermath of the disaster. Still, this work primarily represents the collective talent, dedication, and creativity of the amazing staff of CSU, both professional and peer, those who were present on September 11, 2001, and those who came later, that makes the work we do so successful and rewarding.

Personally this journey has led me to reconnect with two close friends from years ago. One appeared to help with the work, representing a professional organization I am now a proud member of but had not known before. The other appeared at the footprints of WTC during the 2003 memorial, having tragically lost her son in the collapse of Tower 2. Having them both back in my life is illustrative of the oddities of trauma.

It has been a privilege both personally and professionally to do the work I do with the people I do it with. Special thanks are due to friends and family, especially Gordon and Ian, for their support and encouragement. Firefighters are indeed a special group of individuals, and through this time I have had the opportunity to learn firsthand that this is equally true of the women they marry (or plan to marry), the parents who raised them, and the children they have raised. They have enriched my life, and I hope that in some way I have helped to ease their pain.

GRACE CHRIST, DSW

Having just completed a study at Memorial Sloan-Kettering Cancer Center (MSK) of children who coped with the death of a parent from cancer, I immediately thought of what the WTC disaster would mean for the children of the firefighters. My heart sank as I watched the buildings crumble on television. At MSK the children had the all-important preparation, small doses of information that they could integrate over weeks or months. Being prepared is a big help in getting through the profoundly painful process of losing a parent. I knew the firefighters' children would experience a different kind of pain shaped by shock, confusion, and feeling overwhelmed.

Now, as a faculty member at Columbia University School of Social Work and a grantee of the Project on Death in America, I was able to consider interventions and research beyond medical illnesses. My experience best equipped me to help with longer-term needs of families. I knew there would be no "quick fix" to such a profound loss, but the reality turned out to be longer and more complex than anticipated.

In the crisis environment of the first weeks and months the long-haul approach was a hard sell, to say the least! As part of my search I told a colleague at Columbia of my interest. That same day she called Dianne Kane, who was looking for a program to address the long-term needs of firefighters' bereaved families. Malachy Corrigan and Dianne were the only people I met who embraced concepts like *long haul*, a family commitment to bereaved families, an openness to the possibility that visits might need to be in the home, and an acceptance that there was much we did not know but would learn together over time. This is another example of those unique bonds that form during crises, an unexpected gift that brings new dimension and meaning to one's life.

The eventual program team of enormously talented, highly skilled, and committed faculty and doctoral students from Columbia University School of

Social Work (CUSSW) made the work possible as well as rewarding. Their accessibility, reliability, and shared support through the rough shoals of emotion, tragedy, and triumph created the "holding environment" in which so much could be experienced, expressed, and contained. I am deeply grateful for their tireless contribution and their unwavering support. A note of thanks to my husband, Adolph, a child psychiatrist whose wise consultation and support of the team throughout was vital.

Nothing prepared us for the special role a firefighter father plays in the lives of his children and the profound impact of his loss on them. Indeed, we came to know and admire these fathers through the eyes of their children, who often delighted in recounting the details of dad as "Mr. Mom." The qualities of compassion, empathy, thoughtfulness, maturity, and inventiveness the children developed as they met this enormous challenge were extraordinary. We were awed by how the mothers endured the pain of multiple memorials to ensure that their husbands' heroism and sacrifice were fully respected and understood. We will be forever grateful for their willingness to share their experiences, in part to ease the suffering of other souls. There was the widow in the midst of her own intense grief who attended the funeral of a neighbor's young child who had died suddenly: "I just had to show her you can still walk and talk."

SALLIE LYNCH, MA

I first got involved with the FDNY community as an anthropology student studying for a master's degree at Columbia University when I began working with Grace Christ to develop a program to assist families who lost a firefighter father in the World Trade Center disaster. Soon after, I met Dianne Kane and Malachy Corrigan, and later Paul Greene. At the time, I was also recovering from 2001, a difficult year of my life, in which I lost both my father, Thomas P. Lynch, and my uncle, and close family members endured various health problems. Subsequently, the events of 9/11 occurred. This firsthand experience of loss fed my motivation to enter the field of mental health services. Early on, the atmosphere of the Counseling Service Unit of the FDNY made me feel like I was with family, and helping the community through such a difficult time gave me an even greater sense of belonging.

Prior to moving to New York City, I studied cultural studies at Charles University in the Czech Republic, where many changes were shaping the fledgling country after the Velvet Revolution of 1989. During the 8 years I spent in Prague, I developed an appreciation for cultural change and its impact on people and society and learned the importance of culture in connecting people. I also learned how historical events shape the responses and behaviors of particular societies.

My involvement with the FDNY over the past few years enabled me to research the culture of *the Brotherhood* of firefighters and explore the impact of 9/11. I consider myself extremely privileged to have had the opportunity to get to know firefighters and their families, and I want to dedicate this work to them and to share their qualities and experiences with the readers of this book.

It has been an enlightening experience to work with CSU and the many people who responded to the FDNY community with such compassion and understanding. The FDNY/Columbia University Family Program and its many talented clinicians gave a deeper meaning to 9/11—we all learned more about the men who died and the many people who loved them, and we were able to assist them along their path to recovery. Colleagues from both CSU and the Family Program have shaped my perceptions of the kind of professional I would like to be.

Working with the community has also helped me grow and learn how to be strong with my own loss. As personal supports in this journey, my large family, my parents, my siblings, and my friends have been a great inspiration. I am especially lucky to have the steadfast support of my grandmother, Reva, and my fiance, Mike. Most impressive to me has been the cohesion of the FDNY, where the community finds its strength and resiliency, and I would wish that any individual or group affected by tragedy could have this support.

MALACHY CORRIGAN, MSN, RN

The need to provide a mental health response to the extreme trauma experienced by the FDNY members and their families called upon all the skills I have acquired over 30 years of delivering health care. My prior experience with veterans returning from Vietnam helped in constructing a model for responding to trauma, as did my work in a NYC hospital emergency room. But the counseling of thousands of firefighters and their families prior to 9/11 gave me and my CSU colleagues the most important foundation upon which to build a new model of counseling services post-9/11. The strength that members have exhibited facing the trauma of 9/11 not only is a predicate of positive mental health but also creates the environment for the CSU staff to continually seek resources and methods to address the mental health needs of members and their families.

Since the beginning of my work within the FDNY, it has been a rewarding experience to assist members in resolving their mental health issues. It is not a mystery as to why FDNY members responded to the WTC tragedy as they did, for it was their chosen job. It was an incredibly difficult job, done willingly in the company of their FDNY family members. When rescue was not possible then recovery of remains became the mission, consistent with the fire service tradition of leaving no one behind.

I have been privileged not only to serve firefighters and their family members but also to experience the trust and support of professional and peer colleagues. Father John Delendick, FDNY chaplain; Dr. Kerry Kelly, chief medical officer; and Dr. David Prezant, deputy chief medical officer, have continually supported my work in the FDNY CSU.

My own family knows the FDNY well and shared their energy to support my work at the FDNY CSU, which often kept me from home. For their loving support, my thanks to my parents, my siblings, their families, and especially Liz, Patricia, Allison, and Jorge.

Acknowledgments

THIS IS a story about a family at work. Specifically, about how a work family faces a trauma and grows through the trauma. One of the realities of a family is that members learn the strengths and weaknesses of their family. In the text we will discuss the strengths and weaknesses of the FDNY family. Mindful that physical courage is the basis of firefighting, we will focus on the interactions among the members.

The history of firefighting is based on a group model of interdependence and learning from those who preceded the current group of firefighters. This is also true for the writers of this text. We acknowledge that our work depends on all the work of those who preceded us in the FDNY Counseling Service Unit. We especially thank our colleagues both professional and peer who joined with us to provide counseling services to firefighters and their family members.

Our gratitude is extended to two different mayors, former Mayor Rudy Guiliani and current Mayor Michael Bloomberg of the city of New York, whose administrations supported the work of the FDNY Counseling Service Unit. Specifically, we express our gratitude to former FDNY Commissioner Von Essen and current FDNY Commissioner Scoppetta.

In the experience of the overwhelming trauma of the World Trade Center bombing, the FDNY Counseling Service Unit needed help from outside the family. We received help. The federal government through the Federal Emergency Management Administration worked with New York State to create Project Liberty, which provided resources for crisis counseling. The American Red Cross, the United Way, and other nonprofits assisted with resources. Within the extended family of the fire services, the National Fallen Firefighter's Foundation and the International Association of Fire Fighters were among the most outstanding contributors of resources and practical support for the services of CSU.

Within the FDNY family, the Uniformed Firefighters Association, the Uniformed Fire Officers Association, the Office of the Budget, the Bureau of Fire Operations, and the Bureau of Health Services all contributed to the goals of CSU. All organizations need effective leaders. The staff of the Counseling Service Unit benefited from the leadership of Kerry J. Kelly, FDNY chief medical officer, and David Prezant, FDNY deputy chief medical officer, both of whom provided insight, guidance, and personal support to the director of CSU.

Finally, heartfelt thanks to all FDNY members and family members who shared their pain with the hopeful expectation of symptom relief and taught the CSU staff various ways of restoring health as they processed the trauma. The authors acknowledge a deeper level of understanding of the pain of trauma as the privilege of working with FDNY members and family members.

CHAPTER 1

Introduction

A s we write this introduction, we are rapidly approaching the fourth anniversary of the September 11 attacks on the World Trade Center and the Pentagon. March 2006, marks the first anniversary of the Madrid subway bombings. Just weeks ago, four bombs exploded in London's public transport system. It is obviously impossible to predict what may happen before this book is released. Such is the age in which we live. Each time terrorists strike, multiple communities are affected. The everyday experience of life is disrupted with effects that ripple throughout and touch each of the members. This book describes the approach we have used to respond to one particular community and identifies the principles and methods that have helped us in our work and that we believe may be helpful to others responding to their communities in times of need.

The events of September 11, 2001, marked the largest attack ever on the continental United States. In New York City 2,973 lives were lost, countless more were impacted, and many of those remain changed forever. New York is a city organized by communities. Multiple communities within its borders were dramatically influenced by the events of that crystal-clear day. This text documents the experience of one New York City community. It is not a community defined by geography, race, or religion, but rather by profession.

On September 11 the New York City Fire Department (FDNY) community lost 343 of its members. This represents the largest loss of life of any emergency response agency in history (The 9/11 Commission Report, p. 311). Among them were officers of all ranks, firefighters, marshals, and emergency medical personnel (1 chief of department, 1 first deputy commissioner, 2 assistant

1

chiefs, 5 deputy chiefs, 19 battalion chiefs, 19 captains, 53 lieutenants, 4 fire marshals, 236 firefighters, 1 chaplain, 2 paramedics). They left behind wives, fiancées, and girlfriends; mothers, fathers, and siblings; children young and old and yet to be born. They also left behind more than 13,000 surviving members of the FDNY community.

This text is about responding to the needs of the FDNY community. It is the story of a response launched from within the community by the Counseling Service Unit (CSU), the internal employee assistance program (EAP) of the FDNY. It does not reflect the entire FDNY, CSU, and professional community effort, nor does it review all of the pertinent academic literature. Rather, it is primarily the story of how some of the more innovative CSU programs came into being and how they operated, and it draws tentative conclusions on their effectiveness. From that self-analysis and review of available data come suggested principles and practices.

This is the story of bringing help to first responders and their families. It is about reaching out to those who risked their lives that day to help others and as a result suffered the loss of roughly 3 percent of the workforce and 6 percent of command staff in less than one hour. It is the story of helping a group of individuals for whom exposure to the traumatic event did not end on 9/11 but instead continued for 9 long months of digging for the remains of those lost and then having to leave without bringing all of their brothers home. It is the story of designing interventions that supported this ongoing work and respected the firefighters' need to do it. These chapters also tell the story of reaching out to families who lost fathers, husbands, fiancés, boyfriends, sons, and brothers. Their lives were forever changed that day. While each individual's experience of the tragedy was unique, in many ways all members of the FDNY community carried and cared for each other throughout the difficult weeks, months, and years that followed. CSU shaped services in an effort to help them help each other and to enable them to feel less alone.

Terrorism is about fear, not death. It is about rendering those targeted helpless in the face of uncertainty and about their loss of control. As unique as each situation may be, these characteristics are shared, and those who respond to affected populations must understand that organizing the resulting chaos and demonstrating long-term, consistent caring are what helps the community heal. Also shared is the public attention paid in the aftermath of disaster. Those who are left traumatized and bereft in the wake of such an event will likely have to deal with the ongoing public attention paid both to the event and to them.

While this text describes the response of one organization to one affected community it simultaneously describes what it is like from the inside of that organization attempting to create order, safety, and caring communities that help individuals and groups begin to heal. Unfortunately, we believe that some of the heretofore unique characteristics of the 9/11 experience will be repeated. Fortunately, we also believe that some of the principles we applied in developing our response can help those who one day may face a similar situation in their community. Our hope is that this text can assist the reader to be as prepared as possible should that day come, and we describe the elements of response that we believe can be developed ahead of such an incident. Communities in the throes of such tragedies are likely to experience the effects of trauma over a protracted period of time as a result of phenomena such as first responders searching for their own, extensive media coverage, and large groups of grievers who have different relationships to the event and to the deceased.

A number of themes have emerged from the various people and programs that were successful in aiding the CSU response to 9/11. These themes illustrate concepts that can be utilized in response to other situations. They are present in the models we have utilized with particular subpopulations in the FDNY community, and they reflect the philosophy of CSU services and interventions. Perhaps most important is the pivotal nature of the inherent connection people have with one another. Disasters, terrible events, and terrorist acts tear at the human bond we share. Trauma can isolate us, weaken our connections to each other, and weaken the coherence of society. We found that the most utilized programs support and strengthen interaction, communication, and our emotional connections by encouraging safety and acceptance. These programs were able to identify natural strengths within and among people, and made help readily available, often by bringing the services right to the people rather than having people find and travel to the services. CSU identified the following guiding principles as most helpful in responding to 9/11, and they are woven throughout the chapters in this book. They include innovation and adaptability of services, inclusion, multiple service locations, normalization, education, collaboration, and pre-planning.

The *innovative and adaptive* nature of programs and interventions aided in appealing to a broad spectrum of individuals and made it possible to serve a large number of clients. CSU leadership took seriously the findings of previous disasters that rigidly applied traditional mental health approaches were often dramatically ineffective in meeting the needs of highly traumatized and bereaved populations (Allen, Whittlesey, & Pfefferbaum, 1999; Whittlesey et al., 2000). In our experience, continuous needs assessments, feedback, and a flexible application of methods allowed for a creative range of possible intervention models to emerge. Group treatments have proven consistently adaptable to a variety of needs and populations (Yalom, 1970; Buchele & Spitz, 2005). Individual treatments remain a reliable and viable option, especially in a place like New York City with so many talented psychotherapists both internal and external to CSU. In this book we present suggestions about some of the modifications that may be required when the proximity of the event im-

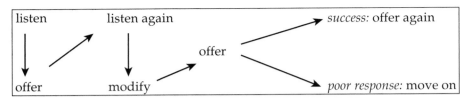

Figure 1.1 Decision tree for program development.

pacts both client and therapist, and when changes in context occurring rapidly and over an extended time period affect the treatment itself. The multiple interventions covered in this volume illustrate one effort to apply the principles of innovation and adaptability. CSU took a bottom-up approach of building on the community's needs starting with the listening process. The nature of service development followed a simple decision-tree format. (See Figure 1.1.)

Maintaining a family atmosphere and a personal bond with the community also facilitated their participation in services. The programs reflect these lessons.

Postdisaster services are consistently urged to *be inclusive* of a broad population of affected groups. A critical challenge in any disaster response is to identify those populations in greatest need of support and to create services they can use in a timely way. After the WTC attacks some risk groups were obvious from their level of exposure and degree of impact—for example, firefighters working at the site and families with young children in which a father was killed. For these groups the challenge was to identify the location and type of services most appropriate to support them in their situation.

When a broad range of affected groups are identified, *multiple service locations* are most often required. We found that outreach efforts that went directly to the client on location were most effective. Chapters 2 and 7 describe on-site approaches specifically designed to support firefighters working at the recovery site. The Firehouse Clinicians program, Chapter 5, did the same for survivors in those firehouses where firefighters were lost. Chapter 8 describes an in-home program developed for families with children in which the firefighter father died. Services were modified over time as the situation changed—for example, the World Trade Center site was closed, firehouse routines returned to normal, and children grew older. Over time, service demands shifted as affected individuals were better able to reflect on all that had occurred. These chapters also address the particular challenges of on-site work, including redefining professional role, adopting a broad repertoire of helping skills, and managing appropriate professional boundaries with those who may embrace you more as a friend than as a therapist. CSU brought services to the workplace and home and decentralized its offices to ensure access to the entire FDNY community, members of which mostly live on the outskirts of New York City. As a result, firefighters could continue to do their jobs and families could continue with their affairs and conveniently utilize CSU services.

Other target populations may be less apparent, but they are important because they comprise critical members of the community and many provide vital support for high-risk groups. Their capacity to help can be limited because the disaster has drastically altered their lives, placing them at greater risk for adverse consequences than might be anticipated. Families of surviving firefighters who are stressed by the demands of recovery emerged as one such critical target population. As illustrated in Chapter 9, for a firefighter to have physically survived the collapse is not to suggest that life at home could return to normal, especially when the recovery effort at the World Trade Center site was ongoing for 9 months after the event. Trauma symptoms affected relationships in many ways and often created distance and discord in family life. To help the process of renewal, CSU brought couples together for a weekend in which they could learn to cope, improve their communication and relationship skills.

September 11 also changed the meaning and implications of the natural pattern of career development within FDNY. Normal transitions, such as promotion and retirement, may become more stressful after such a catastrophic event. The numbers of retirements and promotions, normally celebratory moments, increased because so many had died and those who survived often suffered multiple health problems. Promotions, hastened by the loss of friends and brothers, triggered complicated and ambivalent feelings. Those retiring, often prematurely and without plan, risked separation from the community that understood their pain and could help them heal. As described in Chapter 10, CSU developed programs and community events to address this group.

In most situations, it was extremely helpful to *normalize and depathologize* the traumatic response whenever possible and at the same time support the idea that a broad range of reactions and symptoms are likely, even among a highly resilient population. Anticipating a *new normal* seemed to express an acceptance that life would not be the same as it was prior to 9/11 but that a sense of normalcy would return. Each individual's rate of recovery was appropriate and would lead to their own *new normal*. This helped to restore faith that once again feeling connected would happen. Expecting that day when the new normal would become normal was sometimes referred to as "finding 9/12." We look forward to the day when everyone can find 9/12.

Education is the backbone of all CSU services and a tool for empowering the entire community, including CSU counselors. Education and training improve, prepare, and create best practices and can be mandated, modified, and adapted to changing conditions. Education can offer comfort to the bereaved and traumatized and information as to how to access resources. Training counters helplessness and makes us more likely to be better prepared than we would be without it. The community was offered continuous bereavement and trauma education. Respectful of the experience of clients, this education reduced the stigma normally associated with accessing clinical services and created educated consumers effective in utilizing the services that best fit their needs. Education and training are integral parts of FDNY firefighters' lives, so adding a mental health component to their educational and training regimen seemed to make the information more easily accepted and effective.

Training mental health professionals and peers to educate their defined community of first responders, retirees, spouses, children, and extended families is an important part of the system by which CSU accomplishes its mission. Clinicians were also trained in firefighter culture and were continually clued in on the uniqueness of the FDNY community's experience and effective methods for connecting with members and helping them. CSU staff and collaborators were also given access and encouraged to utilize self-care to ensure their mental and physical well-being. Counselors responding to this disaster risked trauma themselves both from exposure to the event and from the hours, days, weeks, and years of listening to the traumatic experiences of others. Therapist self-care was not orphaned to the personal time of the staff. It was scheduled into their days by creating opportunities for them to talk to each other, encouraging personal and professional growth as part of the workday. This is not only appreciated by staff but is translated into better services. Caring for staff is not a luxury but an important part of an organization's committed, professional response to a disaster that carries so many traumas.

Good people, well trained and committed to the mission, who can institute and follow solid management principles, are vital to success in any endeavor. Mental health systems must be prepared to meet the needs that they hear expressed by their communities by utilizing the talents of their staff and being prepared to bring in additional talent as required. This lesson directs mental health units to establish relationships with a range of outside professionals, which might be better accomplished prior to a disaster than afterward. This book reflects the strong *collaboration* between CSU and its outside partners. The breadth and depth of collaboration efforts is a core principle of CSU, as it is believed to optimize program effectiveness. Collaboration is accomplished through continuous interaction and communication, sharing knowledge, insight, expertise, resources, and actual participation in each other's programs. Collaboration is an especially valuable tool when circumstances create a need to obtain a broad range of services, some never before imagined. This required an approach of openness and proper screening for compatibility with CSU's goals and mission. One illustration of successful collaboration describes how clinicians from the Family Program, Chapter 8, conducted workshops for Kids Connection, a CSU program, and contributed articles for *the LINK,* the

CSU newsletter. CSU staff and members of the Family Program attended various functions and training sessions of both programs and consulted with each other whenever possible. Referrals were continuous, improving access to services and allowing us to respond quickly to new issues and new phases in adaptation. The leaders of CSU established this high standard of collaboration as a requirement. This book is but one more expression of this core principle, an example of the internal and external efforts that have become key parts of the overall community response work of CSU. It modeled for mental health professionals, administrators, firefighters, and families the essential therapeutic ingredient of building and rebuilding human connections.

It is impossible to be fully prepared for any given situation, but FDNY and CSU both have a strong belief in *pre-planning and preparedness.* While the public's perception of the response to a disaster event never fully appreciates the tremendous preparation that already has occurred, disaster workers know the response is all about training and preparation. In the case of FDNY, readiness to respond has always been a core part of the way of life and culture, and this is mirrored in CSU's procedures and the services it has developed. The primary desire and mission of first responders and CSU staff is to be there to help when and if things go wrong. The history and culture of the department in Chapter 3 show the tradition of courage in the face of danger, the acceptance of fear, the loyalty to each other dead or alive, and the incredible cohesion that is the strength of the Brotherhood and the entire FDNY community. From those traditions came the modern CSU response to the 9/11 tragedy. Historical events are the building blocks of FDNY culture, and the World Trade Center tragedy has had a profound impact on that culture. History and culture inform the behavior of a given population, and for CSU, they are intrinsic parts of service creation and delivery. Knowledge of the past history of a community and the events that have impacted its members strengthens the power and effectiveness of services.

The barrier separating order from chaos is shockingly weak and vulnerable in many respects. Only when disaster strikes and that barrier breaks do most people realize how fragile societies really are and how strong and resilient societies can be. Disaster workers know both sides of the barrier, appreciating society's order as well as coping with the chaos that results when social order breaks down. Leaders have to keep themselves mentally clear enough to think and plan. At the same time, they have to keep others functioning well enough to carry out those plans. As soon as the towers fell, firefighters began digging for brothers and civilians thought to be buried in the rubble. FDNY active and retired members immediately flocked to the site. No one needed to tell them to report—it was the natural instinct developed over years of training. They stayed until the place where the towers had been was virtually broom clean. Few stopped to ask why the firefighters led the effort. Subsequently, questions have been raised about civilian leaders' decision to allow firefighters to recover the remains of their own since it is so much more traumatizing to dig for body parts of individuals you know. The reason the recovery stage occurred in this way and that no one openly questioned the process is that firefighters have expected that of each other for more than 200 years. It is important to recognize the historical and cultural demands and appreciate that, in this case, recovering the remains of the Brotherhood by the Brotherhood may have actually lessened the collective trauma. It is our belief that preventing the firefighters from completing their mission probably would have added to their trauma.

This volume primarily tells the story of firefighters. CSU services are also fully available to EMS personnel, and many have utilized them in the aftermath of 9/11. It would be a mistake to minimize the loss and exposure experienced by this part of FDNY's membership because it lost only two members of its ranks on that tragic day. They too rushed to the scene in record numbers. Many got there early and were exposed to the collapse. Many lost friends and colleagues both within FDNY and outside. Many worked at the morgue doing extraordinarily difficult body-handling work. For others the work was filled with the frustration of standing by at the World Trade Center site for hours, days, and weeks waiting for patients who never came and being unable to dig alongside the firefighters, as many would have preferred to do. Our focus on firefighters has more to do with sheer numbers. There are currently 11,400 members of the fire service and 2,800 members of EMS. It is also true that the 1,200 civilian members of the department who suffered loss and additional job stress during this time utilized appropriate services as well.

Finally, a word about language. The people who have gone to homes and workplaces or worked with members of the FDNY community in the office have been referred to with various titles throughout this book. They have been called mental health workers, professionals, mental health clinicians, interventionists, social workers, psychologists, psychotherapists, counselors, peer counselors, and various combinations of these words. Generally, their functions are more similar than different. Different titles are sometimes used to refer to the credentials of the provider, or are attempts to destigmatize services or reflect the titles preferred by those who utilized the service. Not surprisingly, credentials are less important than the willingness, knowledge, passion, and skill to accomplish the daily, sometimes mundane, tasks of helping and not tangling in professional turf and identity.

Almost every culture and occupation has its own language, words, and acronyms that may be frequently used on the job and become incorporated into a shared language. Words common within the culture of the FDNY are defined and explained throughout the text. We have avoided using the term *Ground Zero* when referring to the site of the collapse of the World Trade Center. We note that firefighters generally have said that it connotes a certain degree of disrespect for the World Trade Center site, which became for them hallowed ground, a memorial to their brothers and to the civilians they tried in vain to rescue. No doubt this term is used respectfully by millions around the world and by the tourists who travel great distances to be near the ground where the Twin Towers once stood. However, to those who worked at the World Trade Center site, the term *Ground Zero* could be used to describe the site of any attack and, when used by visitors to New York City as a tourist destination, can unintentionally trivialize the horrific events that occurred there. Within the FDNY, the World Trade Center site is known by several names, such as "the Site," "the Pile," "the Pit," or "the Trade Center," which we have chosen to use in this text. We realize that some of the aforementioned terms may also have a negative connotation for some and do not intend to offend.

CHAPTER 2

Coping with Chaos

ISSION DEFINES a fire department, and the mission that unites New York City Fire Department (FDNY) members is grounded around saving lives and protecting property. Those two core principles shape the entire fire service community. In the United States, just over 100 firefighters die in the line of duty each year (FEMA, 2004). Firefighters know the pain of sudden, tragic loss, the rituals of mourning, and the impact on the community of family, friends, neighborhoods, and towns. However, no one could anticipate the depth of loss that the tragic deaths of 2,973 people, including 343 firefighters and paramedics who perished on 9/11, would have on the FDNY (The 9/11 Commission Report). Roughly 3 percent of the workforce and 6 percent of command staff perished in the collapse. Out of 300 units, 61 suffered the loss of at least one firefighter, and several of those units suffered the loss of 7 to 10 fellow firefighters. Some 240 FDNY members (158 firefighters and 82 EMS workers) were transported or admitted to nearby hospitals, and 75 members lost biological brothers, sons, or fathers (D. Nigro, personal communication to Malachy Corrigan, November 13, 2001).

Firefighters are expected to expend physical and emotional energy in lifesaving events and to bear the pain of unsuccessful rescues without communicating this pain to the outside world. The family-like dimension of the firefighting job, however, creates an environment where that pain can be shared within the firehouse. When questioned, approximately 10,600 firefighters reported that the most important supports in their lives were fellow firefighters, spouses, and significant others (Prezant, 2002). The deep connection firefighters feel with each other was one of the primary factors that determined their response to the events of 9/11 and the recovery effort that followed.

In the history of the FDNY, its members have always recovered the remains of firefighters who died in the line of duty. It was the minimal expectation of many firefighters on 9/11 that they would be able to recover the remains of those fallen. In fact, on 9/11 and in the months that followed, some chief officers of the FDNY proclaimed recovery of remains as the primary mission. However, the destruction of the World Trade Center Twin Towers made it impossible to recover the remains of all victims. Metal desks, metal cabinets, and supporting I-beams were turned to dust in many sections of the two towers. The remnants of these towers, which once stood 110 stories high, now stood only three stories tall, an eerie mixture of pulverized concrete, metal, furniture, orange fires, upright steel structures, and an olfactory imprint that would remain with survivors. All of these sensory overloads contributed to the chaos.

In this chaos and devastation, the firefighters expected of themselves, and society readily accepted, that they, along with other rescue workers, would bear the pain of the loss of 343 family members and accomplish the mission of rescue and recovery. In turn, society was amazed at the dedication and bravery they saw among the workers at the site. Most firefighters described the site as a scene from a movie. Nothing in the cumulative thousands of years of firefighting experience had remotely prepared them for what they saw and the mission that lay ahead. Firefighters had to create order from chaos. At the same time mental health clinicians had to assess psychological needs to restore mental health to those who had been exposed.

THE COUNSELING SERVICE UNIT PRE-9/11

The Counseling Service Unit (CSU) of the FDNY has grown from an employee assistance program serving an average of 600 clients per year to one that has shouldered the concerns, trauma, and loss of employees and family of 343 members of a department of brothers. This metamorphosis has brought about new methods of therapeutic practice and creates the space for more effective future interventions with traumatized and bereaved communities. Founded in 1966 by two active-duty firefighters who were members of Alcoholics Anonymous (AA), CSU initially provided services to help people suffering from alcoholism and addiction who were active-duty members of the fire department. They were not mental health professionals, but they were AA members and translated the 12-step model into the Counseling Service Unit.

Over the years, the department officials made an effort to expand the services of the newly developed employee assistance unit into more of a professional and peer counselor mix. In 1982, when the current director was hired, he was instructed to not lose contact with the original mission of the unit, which helped people stop drinking, and to continue to utilize peers and professionals to talk with firefighters, drawing on each other's strengths. At that time there were many ways in which the job allowed alcoholism to flourish by supporting the tremendous cultural realities that were in place in most firehouses. During 1982, CSU served 75 clients.

In an effort to further professionalize the unit, one of the first things the new director did was to determine who on the staff were really interested in becoming counselors. Those individuals were sent to school to be trained as certified alcohol counselors (CACs), the accepted credential in the field at that time. The first five or six firefighters in those paraprofessional roles who went to school received certificates in approximately 1 year, forming the core of the original staff. In the mid-1980s, others joined the staff, including a retired firefighter with a PhD in clinical psychology, and a person with a master's degree in counseling, specializing in bereavement issues. These additions expanded services further. Bereavement was and is clearly a reoccurring issue for firefighters, acutely because of fatal fires, but also because of the general losses that arise in any family system. It therefore is not surprising that many of the people who came in for treatment of alcoholism also suffered from unresolved grief issues.

Rather than treating firefighters simply as alcoholics or alcohol abusers, CSU sought to increase the quality of clinical care so that people had the chance to get all of the services they needed. Over the next few years, CSU recruited more people from mental health disciplines, mostly social workers, to provide not only addiction services but grief and bereavement services as well as treatment for other mental health issues.

Whenever possible, creative authority to respond to particular situations by developing programs and solutions was encouraged. CSU recognized that the natural environment for the everyday lives of firefighters was the firehouse kitchen. Building on this natural support and using this natural setting to connect with firefighters became the founding principle for initiating effective clinical services. During that time, the average number of line-of-duty deaths per annum was five in the FDNY, and besides those deaths there were multiple injuries. These individual incidents led CSU to develop a skill repertoire that has informed the post-9/11 response. CSU's current director describes one such incident in which he learned the value of understanding exactly what the firefighters at a *bad fire* experienced, but also the danger of having shared their trauma:

> One of the most important fires that shaped my conceptualization was the death of a firefighter, a personal friend. He was an outside vent [OV] and their job is to go up a fire escape and make sure to get a window, so that if your fire-

fighters are trapped, they have a way out. The other thing OVs do is you look in that window and see if there's anybody in that room. I had known him [the OV] quite well for about three years, and he was a leader at his house and had brought many of his other firefighters to be counseled for all different reasons.

He was the OV that particular day, and for this fire the box came in at three a.m., and sometime shortly after that, he looked in that window, and he saw a crib in a fully occupied apartment building. He was pretty sure—we don't know, because he died—but he had to think there's a child in that crib. The room was engulfed in flames. There was no water. There was some problem. He knew that because he had the radio, but his perception was that he could save that child, get to that crib, get that child, come back out that window. That had to be what he was thinking. What else could he have been thinking? He did that, but he never came out. The fire consumed the room and consumed him.

I knew so many people in that firehouse that were working with him that evening, that night at three a.m., that they called me at home—this was before the days of the cell phone. They called me at home and said, "Mal, you gotta come down here, your buddy's probably dead." So I went, literally to that building in South Brooklyn, and they brought me up the fire escape, not the interior stairway, and I looked in that window and saw the crib, what was left of it, and saw what was left of him. And I could understand how a person could make that decision. Another guy I knew had been injured in that fire, but he didn't realize that the other firefighter had perished. So the next job was to go to the hospital and tell this guy that his buddy—you know that's part of the thing that you do—that John had perished.

The guys knew me, and they felt if I saw that [from the fire escape], I would understand more than all the words they could tell me. And I did. To this day that's the most traumatic fire in my mind. To this day sometimes I have nightmares about that. But did it help me with my work? Absolutely, because it made me go to another level of understanding that maybe I could have never reached. Because after that when I speak to firefighters, it's hard sometimes. You can't get them rolling, and ever since that time when I'm in a group of firefighters, when I'm trying to educate them on a topic, and they are welcome to respond—because I know you can't just lecture because it's not going to be effective. And when I've done all the things you do as a lecturer, as a teacher, and they're not working, I say, "Show of hands. How many people remember their first child who died in the line of duty?" I was just getting their attention. I can barely shut them up.

Interestingly, 6 years after the aforementioned event, at the time of another tragedy, a firefighter came forward requesting to talk about the earlier event. After witnessing another tragic line-of-duty death, he was ready to discuss guilt he had carried for 6 years, feeling that he could have done more at the earlier fire. Such is the nature of delayed onset and the value of being there as a consistent presence so that when the time comes there is an available outlet.

Knowing that firefighters respond best in the kitchen, where they are comfortable, is critical to providing services. The tradition of showing up at a firehouse reeling from a *bad fire*—a fire where there was a civilian death, a line-of-duty death, or a serious injury—set the standard for many of the services CSU later developed, including the firehouse clinicians program after 9/11. (For more on this program see Chapter 5.) Of course, it was recognized that it would be necessary to introduce anyone who joined a firehouse at the kitchen table, and peer introduction became the model. Prior to those very early firehouse visits, the perception firefighters had of CSU, despite the name, was that it served only people with alcohol-related problems. The general understanding was that an alcohol abuser would go to Pier A, the building that housed CSU, and from there to "the Farm," a place outside New York City, to dry out. Creating a new perception of CSU as not just an alcohol abuse unit but rather a place where any firefighter could get help for himself and his family was a cultural obstacle CSU staff had to overcome. Establishing a presence in the aftermath of bad fires helped CSU eventually become known for clinical services related to trauma and bereavement and also for being there for the long haul.

It has always been CSU's policy to not engage with clients while they are drinking; the choice is always that they can either drink or talk, but not both. One of the events highlighting this philosophy was not a fatal fire but a young firefighter's suicide. When CSU was notified the night it occurred, many of the guys had already gathered and started drinking before wanting to talk. The talk was postponed until after the internment, when a firehouse meeting was held. Suicide is always an extremely difficult event in the lives of those who knew the deceased.

> At the meeting, 56 of the 57 house members were present. The meeting was held in the kitchen, and I was given a chair in the middle of the room. The officer who had invited me sat across from me, very close, and criticized me for not foreseeing the suicidal behavior. This lasted about 45 minutes without me replying before the officer said, "Well I guess there's no way you could have known that because we never called you. We never told you there was a problem." This opened up dialogue with several people in the firehouse and left a lasting lesson with them. Approximately 12 people from that house eventually got promoted to lieutenant and through the course of their careers, as they moved from that firehouse and worked all over the city, they would still call me to voice their concerns about their fellow firefighters. They remembered that day and promised themselves that they would not be the officers who overlooked any symptomatology in the future.

Another policy CSU has included in its operations is an effort to remain in touch with families over time, particularly when it comes to children of firefighters who die in the line of duty. Throughout the years, CSU staff developed an understanding that issues relating to the loss of a parent can emerge over time as children move through different developmental stages and confront new challenges and milestones. Sometimes children who were very young when their firefighter parent died would seek services when they reached adolescence. It was also not uncommon for a child who lost a firefighter parent to grow up and remember the support and compassion counseling staff at the fire department showed them. Sometimes those children would become firefighters themselves and would then seek services. The CSU tradition, like the traditions of New York City firefighters, is about long-term caring and commitment.

MERGING WITH EMS—TWO DIFFERENT CULTURES

In 1993, the mayor of New York City decided to merge the emergency medical services (EMS) and the fire department. This decision also brought a new group of mental health practitioners to CSU from the Health and Hospitals Corporation's Employee Assistance and Trauma Intervention Program, a much newer program than CSU with one of the first critical incident stress management (CISM) teams in the city. The merger of the EMS program with CSU combined two very different cultures with very different histories. The EMS program started much more as a corporate-style mental health clinic with private offices primarily offering individual treatment. Compare this to the firehouse environment of CSU—guys hanging around, a day-treatment program, the kitchen table, plenty of food, and downtime spent in the company of other colleagues. In contrast, the CISM team responded 24/7 by dispatching a professional counselor and EMS peer to meet on scene with any ambulance crew that had what they considered to be a bad call.

Of significance was the strongly held belief of both programs—services, interventions, and treatments were not mandated, but rather were accessed by request. Each of the programs operated through education and support providing classroom instruction at the separate training academies to those entering the system and those being promoted within it. Both historically included services to family members as part of their mission but saw relatively few family members prior to the events of 9/11. These similarities helped to smooth the transition as a new handful of licensed mental health practitioners from the EMS program joined those already in place at CSU and worked alongside the certified alcohol counselors (CACs) and firefighter peer counselors.

Fatalities and serious injuries were a more frequent occurrence in FDNY than EMS given the nature of the job. CSU was always present for families whenever such an incident occurred. Being there for families was part of the job description of CSU staff. Procedures included assessments of the family's needs, referrals to outside services, and a promise that any issues that might develop in the future could be brought to CSU's attention and that help would be provided whenever possible.

All in all, the underlying principles of the CSU philosophy and the ways of the EMS employee assistance program were not so different. During the 7 years after the merger and before the events of 9/11, CSU continued developing services with an expanded and more multifarious staff and was able to respond to a broader range of clients that presented a larger range of problems. Although knowledge and overall acceptance of CSU services were not anywhere near the levels reached after 9/11, it had become clear that mental health treatment was the core purpose of the combined unit and that a firefighter or EMS worker could come into the office and be seen by a licensed person for treatment for themselves or their family members. The day treatment program for addiction was maintained as a separate program, but it too had a different staffing pattern. It was understood that if CSU did not provide those services at a quality level, the other services and the reputation of the unit would be discredited and not valued by a large portion of the fire service members, who remembered and valued the origins of the program. By September 10, 2001, CSU, which had moved from a location near City Hall to offices at 251 Lafayette Street in lower Manhattan, had a staff of six full-time doctoral or master's-level civilian professionals, six uniformed members—one of whom was also a master's-level social worker—two master's-level social work interns, and two administrative support staff.

THE CSU RESPONSE TO 9/11

When news of the 9/11 attacks broke at CSU, all the staff could do was wait. Although with other events a location was generally given for CSU counselors to report to, this time there was a delay. With a direct view of the horrific event from the rooftop, workers at CSU were in clear sight of a constant and steady stream of civilians walking up Lafayette Street trying to get out of the area. A feeling of helplessness was widespread. Communication between the Emergency Communication Center and the command center for fire service on the ground was down. All those familiar with firefighters' dedication to their jobs knew they would try to get up as high as possible to rescue as many people as possible. This, combined with the communication problems, was an indication that there likely would be many deaths.

Answering calls asking for instructions for CSU, the director, who had taken a personal day off, urged staff to try to stay back so they would be able to help afterward when those who initially went to the site of the disaster would need backup. Realizing the enormity of the event, the CSU director and his wife, a nurse for FDNY, went to headquarters. Firefighters would be brought there for treatment and they believed immediate assistance would be needed at that location. In the absence of patients, the focus turned instead to the many organizational tasks that emerged. A protocol was put in place for families calling in, and a list of names of the missing was started. Planning and organization were two of the most valuable tasks for an event so large that no existing protocol could handle it. Every 2 hours, someone was given the duty of going over any cases that came in by phone that those answering could not handle. There was no script. The phones were ringing continuously, and very little reliable information was available. Even as the list of the missing was updated every 2 hours, it was difficult to determine its accuracy due to the communication problems and the fact that many firefighters were separated from other members of their firehouse once they arrived at the World Trade Center.

Eventually, some time in the afternoon, CSU received a dispatch call from EMS to go to Chelsea Piers, where a temporary hospital was being set up and the expectation was that there would be hundreds of victims. Chelsea Piers garages, located due north on Manhattan's west side from the World Trade Center site, were converted into a staging area for mental health practitioners, EMTs and paramedics, and eventually doctors and nurses, but there were no patients in sight. Many well-meaning mental health professionals had gathered, hoping to be of help. It was apparent by the dust that covered them when anyone standing by had been at the World Trade Center. Again and again these individuals, mostly EMTs and paramedics, were approached to talk. This behavior should be highlighted as what *not* to do in the aftermath. CSU staff began trying to keep people from repeatedly questioning the EMS crews, attempting to give them some space to breathe. This effort continued until after 9 p.m., when people were told to go home and wait for a call if they were needed. One CSU counselor describes the following:

> It was after 11 p.m. when I decided to take the subway, now re-opened, home to Brooklyn. Barely aware that I was still wearing my blue CISD [critical incident stress debriefing] jacket, I got out of the train and made my way to the turnstile. A young guy approached me offering to buy my jacket. Realizing he was serious when he started counting the money in his pocket it took an additional moment to recognize that what he wanted was the FDNY patch that might give access to the site. Things would indeed never be the same. Emerging from the subway, I was astounded to see my neighborhood in downtown Brooklyn covered in ash.

During the first 24 hours after the collapse, CSU placed five peer counselors at the World Trade Center site—four firefighters and one EMT. The CSU office, 1.81 miles north of the site, was staffed by five civilian counselors. At headquarters, CSU's director and command staff continued to compile an accurate list of the missing, convened a death notification team, and set up a telephone hotline for family members.

In the first days after the collapse, CSU decentralized offices to better provide support to families of the missing and deceased. A new location was opened in Fort Totten on September 12, 20 miles east of the site, and another location was opened in Staten Island, 14 miles south of the event, on September 13. Also in the first days, CSU continued to provide support at the World Trade Center site and other fire department locations. This support focused on attending to the practical needs of the workforce and identifying individuals in need of immediate assistance. From September 13 to 16, the International Association of Firefighters (IAFF) and the National Fallen Firefighters Foundation (NFFF) began to organize peer teams from around the country to assist with supporting the first responders.

ASSESSING THE COMMUNITY

For the purposes of understanding the strategy that CSU used to cope with the devastation of 9/11, four concepts need to be described: community, chaos, crisis, and change. *Community* here is defined as a basic concept formulating a plan within a workplace environment. Employee assistance programs (EAPs) are built on the premise that work has meaning on an organizational level but also on a personal level (Bureau of National Affairs, 1987). The product of the organization requires workers to interact in varying degrees to achieve the primary mission. The workers utilize a variety of tools to achieve the mission, and in the fire service, all of the tools require teamwork. The basic team of five firefighters forms a community at work. Tasks at the firehouse are shared, personalities add the psychological element, and five groups of five members form the fire company. Firefighters identify themselves first and foremost as members of a fire company. This strengthens the bond, which preserves the unit in physically challenging and psychologically threatening situations. Community is created in a company by an individual's response on the fire ground and an individual's interactional skills in a firehouse. Trust is formed, a new member is accepted, roles are assigned to each member, and a family dynamic is formulated. As time affirms the value of interdependence, the community is extended to other firefighters.

Chaos, for CSU purposes, is created when a situation occurs that is outside of one's normal experience of reality. An essential element is that the situation appears to be out of control. Physical danger adds an element of unpredictability. One of the basic methods of firefighting is the *size-up*. The size-up is an initial assessment of the nature of the fire or emergency situation, the first attempt to control the situation. Chaos is the antithesis of the size-up. Action provides psychological relief for firefighters, while chaos promotes the possibility of action but restricts the psychological size-up of individuals and groups. Crisis ensues. A mission-driven community is in chaos when physically and psychologically the members are in crisis.

A *crisis* is created when the resources available cannot accomplish the goal of the life-critical task, and a crisis can occur on multiple levels—physical, psychological, spiritual, and moral. Resources must be supplied to allow the workforce to begin to take control of the chaos, or the chaos gets worse. When the customary tools for fighting fires are destroyed, the *bucket brigade* begins, meaning firefighters adapt and go back to basics. Firefighters need purposeful action; the mission is rescue, and the buckets represent the first step to control, the first step to creating a size-up and a workplace in the chaos. Temporarily, the crisis persists. However, the first level of control is exerted at the work site. Until sufficient resources are applied, at the firehouse and in the family home, the community remains in crisis. The confusion related to the perished, the pain in the firehouse family, and the pain in the family at home bonded the firefighters and the families of the perished in a state of painful confusion.

When change is rapid, constant, and prolonged, it is experienced as permanent. Change became an appropriate part of healing and was accepted in this insulated workplace community. At the site, members often expressed their happiness to be alive but simultaneously their guilt to be alive. This was clearly the beginning of a psychological needs assessment from mental health practitioners. Just as when the customary tools for firefighters are not available, mental health practitioners needed to create a bucket brigade of their own—CSU needed assessment tools.

On 9/11, accurately assessing the chaos of the workplace was also the first step in managing it (Figure 2.1). Accurate information would allow workers and victims to control their internal perceptions of the chaos, dispelling rumors and misinformation. However, compiling an accurate count and determining the identity of the missing and hospitalized were complicated by the number of FDNY members of all ranks who rushed to the towers to help, often without official gear or dispatch. The time of the attack, when some were getting off work and others just arriving, meant that even more members than usual were nearby and instinctively rushed to the scene. The location of the attack, less than three miles from FDNY headquarters, meant that many top-ranking members as well as those waiting at the medical office also rushed in. Many had subsequently perished in the attack. Many who survived had narrowly escaped. Losing so many close coworkers so rapidly made it difficult for those at headquarters to continue functioning in their positions, especially when their workload had just increased exponentially. Accepting that the missing were, in fact, deceased would take even longer. To do so broke with

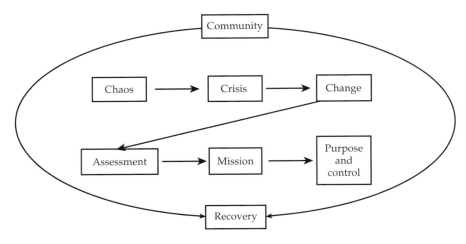

Figure 2.1 Helping a community in crisis.

FDNY tradition, in which firefighters do everything they can to rescue a fellow firefighter no matter how long or how dangerous that becomes.

The CSU director worked with FDNY staff at headquarters on the task of compiling a list of the missing.

> In the first post-impact days, when the mission was recovery of live bodies, no one knew who or how many were missing. Consciously thinking of them as anything but missing wasn't allowed, yet it was unavoidable. Speaking of them as dead was unacceptable. We started a list of the missing at headquarters to keep track so we could inform family members who called in on the status of their firefighter.
>
> When the first 50 names were on the list, I realized that I personally knew 10 of them. I stopped writing on that page and started a new page because I knew I couldn't bear to see another face. As more names came in, the list grew to seven pages of 343 names, with no more than 50 on each page. The pages were splattered with tears. The list of the missing, of course, eventually became the list of the perished.
>
> I did not look at the full list of names again until the first anniversary of 9/11 came around and I was to attend a commemoration ceremony a few days before the anniversary itself where I knew they would read the names and show the faces of the men who died. The night before the ceremony, I read every name and pictured the deceased in my mind in an attempt to desensitize for the next day, when I knew I would have to be more composed.

Sometimes disaster workers have to make small and large decisions based on their ability to function. Above all, mental health workers who are going to respond to major disasters have to be mentally and emotionally able to function. For this reason, they have to limit their own personal exposure to trauma and be mindful of their own limits in whatever manner those limits may appear. (For more on self-care see Chapter 4.)

RECEIVING OUTSIDE HELP

Given the nature of the event, all firefighters were recalled to work on 9/11; hence all were exposed to the psychological trauma of the collapse of the towers. It was immediately apparent that CSU would need to expand its base of professional and peer counselors to begin to organize an effective response.

In these early stages of the response, CSU managers were inundated with phone calls and messages from trauma and grief counselors and other mental health workers eager to help. CSU did not have a system or procedure in place for sifting through these offers and choosing which people to utilize and how. Most often, responding to such offers took time and energy away from other, more pressing tasks. In the earliest days more calls coming in to CSU were from helpers than from those requesting help. Staff recall working out a system to handle the sheer number of people offering assistance.

> At one point I got the idea to ask those offering help to post their offer via e-mail to a mailbox we labeled "CSU help." This helped reduce the number of telephone slips waiting for a call back, we didn't even have voice mail at the time, and gave the volunteers who came in to help answer our phones something clear to tell the callers. Ultimately it was only minimally helpful as the mailbox filled quickly, responses had to be sorted and acknowledged, and more importantly an effective method of assessment remained elusive.

While knowing that, in the long run, local helpers would be most beneficial, it was much more expedient and efficient for CSU in the early weeks and months to accept the out-of-town help offered by the IAFF and the NFFF. These visiting teams of mental health workers and experienced peers came from all over the country and beyond.

These helpers came pre-screened. They arrived in teams of mental health workers, firefighter/EMS peers, and chaplains. Uniformed peer counselors provided outreach at the World Trade Center site. Clergy were particularly effective in supporting the workers in the morgue. Mental health clinicians assisted at CSU locations and at the Bureau of Health Services. This assignment pattern of separating peers, mental health workers, and clergy was different from the typical deployment of CISM teams who arrive at the scene of a major incident to offer help. There were multiple reasons for this pattern

of utilization related to both the need for professional help in multiple locations and the belief that peers and clergy would be most effective at the
site. This followed and supported the preexisting pattern of response utilized
by CSU.

CSU by this time had three office locations with no additional professional
staff. The mental health professionals who arrived as part of CISM teams
filled a critical gap in staffing. Most of these mental health workers had done
some on-scene disaster work previously, a definite plus; however, they came
for a defined, relatively brief period of time, most often a minus. Those who
showed disappointment when asked to perform work that was not directly
with clients were less helpful than those who came willing to do any task that
was needed. Many brought a skill set that went beyond direct counseling and
included administrative and organizational skills much needed in the earliest, most chaotic period. As CSU's assistant director recalls:

> Once the mental health person accepted that we were not going to utilize
> them in the more traditional manner of dispatching them to the scene along
> with their peer team, most were open to whatever challenge they were given.
> They staffed our newly opened offices and went on family boat trips. They an-
> swered phones, designed new forms, and made sure we took a break to eat.
> They became New Yorkers when, with great trepidation, they were handed
> a Metrocard and a description of how to get from midtown down to SoHo.
> Many sent cards and left messages of support for months after they left. We
> are indebted to each of them.

In addition to providing support at the World Trade Center site, new teams
composed of FDNY retirees, visiting uniformed peers, and clergy were dispatched to firehouses and EMS stations. These peer teams were used primarily for case finding and education due to their natural cultural informality
and closeness with fellow firefighters. Peer counselors created an environment to encourage the venting of feelings and educated firefighters about basic emotions and basic critical incident stress management. In performing
case-finding functions, peer counselors helped to identify working members
who exhibited signs of acute stress reaction, and, perhaps most important,
they provided information about where help was available. Members were
encouraged to see a professional counselor at CSU when they were ready.
These crucial assessments helped to identify and encourage members who
needed some time away from the duties at the site to do so. This system of assessment and referral was effective. It allowed peer counselors to use their
credibility with other first responders and facilitate referral to a professional
counselor when appropriate.

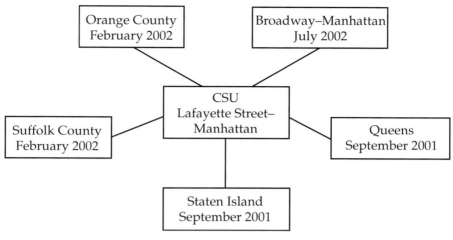

Figure 2.2 CSU office sites.

In addition to this very critical *hands-on* assistance, CSU also benefited from the financial support offered at this time by both the IAFF and the NFFF.

CSU EXPANSION

By October 2001, CSU had received an additional funding injection from the Federal Emergency Management Administration (FEMA) and Project Liberty. This enabled CSU to increase its staff and begin providing support groups for the FDNY community. FEMA and Project Liberty funding also enabled CSU to expand to six offices, opening a Suffolk County location and an Orange County location in February 2002 and moving day treatment to an office on Broadway in July 2002. When expansion was complete, CSU had a core staff of 29 civilian mental health professionals, 30 uniformed crisis counselors, and 17 support staff, as well as hundreds of consultants providing counseling services. By February 2002, the organization was structured as shown in Figure 2.2.

By November, CSU was receiving support from a broad range of global sources.

CONNECTING WITH THE FIREFIGHTING COMMUNITY

The amount of loss was overwhelming. While, as a group, firefighters are experienced with loss and bereavement within their work lives, the catastrophic events of 9/11 went far beyond their experience. Disbelief, anger, and mistrust of authority were normal responses, primarily due to feelings that something had failed—something must have for things to have gone so horrifically wrong. The priority of the workforce understandably remained the recovery of the remains, and that mission was the central focus of physical and emotional energy. Confusion about the place of these conflicting feelings in a dedicated workforce was all too common and too powerful to be contained by previous workplace bereavement education or intervention.

In an effort to address some of these needs, CSU worked with fire operations to offer a series of firehouse meetings in the fall of 2001 to those units wishing to participate. In each firehouse the officer issued an invitation to all members on the roster to report to the firehouse at a specific date and time. Traditionally such meetings are held when something of importance to the entire house needs to be discussed. At CSU's request and with the cooperation of headquarters, units were put off service during the time of the meeting to ensure that it would not be interrupted by a run. The meetings were primarily educational. A professional generally began the meeting by providing some information to the entire group about grief and bereavement, including typical signs and symptoms following a traumatic event. Equally important was that the meetings, which averaged between 48 and 58 members per house, brought the entire house together in an organized way. Following this general presentation members were divided into smaller groups of 8 to 10 members to allow for discussion and case finding. A peer and a professional counselor from CSU co-led these small groups to demonstrate unity, facilitate the process, and support each other in what could be a dramatic expression of anger.

The primary goals were education, normalization of reactions, and offering members a forum for expression of the very intense, most often angry, feelings they were experiencing. It was hoped that this early, more direct exposure to CSU staff would begin to destigmatize the use of in-office services—if not immediately, then later on in the process. An unanticipated outcome often expressed by members was that these formal meetings were the first opportunity for the entire firehouse family to be together after the events of 9/11. Members also expressed satisfaction that this was the first time someone outside of their immediate firehouse family had listened to their concerns. Consistently following the meetings, members of the participating units would inform a peer or professional counselor about concerns for a coworker. While these were informal communications, they reinforced the value of caring for each other in the fire service. These early firehouse meetings were different in form and had a different purpose than the Firehouse Clinicians Program, which is outlined in Chapter 5.

CONNECTING WITH FAMILIES

The official response to the families of the missing was a series of family meetings organized by FDNY. These informational meetings were held at a hotel in midtown Manhattan 1 and 2 weeks after the event. CSU was invited to attend in anticipation of the need for support to the family members. The turnout exceeded all expectations and the meetings helped CSU staff begin to assess the size of the greater community they would be providing services to and helped them determine how to shape those services. CSU announced at these meetings its commitment to providing services that would meet the families' needs for the long haul.

At these family meetings, the enormity of the event again became clear. It was difficult not to feel overwhelmed in the face of such catastrophic loss. Clinicians are taught that when working with a client who is feeling overwhelmed it is useful to help them partialize the situation and begin to work with one component at a time. How does one begin to create some degree of organization in the overwhelming task of assessing the needs of 343 bereaved families? Initially CSU knew almost nothing about them. Was the member married or single? Was the address on record correct? Did he or she have a girlfriend, boyfriend, fiancée, domestic partner? How many children? How old? What about his or her parents and siblings? Suddenly, in a matter of days, CSU had three offices, not one. How would staff keep track of who was in contact with whom? Who should reach out and how? Certainly at that point in time CSU's technology system could not support such an effort.

At the large family meetings held in Manhattan, all CSU helpers carried small notebooks in which to record any information they learned about a particular family and its needs. These were purchased the day of the first meeting and turned out to be an effective way of recording new clients for counselors to follow up with when they returned to the office. But what to do with those notebook pages? How to keep organized in a way that would be helpful? How to begin to gather necessary information on so many unknown people? To CSU's assistant director, the answer seemed obvious: Mental health practitioners are accustomed to keeping their work organized in case files. Perhaps a file folder for each family would begin to help.

One of the legal services departments at Headquarters had offered to help any way they could. They were known to have a staff that was responsible and organized. I asked if they could perhaps make manila file folders for each family, ideally coded in some way by geographic location of the family residence. I thought this would help us to get the file to the closest CSU location to begin to assess needs more efficiently. A few days later three firefighters arrived at CSU asking for me, each carrying multiple large cartons. The files requested had arrived. They were placed in my office. I began to sort them out, separating them by geography. It had not occurred to me to specify letter-sized files, so instead I now faced 343 legal-sized folders organized alphabetically. I sat on the floor in my office sorting the files by location, Staten Island, Nassau and Suffolk County, Queens, Orange County and the other upstate locations, Manhattan, Brooklyn and the Bronx. The piles grew unevenly. I was called away to attend to another task. I returned. Suddenly [came] the realization that each of these files that so filled my office floor represented the life of a person from within our community that was no more. At that moment it was impossible to not feel overwhelmed.

Identifying the services required for families of the deceased by geography enabled the decentralized offices to begin providing a broader range of services to their local communities. Following the larger informational meetings, family group meetings were then held at locations near family homes, and those informal gatherings eventually led to more formal group meetings, which are covered in Chapter 7.

Following that Thanksgiving, CSU initiated outreach for children's bereavement services. The timing of these services coincided with the holidays, which were a painful reminder of the absence of a firefighter father in the home. Throughout the fall, Father John Delendik, head of the FDNY chaplains, transported families to and from the World Trade Center site by boat. This service organized by the department was supported by CSU, who assisted in staffing the boats whenever possible, frequently assigning one of the out-of-town mental health helpers. During this time many family members wished to visit the site where the towers once stood and where their loved one had died. It was a difficult trip to make. The magnitude of the area and the amount of debris among which were scattered the remains of so many were astonishing. Somehow, arriving at the scene by boat had a calming affect on most. A memorial area near the point of disembarkment allowed family members to leave flowers or candles or words behind. Firefighters were able to help those who wished to regain a visual perspective on where the towers stood and how the recovery operation was structured. Those not wanting such information could remain at the memorial or return to the boat. These trips, along with the prayers offered by Father John, were healing and comforting to many.

FAMILY LIAISONS

Despite advances in firefighting equipment and training, as stated earlier, more than 100 firefighters die in the line of duty each year in the United States. Of these on average five are members of the FDNY. Many external groups respond to a family when a firefighter perishes in the line of duty. In New York City, often the local community around the firehouse responds immediately with cards, flowers, prepared food for the firefighters, prayers, and donations for the family of the perished. Local organizations, including Silver Shield Foundation, Fallen Hero's Heroes Fund, and Rusty Staub Foundation, to name a few, respond to future educational needs, meet immediate financial needs, and help sponsor social events for the family members. Organizations external to the FDNY, but within the firefighting community, also reach out to the family of the perished. The NFFF and the IAFF, as demonstrated by the help provided to CSU and the FDNY after 9/11, are the most prominent organizations that respond to every family whose firefighter dies in the line of duty. All the organizational resources within the FDNY, including the Uniformed Firefighters Association (UFA) and the Uniformed Fire Officers Association (UFOA), also focus their attention on the family of the perished firefighter.

In the crisis of the horrific experience of a line-of-duty death, someone needs to personalize both the firehouse family and organizational support to the family of the perished. That person is known as the *family liaison*. A family liaison is a firefighter or fire officer, generally known to the family of the perished, who volunteers to work directly with the family. The work is extremely personal. It involves assessing and meeting the practical needs of the family on a daily basis while mediating the services that the FDNY has available to the family. The family liaison must be an advocate for the family while being mindful of all the resources available to the family. In emotional turmoil, even the best organizational intentions can conflict with the family's desires. The family liaison is part of the cultural tradition of the FDNY and exemplifies the moral obligation that each firefighter feels to care for the family of the perished firefighter.

Over the years it became a tradition that one or two firefighters volunteered to perform the family liaison role and would be detailed to the family following the death. This system was effective in meeting the immediate needs of the family in the initial aftermath of the tragedy and at the time of the formal funeral services. Typically, line-of-duty deaths come with no warning. In the public process of the funeral and burial there coexists the private mourning. The out-of-town relatives need to be considered, the children may need funeral clothes, the home is often undergoing some renovation, and someone needs to organize the enormous volume of greetings and food from well-wishers. Funeral directors are often a great resource for the family and the family liaison, but they too will participate in a unique experience when 4,000 uniformed members stop by to offer their prayers and condolences.

The family liaison represents all the members of the firehouse family who need to express their commitment to assist the family of the perished. These family liaisons know the tradition of the FDNY and can interpret the traditions to the family. More critically, the family liaison can represent the decisions of the perished family members to the FDNY so tradition does not overwhelm the desires of the family to conduct a funeral and burial within the customs of that specific family. This type of contact fosters an emotional bond that is both reassuring and fragile. The interpersonal issues of a grieving family are exposed to an outsider. Family secrets are revealed. Fragile interfamilial bonds are obvious to a family liaison, and in this emotional turmoil, the boundaries of personal intimacy can pose a risk.

The tradition of the family liaison was in place at the time of 9/11. However, the system as it existed had never been put to the test of dealing with multiple deaths from multiple units all at the same time. In some situations, one family liaison was assigned to more than one family. In other situations, two family liaisons were assigned to one family. The disparity in assignment created confusion, and the length of the assignment was unclear. In previous line-of-duty deaths, remains were recovered and the family had a funeral and burial within 4 to 7 days. In the aftermath of 9/11, most families initially had no remains, so they often chose to have a memorial service. Later, for the fortunate families, funeral and burial services were held following the recovery of remains. These variables left the family liaisons with no guidelines to assist families in these painful areas, which were new experiences for both the members of the FDNY and the families of the perished.

Some fire units suffered the deaths of multiple members, which pressured some surviving members into service as family liaisons who under different circumstances would not have chosen such personal service as a role in a line-of-duty death. The other consideration was that most of the family liaisons had survived the event that took the life of their fellow firefighter. Issues of personal safety and survivor guilt were repressed by many liaisons in order to perform their role in assisting the family of the perished.

The majority of the family liaisons had their own marital families who feared for the physical and emotional health of the liaison. At a time when the family liaison could have benefited from the support of their families, the attention was focused on the family of the perished. Some family liaisons, especially those whose children were college age and young adults, included their spouses as part of the support for the family of the perished. Often this promoted a base of support that included health care and social issues for the family of the perished. Frequently in the firefighter family, the spouse takes responsibility for scheduling health care appointments and social schedules. In these situations where the family liaison and his spouse worked together, a variety of issues could be effectively addressed with support from both people.

In other cases, especially when members were pressured into service as family liaisons, an individual liaison did not have the specific support to be appropriately emotionally detached from the pain of the widow. These relationships were identified in the press and resulted in painful experiences for all involved. The family liaison, the widow of the perished, the spouse of the liaison, and the children of both families all bore the pain of public scrutiny. Efforts to reach out to the family liaisons involved in these few situations were not productive. Often these relationships were in place for months when the relationships were revealed.

In planning for the future, it would be advisable to formulate some guidelines. These might be helpful to other services faced with line-of-duty deaths.

Guidelines for Family Liaisons

- Family liaisons should be selected by a company officer from volunteers.
- Two family liaisons should be assigned allowing for coverage and promoting time off.
- Assignments should be time limited to 1 or 2 weeks. If situations require, different family liaisons can be selected in specific family situations.
- Company commanders should interview family liaisons at specific intervals to learn the needs of the family of the perished and to assess the family liaisons' ability to perform the tasks.
- After the formal mourning process, the family of the perished should be assigned a firefighter to be the company contact who can report on family needs at a firehouse meeting. Appropriate support involves multiple company members in meeting the needs of the family.
- Family liaisons should be informed of additional resources available for support of families of the deceased as well as for themselves and their families, including appropriate employee assistance units.

MOVING FORWARD

Assessment of the impact of 9/11 helped CSU staff to identify individuals and groups in need and begin to create services for them. Understanding the affected community, its culture, and its way of life informed the development of effective patterns of service delivery and outreach. CSU services were consistent with its overall mission to remain connected to the lives of FDNY members and their families. It was understood that service needs and modalities differed over time but that community always needed to be preserved. The initial response consisted primarily of education, mostly around trauma and bereavement; case finding in the workplace and home; and general strategies to promote listening, ventilation, acceptance, and retelling.

On November 11, 2001, 2 months after 9/11, another tragedy struck the FDNY community when American Airlines Flight 587 crashed in Far Rockaway, Queens, killing all 260 on board and 5 on the ground, and destroying several houses in an area densely populated by firefighters. CSU was central in providing on-site response to that disaster, organized immediately by firefighters who lived in the area. This additional tragedy so close on the heels of

9/11 increased the traumatic response of many who were holding their reactions at bay while they continued to work on the recovery of remains.

The systems and procedures CSU put into place in those first days, weeks, and months after 9/11 formed a base for the services that would emerge over the next few years. They continued to introduce new innovative services in response to the needs presented by the FDNY community. Outreach was conducted via newsletters, videos, and mailings, and the programs developed supported the community through memorials, funerals, and anniversaries. (For more on program development see Chapter 4.)

After the initial phase, services were more focused around structuring groups and individual treatment, identifying premorbid factors likely to increase traumatic response, and providing psychological evaluations and more complex treatment strategies. As needs were identified, programs were developed for addressing family changes in survivors, developmental changes in children with new understanding and additional questions about the events of 9/11, and organizational changes resulting from the unprecedented numbers of retirements, promotions, and special assignments. These and other emerging needs created an adaptive pattern of CSU services, committed to long-term connection to the community.

DEFINING A TIMELINE FOR YOUR COMMUNITY

While the dynamics of each community are different, certain lessons from the CSU experience can help any employee assistance program or team of mental health professionals responding to a community in the aftermath of disaster. Principles that informed the CSU strategy and those that have evolved as a result of this experience include the value of long-term commitment, on-site services, whole-family support, and need-driven assistance. Understanding the community's culture and identifying and utilizing the natural resources of the community to provide strength-based interventions can enable service providers to assist workers and families when needs are identified. For CSU, disseminating information about its purpose and mission has proven effective. Counseling has now become widely accepted within the FDNY, and inhibitions about utilizing these services will never be the same. From September 11, 2001, to June 30, 2005, CSU and its outside consultants saw 10,741 clients.

Any employee assistance or community-based program serving first responders should attempt to make itself known ahead of time so that those who may have need of it in the aftermath of a disaster will know to access services. Becoming a known entity in the external provider community via participation on committees and the like can help an internal organization legitimize itself ahead of time, which may ease the difficulty of securing funding for needed services when the time comes.

Important in developing successful collaboration is to identify outside partners who have a commitment to provide services for the entire duration that they are needed and to combine well with the preexisting skills of an organization. The first step in this process is to understand the gaps in services. Aside from outside partners, natural supports for assistance may also emerge. For instance, widows from previous tragedies showed up to provide support at some of the informal family meetings CSU organized in local offices. They offered to help with outreach and informal events where they could assist and share their experiences with others. A second step is to screen the outside partners offering services to understand their role and assess their skills. This required detailed organization to maximize services and focus attention to the community's agenda, rather than imposing a new one. The most successful collaborations emerge from programs that have a skill set to provide a service the internal organization does not readily have the means to provide and from outside partners who enable open communication.

Organizationally, good principles for management, communication, strategic planning, and delegating responsibility are essential. CSU was relatively small when 9/11 occurred, which inhibited spending and use of resources in some ways, while in other ways it necessitated the range of creativity that allowed for adaptive programs to emerge. In a crisis situation, knowledge of one's own organization can help circumvent worst scenarios. A helpful exercise in crisis management planning is to envision worst and best scenarios in a workplace and a community. This can give insight into politicization, competition for resources, funding snags, and other issues that could emerge and hinder program development. Knowledge of one's own organization and outside resources can also help when program developers and coordinators need to conserve their energy and choose their own battles. From its early days as a counseling unit for alcohol abuse, CSU still has the Serenity Prayer on the refrigerator in the kitchen, which serves as a reminder to accept what is beyond one's control when trying to respond to chaos and crisis.

When faced with a crisis, the inevitable feeling of helplessness should be turned into planning, and leaders should be pulled into a room away from the chaos to plan. This can help reduce the frenetic feeling of rushing into everything and accomplishing little, which is so common when responding to such events. If services are needed on a large scale geographically, as was the case for CSU after 9/11, it is important to decentralize services or otherwise adapt to make services readily accessible to the community. CSU focused on creating a strategy for defining and assessing the community, determining who needed what services, and when and how these services would be provided. Needs were identified utilizing both peers and professionals from the CSU staff, with a primary mission of supporting and reinforcing the natural resiliency of the community. While it is anticipated that help will continue to be needed to for a long time to come, it is equally important to recognize and credit the internal strengths of both the individuals and the organization and acknowledge the gains that are made as the entire community moves forward.

CHAPTER 3

Understanding Culture

In the firehouse, the old expression is, if he's thin skinned, you keep hitting him, until he learns to toughen up. You can't be thin skinned in the fire department. You have to have a real thick skin, because that's what we do.—high-ranking chief

They break your chops when you're new. They break everyone's chops. Everyone gets it, buckets of water from the roof, you know, they make you start the saw when you're doing the rope, and they dump a five-gallon bucket during the warm weather, and everyone is fair game. You know, everyone gets it. They dump it on the bosses here. You always have to look up when you're walking in from a run, because the other company—it's like company rivalry—who can get each other? When you're a probie, they flour you. They Saran Wrapped me to the table for my birthday and put the cake in my face. But if you can't handle that—if you can't handle having your chops broke, being embarrassed—you're not going to be able to handle it in a really bad situation when you're placed on the line, there's a kid screaming, the fire's coming down the hallway, and you're like, "I can't do this." And they're screaming at you, "Let's go!" That's why they do it, but they're not going to tell you that. They just see if you can handle it.—young fireman

WHILE MEMBERS of the community of the New York City Fire Department are no strangers to the imminent presence of death, the enormity of losing 343 men in one day, unprecedented in the history of firefighting, continues to reshape the cultural framework of life within the organization. In the entire United States, there was an average of 116 line-of-duty firefighter deaths per annum between 1977 and 2000, compared to the 446 that died in 2001 (including the 343 who died at the World Trade Center; FEMA, 2004). In the FDNY, approximately five firefighters die per year in the line of duty.

In order to provide effective mental health services to any community, a thorough understanding of the culture and way of life of its members is essential. Traditions founded in the history of firefighting in the city, the formal and informal code of ethics by which the FDNY lives today, the familial structures both in and out of the firehouse, and everyday experiences of firefighters and their families form the key that unlocks the cultural identity of the FDNY. The nature of the FDNY and the community surrounding it form a specific culture forged in the common history, tradition, and way of life of its members. Many of those cultural traits have been altered by 9/11 and its effects.

The experience of that community since September 11 is also unique and adds to the pool of historical experience that shapes FDNY culture. The unremitting media attention paid to the survivors has been astounding and continues in a new strain, though not always as positive as in the immediate aftermath. The politics surrounding the 9/11 tragedy, which have led to the war on terror, remain another constant reminder of the grief of the FDNY. A very public community of mourning was formed within the United States and in other countries, providing both support and a sort of celebrity status to many firefighters, as well as families and friends of those who died. The sheer number of families who lost a firefighter father, husband, brother, or son that day creates a phenomenon the likes of which has never been seen before in the continental United States. Most of the fathers who died were, in fact, very present in the home due to the two 24-hour shifts they worked per week (known within the FDNY as 24s) and played a co-primary-caregiver role with their children. The loss of so many in one workplace and in such a family-oriented community where generation after generation joins the department is also unique and demands our attention.

The cultural norms of the FDNY dictate a tendency to reject outside help. This tendency stems from a cultural attribute that prevails throughout the FDNY community—incredible fortitude. However, this resilience and calm under pressure also has aided in the recovery of the FDNY community. The concept of "the Brotherhood" and the close, family-oriented community that binds firefighters provide an unusually cohesive support network. There is natural cohesiveness in life-threatening work and in the shared experience of traumatic events, and, as stated in Chapter 2, firefighters generally identify their firehouse and others within their community as their primary supports. For this reason, recovery efforts that came from within the community and embraced FDNY traditions, morals, and sentiments have been the most utilized. Programs such as the Firehouse Clinicians for active-duty members, the FDNY/Columbia University Family Program for families of the deceased,

Couples Connection for families of survivors, and Stay Connected for retirees are featured in this book and illustrate the effort to build on preexisting strengths of the community. This strategy of providing support through existing family and community networks has been found to be effective in disaster response efforts (Zinner & Williams, 1999).

Some of the ripple effects of 9/11 that have reshaped the culture of the department include the restructuring of the demographics of the department, a reworking of familial relationships, changes in procedure, not to mention the immeasurable psychological toll. One firefighter who was active in the recovery effort at the World Trade Center commented that the FDNY will not return to normal until the last guy present at the World Trade Center retires, which could be 20 years or more (Linkh, 2005). Mass retirements after 9/11 have brought a younger group of firefighters into the houses. Many firefighters have moved more swiftly up in the ranks due to the large number of officers who perished, 6 percent of the total command staff, and those who retired, nearly 11 percent of the total command staff. Family members once kept in the dark about the dangers of the job have become rapidly aware of the experience of the firefighters, and discussions at home often contain more realistic details and sentiments. Nonetheless the horrific details of 9/11 and the many months of searching through the rubble have left scars in the minds of the firefighters that only they can own. Their shared experience and shared grief has both challenged and strengthened their bond and the bond of the community that surrounds them, now encompassing the pain of losing so many. This familial and cultural closeness both intensified the pain and helped heal it.

CULTURAL IDENTITY

While most historians, authors, and journalists who write about the FDNY speak openly about the existence of an FDNY culture and firefighters themselves refer to their jobs as a "way of life," in writing an ethnographic exploration, or cultural interpretation, of the FDNY, it is helpful to explore some of the varied ways in which anthropologists define and examine culture. British anthropologist Edward Tylor attempted to create a technical definition of culture in the 19th century, calling it "socially patterned human thought and behavior" (Bodley, 2000). Anthropologists vary greatly in their understandings of the meaning of culture, and most choose to focus on one or a few elements of culture or a particular definition of culture in order to understand the group they are studying. Narrowing down the many definitions is a task in itself, and the complexity of culture is easily misinterpreted.

"By 'culture' anthropology means the total life way of a people, the social legacy the individual acquires from his group," said anthropologist Clyde Kluckhohn (1949, p. 24). He sees a close relationship between cultural and biological determinism in forming the way an individual lives. "All men undergo the same poignant life experiences such as birth, helplessness, illness, old age, and death. The biological potentialities of the species are the blocks with which cultures are built," he said. Kluckhohn's notion that "culture channels biological processes" is based on the assumption that societies create and transmit culture. With its intangible nature, culture can only be seen in the "regularities in the behavior or artifacts of a group that has adhered to a common tradition." The FDNY certainly has a common tradition and transfers it to future generations, thus carrying on its way of life from "a storehouse of the pooled learning of the group" (Kluckhohn, 1949). The events of 9/11 and the shared experience of trauma and loss have added to that pooled learning, and they also are being passed on to future generations and somewhat modifying the society's cultural practices and way of life to fit the new circumstances.

Raymond Williams, an early pioneer in the field of cultural studies, emphasizes in his writings the everyday lived experience of culture. "A culture," Williams said, "has two aspects: the known meanings and directions, which its members are trained to; the new observations and meanings which are offered and tested" (Williams, 1958). In this text, *community* is used to describe both the FDNY workforce and their extended family and friends in their places of work and neighborhoods. Anthropologist Margaret Mead refers to an Anglo-Saxon ideal understanding of community

> in which people live together in voluntary co-operation, helping each other, caring for the widows and orphans, and keeping themselves unspotted from the world. . . . (Mead, 1966)

Mead's definition captures the support structures alive within the FDNY community. For the purposes of this ethnography and this book, the FDNY community should be understood as a social system within which firefighters, their families, and friends live and through which FDNY culture manifests.

Clifford Geertz emphasizes the importance of the interpretation of meaning in studying culture. Geertz, an anthropologist, sees systems of meaning as the collective property of a group that makes up a culture. According to Geertz, a deeper understanding of culture is necessary, and this is only to be gained through "thick description" or a cultural analysis of the individual's experience in a particular culture without superimposing the cultural framework of the observer. The analysis, Geertz says, should be "not an experimental science in search of law, but an interpretive one in search of meaning" (Geertz, 1973). Throughout its history, CSU has sought this meaning, taking the needs of the FDNY community first and designing interventions around them, and outside helpers have been taught to work within the cultural framework of the community.

We learn culture from belonging, and we share that learned behavior with those who belong to us, and it becomes our social legacy. Our culture determines how we will behave in certain situations and is the prism through which we interpret the behavior of others. While it is important to understand that culture is not the universal determinant of the path of an individual, its power to regulate our behavior and our everyday experiences can be on a subconscious level and therefore should be accounted for in providing therapeutic services. Kluckhohn writes:

> Culture regulates our lives at every turn. From the moment we are born until we die there is, whether we are conscious of it or not, constant pressure upon us to follow certain types of behavior that other men have created for us. Some paths we follow willingly, others we follow because we know no other way, still others we deviate from or go back to most unwillingly. (Kluckhohn, 1949)

In *Mirror for Man*, Kluckhohn likens culture to a map, which when properly drawn can help one accurately chart a course through the life of a society. In exploring FDNY culture, we attempt, as accurately as possible, to map, in a particular period in history, the lives of individuals belonging to that society and carrying on the subconscious and conscious aspects of its culture every day. The learned behaviors of FDNY firefighters and their families stem from a long history and tradition in New York City and beyond, a regimented lifestyle dedicated to altruism and control over one of nature's most deadly forces set loose in an urban environment, as well as many ethnic and religious commonalities.

The FDNY's experience with the events of 9/11 also should be seen through the prism of history and politics as the context in which the stories of the individuals in the community take shape. Culture can be seen as a fluid process shaped by many elements, including history. "The difficulty with naive interpretations of culture in terms of individual behavior is not that these interpretations are those of psychology, but that they ignore history and the historical process of acceptance or rejection of traits," writes Ruth Benedict (Benedict, 1934). Historical events have a profound effect on behaviors within cultures at any point in time. The experience of the FDNY community is best understood using Geertz's model of "thick description" and interpreting the meanings of culture through the eyes of those who are living it day to day. The changes occurring within the FDNY, as with any group, should be examined in their cultural, psychological, historical, and political context. In interpreting the culture of the FDNY as a Brotherhood, it is helpful to quote Benedict, who said, "What really binds men together is their culture—the ideas and the standards they have in common" (Benedict, 1934).

APPLYING CULTURAL IDENTITY TO INTERVENTION

Internal community responses to disaster have an advantage in that the culture of the affected population is already interwoven with the experiences of service providers. CSU put that advantage to good use, but given the huge scope of the event, people outside the department also had to be trained to understand the ethics, mentality, and culture of FDNY firefighters and their families. Methods of such training should include an initial cultural analysis to better comprehend the threads that make up the fabric of the community and, of course, peer introduction, which CSU employed.

For any community affected by traumatic events, mass violence, and disaster, interventionists should take into account family structure and relationships, workplace interactions, history, social status, ethnicity, and tradition. The primary way to understand such aspects of life within a particular culture is through observation, ideally as a participant; deep immersion into a culture can provide such insight.

In the case of mental health services, where the ultimate goal is to provide interaction that will inevitably modify the experience of members of a particular culture, one should anticipate apprehension. The approach therefore must be nonthreatening and adaptive. The innovative programs of CSU demonstrate methods of accessing and assisting a community without threatening its way of life.

Checklist for Understanding the Culture of a Community

✓ Understand the history and traditions
  • Use written and oral history, legends, personal stories.
  • Explore historical events that have shaped contemporary everyday life, attributes, and traditions a community has adopted.

✓ Process of enculturation (process of learning a culture and assimilating)
  • Gain acceptance and trust through direct participation or peer introduction.
  • Be nonthreatening and adaptive, open to new ideas.

✓ Understand everyday life
  • Different settings (i.e., family, workplace).
  • Behavior and customs (i.e., learned behavior of a group, support systems, ethics, values).

✓ Understand additional cultural factors
  • Ethnicity, religion, economy, gender issues.
  • What increases group cohesion?

✓ Understand interaction of culture with other groups and communities

✓ Understand cultural influences that affect individual behavior

---

Exploring the Culture of the Brotherhood and the Impact of 9/11

To grasp a better understanding of "the Brotherhood," the name firefighters use for their culture, this cultural exploration aims to answer the following questions:

- What are the personal stories of community members?
  How did they become involved in the FDNY or the community?
  How long have they or their family been in the department?
  What was their experience within the FDNY like?
- FDNY tradition
  How do members understand the code of ethics?
  What are some examples of written and unwritten laws?
  What taboos, expectations, and learned behaviors are there?
  How does the Brotherhood function as an organization?

A second set of questions relates to the impact of 9/11 on the community:

- What changes have occurred in everyday life in the firehouse and community?
- What procedures, written and unwritten laws, taboos, and norms have been tested or modified by the event?
- How has the media attention to the event and the hero status given to firefighters been perceived?
- What supports have firefighters relied on?
- What impact did the prolonged recovery effort at the World Trade Center site have?
- Has 9/11 strengthened the bond of the Brotherhood and the community?
- Did 9/11 cause any permanent changes to FDNY culture?

Most in the FDNY lost family members or close friends at the World Trade Center, and all had felt the sorrow and pain of the community that surrounds them. It is important to note at the outset that the impact on the FDNY is immeasurable and ongoing and therefore difficult to interpret or analyze so soon after the event.

FIREFIGHTING HISTORY AND TRADITION IN NEW YORK

Most people within the FDNY today maintain that firefighters would do their jobs even for nothing, and in the humble beginnings of firefighting in the city they did. Firefighting in New Amsterdam was initially aided by the entire community. Although there were eight official wardens, each male citizen was required to take a turn on watch. Fires at that time were fought with buckets, hooks, and ladders, paid for by fines for dirty chimneys in accordance with the Fire Ordinance of 1648. A night patrol known as "the prowlers" and sometimes called "rattle watch" checked for fires at night. In 1658, 250 leather buckets were provided by Dutch shoemakers to form the first bucket brigades (FDNY, 2005). In colonial New Amsterdam under Peter Stuyvesant, the first firefighters, volunteers, were primarily Dutch immigrants. Residents of the city would leave buckets of water outside their doors for firefighters to collect and would be able to pick them up outside City Hall when the fire had been extinguished (Golway, 2002).

In 1731, the Common Council of New York appointed two people from each ward as "viewers of Chimneys and Hearths," as the increasing size of the city and value of the property on the island of Manhattan required a more organized system. In an attempt to prevent fires, the city began issuing fines of 40 shillings to residents whose chimneys caught fire. The city obtained two hand-pumped engines in December 1731, named Engine Co. 1 and Engine Co. 2. Still, fires were fought by citizens. Alderman John Roosevelt was named overseer of the engines with 12 pounds as his annual salary, and the first two firehouses were built near City Hall. In 1737, the Common Council created the fire department. It had approval to hire 42 "strong, able, discreet, honest and sober men" as firemen (Golway, 2002). While the firefighters were now trained, they were still without salary and held various day jobs as everything from blacksmiths and carpenters to bankers. The firemen were compensated with exemption from militia and jury service. The number of firefighters gradually increased throughout the 1700s, as did the number of engine companies.

Many of New York's firemen enlisted with the American patriots during the American Revolution and fought for independence from Great Britain. When the British took control of the city on September 15, 1776, so many of the city's firemen were in rebel camps north of Manhattan with George Washington's army that when a fire broke out in the Fighting Cocks tavern on September 21, the city lit up and the blaze destroyed more than 500 buildings, roughly 25 percent of the city, and left thousands of residents homeless. The Americans took control in 1783, and in 1786 a new fire department was formed, consisting of 300 men, 15 engine companies, and two hook-and-ladder companies. Most of the hundreds of firefighters who had stayed on duty under British rule were ousted from the department, although a handful remained. One engineer who had remained loyal to the city, William Ellsworth, eventually got the title of chief engineer, equivalent to the chief of department today (Golway, 2002).

POLITICS AND DEFIANCE

Firefighters throughout history have been known to be at loggerheads with politicians. It could be said that the separatism and political defiance that still exist within the department today were initially forged after the American Revolution when fire companies were given the privilege to elect their own foremen in 1792. Historian Lowell M. Limpus referred to this system as a "miniature republic" within the fire department (Limpus, 1940). Firemen shared a strong bond with their foremen, just as firefighters today share a similar bond with their officers due to the common dangers of their jobs. The firemen also set up and controlled a special fund at the end of the 18th century to raise money for families of disabled firemen (Golway, 2002). This is an early example of the tradition of taking care of families of fallen firefighters; the UFA today has a fund for widows and children of firefighters who die in the line of duty.

Despite the new ability to elect foremen, firefighters were still under the command of politicians at fire scenes until 1805, when chiefs were given authority. Fire brigades still traveled on foot, with company foremen using speaking trumpets to clear the streets. After a large fire in late 1796, the Common Council began buying the department better equipment, including hoses. In the early 1820s, the department had grown to include 1,200 firefighters, 46 engine companies, four hook-and-ladder companies, and one hose company (Golway, 2002). Throughout history and today, bad fires inspired necessary innovations in equipment. In January 2005 three firefighters had to jump from a burning building and two of them perished, causing the fire department to issue new ropes.

As New York City expanded, the fire department grew along with it, and throughout the years, the dangers of fires and the job of preventing them grew. On December 16, 1835, a terrible blaze destroyed some 674 buildings in the financial district of the city and left thousands out of work, two dead, and 52 acres of lower Manhattan in seared ruins. The fire of 1835 could not equal the devastation of September 11, 2001, which covered 16 acres and had an exponentially higher death toll. Nonetheless, there were some similarities. The stock exchange stopped trading for 4 days, and the nation rallied to support New York. The 1835 blaze became known as the Great Fire (Golway, 2002).

Even during such times when the fire department was so needed in the city, politicians and firemen continued to butt heads. The Great Fire, it seemed, had even fueled the negative opinions politicians had toward the firemen. The city believed the young boys who hung around the firehouses were unruly and escalated criminality at fire scenes. However, firemen often defended those boys from criticism due to the help they provided and the fact that many of them eventually joined the fire department (Golway, 2002).

In 1836, the problems between firemen and politicians turned violent when the authority of Alderman Samuel Purdy was defied and he was assaulted by members of a fire company rushing to the scene of a fire. The brawl led to the arrest of two firemen, Luke Usher and John Lightbody. A large group of firemen attempted to rescue Usher and Lightbody by storming the city's watch house but were turned away. A resolution that required the fire department "to prevent all persons not belonging to the department, and especially boys, from entering any house or handling any apparatus belonging to the department" was ignored by even the highest-ranking man in the department at the time, James Gulick. In May of the same year, after an outburst in opposition to criticism of the department at a meeting of the Common Council, Chief Engineer Gulick got word of the city's plans to fire him and walked away in protest from a blaze in the city. The firemen at the scene reversed their hats in protest of the city's plans and left the fire burning, declaring that they would not work without Gulick. After that, Gulick was removed from his post and replaced with John Riker, who was formerly an assistant engineer, one of the few paid jobs in the department at the time, with a salary of $500 a year. Livid ranks of firemen drew up a petition to reinstate Gulick, protested throughout the summer, and on September 21 carried out their threat to walk off the job. Between 600 and 800 firemen, roughly half the entire force, marched to City Hall to resign. When the city still refused to fire Riker and give Gulick his job back, the Resigned Firemen's Association was created, and the firemen went into politics, nominating Gulick for the post of city register. In an unprecedented upset helped by the support of the Whig Party, Gulick won the election.

By December of that year, another fireman, Morris Franklin, who Gulick had rescued from a blaze in 1832, was elected to a seat in the General Assembly, again with the help of the Whigs. The next spring, the Resigned Firemen's Association backed the Whigs again and managed to get Tammany out of the mayoral seat and deplete its majority in the Common Council. Riker was fired, and a friend of Gulick's, Cornelius Andersen, was made chief engineer. The city repealed the annual salary given to assistant engineers, which many firemen saw as an insult to the job, and many of the resigned firefighters once again joined the force (Golway, 2002).

Firefighters still do not hesitate to stand together and fight for what they believe in. In October 2001 the city decreased the number of firefighters allowed at the World Trade Center site to 25 workers from 64. Firefighters were reluctant to leave the scene, determined to continue at the same pace to recover the remains of all of their fallen brothers. On November 2, 2001, they held a protest at City Hall, and a fight broke loose between the New York City Police Department (NYPD) and the FDNY. Police began arresting firefighters, and among those in danger of being arrested was a young firefighter. The officers at the scene knew he would lose his job over such a violation while they, with more seniority, would only be reprimanded. To protect the young firefighter, they told him to run and distracted the police. In the end, 18 were arrested for harassment or criminal trespass and one for assault. All charges were eventually dropped by the city to patch up relations between the NYPD and the FDNY, which had grown closer than ever in the weeks after 9/11 (Cardwell, 2001).

COMPANY RIVALRY

After the firemen's move into political life in the 1800s, New York's streets were filling up with gangs and street brawlers. Many of the firemen also were involved in the politically and otherwise motivated gangs, including William M. Tweed and the most famous firefighter of the era, Moses Humphreys, otherwise known as "Old Mose," leader of the Bowery B'hoys. Old Mose became a legend in New York and the subject of plays. "He swilled beer from a fifty-gallon keg attached to his belt, and he feasted on copious amounts of oysters and beef, leaving the rest of the city in short supply" (Golway, 2002). Moses Humphreys was an Irish-American fireman in a time when the Irish made up only 7 percent of the department. A tradition still alive today was prevalent in the time of Old Mose—fire companies gave themselves nicknames. Humphreys worked for Engine Co. 40, which called itself Lady Washington's Company. That company became famous for brawling with other firemen in the chase to get to fires first. While Gulick had tried to stamp out "firehouse rowdies," the era of gang warfare in New York City was strongly reflected in the ranks of firemen. Historian Terry Golway describes the enthusiasm with which rival companies raced to a fire first:

> The first company at the fire scene was accorded the honor of extinguishing the blaze. Trailing companies, if they were needed, were deployed to the drudge work of delivering water from a reservoir or cistern through a relay system of pumpers. So when an alarm sounded and firemen hitched themselves to their wagons, the race, a real race, was on. Many companies, when confronted with crowded streets, jumped curbs and hauled their engines along sidewalks, to the dismay and occasional horror of the general public. Some firemen, to get a jump on the competition, began sleeping at firehouses. (Golway, 2002)

A legendary brawl ignited between Engine Co. 15 and Lady Washington's Co. 40 in the summer of 1838. The members of the two firehouses, who regularly raced one another to fires in lower Manhattan, decided to settle their disputes after battling a prolonged blaze near Wall Street. The fight broke out around Mulberry Street, near Engine Co. 15's firehouse, and stories claim that anywhere from hundreds of men to a thousand were involved in the brawl. The great brawler Old Mose was knocked out by Henry Chanfrau from Engine Co. 15, which finally ended the fight. Similar brawls continued to ensue throughout the mid-1800s, and the gang violence within the city became loosely affiliated with certain fire companies (Golway, 2002).

To a lesser degree today than in the great brawls of the 1800s, rivalry between companies is still much a part of firefighting. The primary arena for playing out this rivalry today is through sports, but the competitive feeling still sometimes works its way into emergency response duty. One rescue company is known for stealing other companies' lines at fires. Inevitably, when they do this, a fistfight breaks out. When they finish using the line, sometimes after having unraveled the hose and dragged it through a building or up a staircase, they close it and leave it there for the other company to pick up. Another company, known as "the gentlemen of the rescue teams," is known for sending more guys up, two to hold the line and two to fight off the rescue company trying to steal their line.

In general, racing other companies to fires is fairly uncommon in the department today. While some speed is necessary in getting to a fire, most would let the company ahead of them take the fire. Companies are still competitive about response time, however, the statistics for which are recorded in department reports and in newspapers. Still, racing to fires is not unheard of. On the "housewatch," or the duty chart in the firehouse, each company receives tickets telling them whether they are on first or second due. First-due assignments tell that house it should be the first to respond to a call, whereas second due means the firefighters should be there to help the company on first due. There are some tickets, or boxes, for which both firehouses are called and the first to respond performs the first-due tasks. One firefighter described a race to a fire that took a dangerous turn for the company involved:

> Some other companies, not to name, some other boroughs, race to boxes, because they don't have enough fires. They're very gung ho, which is not a bad thing, but they race. They're speeding too fast some times. A friend of mine, who was covering out there, first tour as a captain, they go into a second-due gas leak, which is most of the time a stove that has to be shut off. It's an emergency, but it's not life and death right away, unless they say fire and gas. This company lost control of the rig, the fire truck, and went careening into a building . . . all for nothing, to race another company when they were second due.

Needless to say, the brawling of the 1800s did not soften the harsh criticism the department continued to receive from city officials. Several chief engineers tried to push for reforms in the department and often blamed the government for the problems of violence and fighting. Volunteer firemen in the city began to receive extensive criticism in the press about their methods of fire protection throughout the Civil War, when riots were common in the city, and there was a new push to establish a professional, paid department. The *New York*

Times called the existing volunteer department a "hot-bed of profligacy and crime" (Golway, 2002). Though the department fought against a bill set into motion to disband the volunteers and establish a paid fire department run by the state rather than the city, business interests, concerned primarily about insurance, prevailed, and the Metropolitan Fire Department took over in 1865. Though the volunteers were out, their influence on firefighting in the city would remain:

> They were often their own worst enemies. But they offered their service with no strings attached, no demands for rewards other than public recognition. They sought excitement, yes, and sometimes took advantage of their celebrity, but they remained, in their public image, selfless men who dared to face and defeat a relentless foe. The new Department would have to live up to that legacy. (Golway, 2002)

MODERN FIREFIGHTING IN NEW YORK CITY

Today, the FDNY is very much an institution with a history rooted in and intertwined with the economic growth of New York City. The bravery and camaraderie of the early volunteer firefighters, as well as their machismo, abhorrence of politicians, and separatist nature, are very much a part of the culture of the Brotherhood today. As seen in the political strife of New York's past, firefighters have always played an important role in American history, and the department has always been impacted by historical events. Their popularity among young men in the city is still a driving force enticing new blood to enter the ranks each year. It is still especially common for young boys to hang around firehouses, ride the rigs, and become captivated by the legendary New York City firemen. Their role in 9/11, their exploitable fame after the event, and their place in the headlines of local and national news media are of historical significance and can reshape the organization and its culture.

In a city so sprawling and so modern, the tasks of firefighting are incalculably great and require a well-oiled organization. While most firefighters will say that their own firehouse is the best place to work, some thrive on working in midtown Manhattan, and others prefer the outer boroughs. The job differs greatly in those locations. Midtown Manhattan does not get as many calls, but when firefighters are called to a fire it is generally a more difficult task to put it out, not simply because of the enormous size of the buildings, but also because of the cost of the structures. Firefighters working in the outer boroughs see themselves as envied by other firefighters due to the fact that they receive a greater number of calls. Rescue 2 brags on its web site that it operates in "the Boro of Fires," Brooklyn, and the web site contains statistics of the large number of runs the company has per annum. Most fires outside Manhattan are in residential buildings, and firefighters generally do not have to worry about breaking down a door to get inside or breaking a window to help subdue the blaze. In Manhattan, however, they have to be more careful and often have to wait for expensive doors to be removed before they can get at the fire.

A firefighter stationed in the Bronx, whose father was a captain in a Midtown firehouse before his death at the World Trade Center, explained the difference between work in the Bronx and Midtown:

> We're very informal here. I mean downtown, they're in a different atmosphere than up here, as you see. They're dealing with people who are important, and not that these people aren't important, but people who are important to the world, people in suits. They can't break doors randomly, not that we do. It's tough to describe, but they have to step back sometimes, unless it's a fire emergency. They have to go about it the wrong . . . you know, maybe wait until the guy unlocks, because it's a $1,000 door or $3,000 door. Here, you know, we break the door. The cops stay there. The super comes in and replaces the door. It's all covered in the rent. This is 99 percent residential, but it's a very downtrodden area. This is where most firemen want to work. It's busy.

During what are known in FDNY history as "the War Years," the Bronx was in fact the busiest borough of the city for firefighters. From the mid-1960s to the late 1970s, many fires were deliberately set in the Bronx for insurance payoffs, and firefighters were constantly responding to alarms (Golway, 2002). The variation in the job requirements in working in different areas in the city attest to the multiple differences in the workplace of individual firehouses. The fire department currently consists of more than 11,400 officers and firefighters, 2,800 EMS workers, and 1,200 civilian employees. There are 203 engine companies and 143 ladder companies, as well as the marine division and special operations (Council of the City of New York, 2003). Each battalion chief oversees a number of firehouses in a given area, and each captain, lieutenant, and firefighter must know the fire response required of the area he or she works in.

One important fact about the job of firefighting in the City of New York today is that firefighters have an unprecedented dedication to their jobs, even when not on duty. While nearly all FDNY firefighters, both on and off duty, rushed to help at the World Trade Center tragedy, this ethic was true even before September 11 and could be seen in the fire that took place on Father's Day a few months before 9/11, when firefighters who were not on duty heard what had happened and went straight to work. Three firefighters perished in that fire. Responding even when not on duty is very common, and according to people working within the community, one of the main reasons so many firefighters died on 9/11 was that the timing of the attacks on the Twin Towers coincided with shift changes. Firefighters who were just going off duty quickly jumped on the rigs and raced down to the scene with their brothers. Others who were off duty, at home, or even on vacation raced to work to help in any way they could. Many retired firefighters also responded, and of these, sadly, one retired captain and two retired firefighters perished responding to the tragedy. Firefighters love their jobs and love fighting fires, and most share the sentiment that whenever they can be there, they will:

> These guys would go into a burning building to save a life if you paid them peanuts. That's how we are. If we're driving home and the fire's out the window down the block and the companies aren't at the door, you know we're going to go in. We're going to go in the building, with our civilian clothes, and do what we can. I love my job. I love going into a fire. It's also a Catch-22, because I don't want somebody's apartment to burn, so the best way I can say it is: we, as a fire department, want to be there when things go wrong. We don't come in to work and pray that somebody's house [burns]—because somebody's tragedy is our happiness—but we also don't want to come into work and sit around on our behinds, because it gets monotonous, you can only pull so many tools out and do so much during the day, clean so much, cook so much. . . . On the other hand, I don't want to be pulling three-year-old infants out, but we want to be there because we're trained. If somebody's having a problem, we want to be there, and I want to be the one there. You know, if I could go citywide, I would, every fire.

THE FDNY AS A PARAMILITARY ORGANIZATION

The FDNY often has been defined as a paramilitary organization. Military discipline was established due to reorganization in the department in 1866 under the command of General Alexander Schaler, which reduced fire losses at a time when major fires had caused insurance rates to increase (FDNY, 2005). Firefighters agree with the paramilitary comparison and readily point out examples of the camaraderie that exists within the firehouse, the duties they are required to perform within the rank and file, and their reliance on each other for safety. The paramilitary terminology within the organization illustrates the visible presence of that mentality, with firefighters referring to "the civilians" running the show (i.e., the commissioner and city officials), "the job," working "detail," "probies," "officers," and so on. Undoubtedly, uniformed forces that work together and rely on each other, whether fighting a fire or an army, share a similar mentality and a bond.

One clear distinction between most military action and firefighting is in the chain of command. While in military forces the high-ranking officers generally do not fight on the front lines but issue orders and send their soldiers into the fray, in FDNY procedures, the captain or highest-ranking officer of a firehouse is the first one into a burning building or dangerous situation and the last one out. The probies, or youngest members of a firehouse, are always side by side with the officer, and the captain or chief takes great pride in defending his firefighters. Thus, in action, the paramilitary makeup of the FDNY can be seen as a sort of reverse of a military chain of command. The firehouse captain's actions at fire scenes strengthen the bond between him and his brother firefighters. Thus, the respect firefighters show their captain is warmer and more like a heartfelt familial connection than a strict admiration or requirement to honor military code. Family in the firehouse can be interpreted as a strong bond to get through tough situations together and help each other out, not just in fires.

In relation to the organization's connection to firefighters' families, the FDNY also differs from most military organizations. Long after a firefighter has perished, the department maintains contact with the family and generally continues to support them. In most military establishments, however, the government will take care of a veteran, but shortly after a service person dies, the connection with the family is severed.

EVERYDAY LIFE IN THE FIREHOUSE

The communal table of the kitchen is the heart of the firehouse home. At the table, brothers convene for meals and discuss politics, women, and their daily antics, rile one another, and, in a very familial setting, plan the workday and life events. Firefighters are known for their superior cooking skills, which they demonstrate in the firehouse and in their own homes with their families. In an environment where the alarm could go off any minute calling firefighters to duty, moments at the communal table are cherished. At the table, probies and officers sit down together as brothers.

The work ethic within the firehouse is extremely strong. Each member knows the task expected of him, or in some cases her, and that it is to be completed without reluctance or resentment. This regimented style matches the way firefighters perform their duty when called out on a run. Each man knows his place and his task and relies on the others to know theirs. The cohesion of the firehouse is strengthened by a series of rituals, which of course vary from house to house. These rituals help build a family atmosphere in the house over time and a loyalty to that house, hence the disruption that can occur when the firehouse faces the loss of a member. While rank is important in the firehouse, each firefighter takes pride in his job and would defend his ability to do that job well even to a higher-ranking brother. One young firefighter, referring to his respect for the captain of his firehouse, said jokingly, "Even if it was the captain, and he tried to take my tool, I would probably hit him over the head with it," emphasizing the pride he takes in his work and the importance of the captain's trust in him to do it well.

Within each firehouse, there are unwritten rules for jest and respect regarding the captain of the house. Each member of the house knows how far a prank is allowed to go and allows a certain amount of horsing around without crossing the lines drawn by the head of the house. The captain of the house, as history has shown, generally defends the members of his house in any situation, including those where politicians or even higher-ranking officers within the department dish out criticism. The role of the captain can be paternal in the house of brothers, and generally even nonranking senior members of a firehouse also claim a right to unofficial authority among the brothers.

Within a firehouse, brothers take care of each other in any way they can. Since firefighters' wages are very low—the average being around $35,000—many of them have second jobs. The UFA managed on November 15, 2002, to get a 2-year retrospective pay increase of 10 percent for employees of the FDNY, raising starting annual salaries of firefighters from $32,724 after a 2-year stalemate without a union contract. Firefighters in Britain have a starting salary of approximately $34,100. The highest FDNY firefighter salary is $49,023, possible after 5 years but still the maximum even after 20 years and only the seventh highest for U.S. cities of more than a million people. Veteran firefighters in Los Angeles, CA, earn $65,748, in Yonkers, NY, $54,211. Veterans in Newark, NJ, and Jersey City, NJ, also earn about $10,000 more, according to the UFA. Union firefighters in Britain are demanding about $10,500 more than the UFA (Burkeman, 2002; Weissenstein & Williams, 2002). Second jobs held by firefighters cover a broad range of skills—some work in construction or carpentry, while others work as substitute teachers. In such situations, firefighters often have to swap duty with other firefighters in order to make ends meet. This is done very casually and usually does not go through the job, meaning no official departmental approval is requested. Firefighters trading, shortening shifts, or filling in for each other call such favors *mutuals.* On a similar note, firefighters needing extra work will often mention something to the others at the firehouse who will make an effort to provide connections for odd jobs they know of.

As true brothers, firemen within any given house generally also spend time together socially. Firefighters often play sports as a house and compete against other companies. Most firehouses feature a display of trophies won at such events. Some firehouses display their pride in other collective successes, such as pipe and drum band trophies and awards. Also common among firefighters is an ethic to help each other with work on their homes. Such a group activity is usually conceived of as a sort of social gathering, complete with food, drinks, and family. All in all, firehouses emanate a feeling that can usually only be found in large but close families, and many firefighters consider their firehouse to be their second family. This feeling, natural to their line of work, includes a shared passion to rescue. For example, in one case when a firefighter's house burned down, the others helped him rebuild completely. The cultural obligation to provide this kind of assistance, as well as the mutuals in the firehouse, increased after 9/11.

RITUALS AND RANK

Probationary firefighters, or *probies,* are firefighters that have not yet completed their first year in the department. New firefighters initially are stationed at a house and then begin a process of rotation, in which they are trained and serve at different houses in order to get a feel for the job. When a new member joins a firehouse from the fire academy, otherwise known as The Rock, the probie is generally put through a series of rituals before he or she is accepted as an experienced firefighter. While some of it is intense training and drilling that all firefighters must do, the initiation can also be seen as ritual hazing. After the rotation period, a probie is given a permanent placement in a firehouse. Even after their first year, and throughout their careers, firefighters are still subject to a certain degree of hazing.

While these rituals may seem like brotherly pranks and may at times even seem extremely cruel, members of the FDNY understand them as a way to test probies and firefighters to make sure they can remain calm under pressure. The degree and range of hazing vary from firehouse to firehouse, but the purpose is understood throughout. For members of a firehouse to be certain that a probie will not lose his or her cool in a burning building where people need to be rescued, the hazing rituals provide reassurance and a certain level of trust, firefighters say. Obviously, such rituals could lead to confusion or resentment if the probie does not understand the FDNY's unwritten code on the matter.

Of course, hazing is common in many fraternal organizations and men's clubs, including ball clubs and military organizations, and is generally widely accepted when it serves as a means to an end in a society. Whatever hazing symbolizes for a particular organization—bonding, trust—the public and authority figures generally view it as good, clean fun, at least until a line is crossed. With the great rise to fame the FDNY experienced after 9/11, the image of some firefighters has now taken a fall, and they are often scrutinized for the instances of brutality that rarely emerge in the hazing rituals of firehouse culture. Stories of the wild behavior of firefighters make the front pages, and readers look for someone to blame. The innocence society expects of heroes sometimes falls short with the firefighters, who have long lived in a tradition of daring machismo. The nature of the dangerous work firefighters do every day perpetuates the need for humor to ease the tension on the job and enhance camaraderie.

In the procedures at the FDNY Fire Academy, or "The Rock," located on Randall's Island in the East River, probies, regardless of their background, are taught that they are all equal. Former stockbrokers, investment bankers, and CPAs are trained alongside carpenters and construction workers, cops, sanitation workers, and corrections officers. The training is focused to extinguish any superior or inferior sentiments in order for firefighters to function as a team and rely on one another to ensure each other's safety. The training facility is much like an army base in appearance and atmosphere. The buildings are structured with entrances hidden in enormous pipe shafts. Inside there are sayings on the wall to remind the probies of the codes of the organization and their dedication to their fellow firefighters and old firefighting equipment is on display to remind them of the many who served before them. One firefighter described the experience probies have at The Rock as a sort of boot camp:

> It's very militaristic. Some guys make fun of it, but they need to [have it that way. If] they have 250 guys running around not structured, it would be a nightmare, so they yell at them, they make them do pushups if they screw up. They don't know where they're going . . . if they ask them a question about firefighting, they don't know it—"Get down and give me 20." It's like a boot camp, but it's good, it kind of brings everybody down to the same level. Some guys are bankers. A kid that was in the academy with me, was a CPA or something like that. Took a huge pay cut to get on this job because his father was in this job. He came down, he wasn't happy. You know some guys think they're better than others, so they hammer everyone to be the same, because we're all the same.

The importance of following leadership is taught in this early education and throughout the firefighter's career, and the 9/11 response reflects this.

Probies initially often rotate among several firehouses. When a probie first begins working within a particular firehouse, he or she is generally given the least desirable chores around the house first, such as washing dishes, followed by stripping the beds and washing the sheets. On the engine or ladder (*ladder* is the official name, but in general firehouse vernacular, the ladder is referred to as "the truck"), the probie has the lowest task and slowly works up level by level to use higher-ranked tools. Probies accept their assignments and strive to gain the respect of the brothers in the house by reacting to hazing rituals with a clear head and cheerful spirit and performing the tasks designated them to the best of their ability. A high-ranking chief described the probie's experience in the firehouse this way:

> It's department-wide, because you're being brought into this fraternity, this Brotherhood. It's really, you know, now you're accepted, you're getting doused

with a bucket of water, or you're cleaning the dishes for the first six months that you're in there, or you're doing all the chores around the house. That has a dual purpose—doing all the chores around the house. It shows two things. It shows that, hey, you're down at the bottom of the totem pole right now, but it also gets the probies familiar with all the tools that are on the rig. It shows them exactly how each tool is cleaned, how you use it, so it's got a dual purpose. While people think it's a hazing, it's really getting them familiar with the tools, but telling them, hey, you're cleaning all the stuff for a while.

It takes years to really know the job, and the constant training and support from officers enable firefighters to reach that level. After serving a few years as a firefighter, the next step in moving up to the position of officer is to take the lieutenant's test. Of course, some firefighters prefer to stay firefighters all their lives and never become officers, but many do take the test and move up in the ranks. The next step after lieutenant is captain, then chief. One high-positioned chief who moved up in the ranks described his path:

> I was a firefighter. I was appointed in November of 1969, and naturally having a brother in the fire department that was a lieutenant, he sort of got me interested in studying, had my books set out, so I set to studying right away, got promoted to lieutenant in 1977, captain in 1984, battalion chief in 1987, deputy chief in 1993, and then the rest is history. And September 11th, after the tragedy, I was promoted [again] the following Sunday on September 16th.

Officers in the FDNY are respected, primarily due to the experiences they share with the firefighters they serve. The protection provided by officers strengthens the bond of the Brotherhood. Due to the dedication of officers to their firefighters, officers often find themselves in the most dangerous situations at any given emergency that a fire company responds to. Even with the highest-ranking chiefs, overseeing multiple firehouses in a city of roughly 11,400 firefighters, the tradition of officers protecting their firefighters is still visible:

> As a chief, I gather that's why we lost 21 [26 with posthumous promotions] chiefs September 11th. We are where everybody else is, you go where your men are and that's what we do. . . . If I'm working on front lines with one of my guys, even at this rank, then they know that they can depend on me, they know that I know what they're going through, like my smallpox shot that I took. If my guys are going to take it, I have to take it, because it shows that if they're going to do it, I should be able to do it, and that's what we do. From September 11th on, all the hours we spent at the site knowing what they were going through, they knew that I knew what they were going through, and it's important, it was important to them to know that I experienced the exact same thing as they did. That's why we're so close.

At the time of this interview, the UFA had succeeded in getting the fire department's approval for all firefighters in the City of New York to receive a smallpox vaccine due to the terrorism alert in the city and the perceived threat of possible exposure to the virus in the workplace. Firefighters were in the process of being vaccinated.

Throughout history, officers have demonstrated their allegiance to the firefighters below them and defended them in every situation they could. In return, firefighters perform their duties with precision and respect the instructions of their commanding officers while maintaining a closer relationship with them than the ranks of most other military organizations. On September 11, the chief of department, the first deputy commissioner, 26 chiefs, 19 captains, and 53 lieutenants died after leading their ranks to battle the fire at the World Trade Center. Four fire marshals, 236 firefighters, 1 chaplain, 2 EMS personnel, and 3 retirees also were among the fallen.

EMS CULTURE

Emergency medical service personnel merged with the FDNY in 1993 and, as described in Chapter 2, EMS and fire service brought two very different cultures together in one department. EMS culture is more comparable to police culture than firehouse culture. EMTs and paramedics work in pairs generally in teams of three, with two of the three partners working a given shift. This is similar to police, who work as partners, compared to firefighters, who work in a team of five on a rig at a regular firehouse. The management structures of the services are also different. Similar to the police department, EMS officers stay back and are not on the front lines. This easily leads those emergency personnel working on the street to the feeling of being constantly scrutinized to ensure that they do not make a mistake. In contrast, in the fire service the job of a lieutenant or captain is statistically more dangerous than that of a firefighter, because they enter the fire first. For firefighters, the perception of being watched and not supported tends to be reserved not for their own bosses but for the higher management of the fire service, mostly referred to as headquarters.

The physical dangers of the jobs are also different. Loss of life within EMS is thankfully rare. EMS workers may suffer career-ending back injuries just as firefighters suffer lung, shoulder, and other job-related injuries. However, within EMS, trauma exposure is extremely high. For EMTs and paramedics, every call is likely to have action and incidents that require intervention. Their work repeatedly exposes them to loss of life and other human suffering, as compared to fire service, where not all calls are fires and not all fires involve loss of life. After the merger, EMS workers and firefighters were more exposed to each other's work and began to understand and respect the difficult tasks and challenges they both face. In most U.S. cities, fire and EMS services are combined into a single delivery system. New York City's is the largest combined unit of EMS and fire service.

COMMON BONDS

Most firefighters in the Brotherhood are also bound by a common heritage, gender, and religion. Ethnically, the FDNY today is overwhelmingly Irish- and Italian-American. While the first firefighters in New York City were Dutch, the history of Irish immigrants in the city intertwines with the history of the fire department from the middle of the 19th century and continues today. Immediately following the anti-Catholic movement within the city in the early 1800s, in which Irish immigrants were a primary target, the Irish filled up the ranks of the department, bringing their percentage from 7 percent in 1830 to almost 40 percent in 1860. The influx of Irish immigrants into the FDNY culminated in 1889 in the appointment of Hugh Bonner, a prominent immigrant firefighter who survived the Irish Famine, to the highest uniformed position, chief of department (Golway, 2002).

The Irish firefighters of the 19th century brought innovation to the department, releasing very detailed annual reports of fire safety statistics. The separatist mentality that the fire department always had within the city seemed to fit well with Irish immigrants, who were forced into a guarded existence by violent attacks on them by the Protestant elite just decades before. The Irish, well known for their participation in gang warfare, filled the ranks of the department and, through their status as firefighters and by introducing much-needed reforms, defied a government that had been against them for so long. New York City's 19th-century Irish had their own schools, hospitals, and other services to protect themselves and their children from Protestant social reformers, who often tried to convert their children, and from Protestant mobs prone to attack them (Golway, 2002).

There is still a strong presence of the Irish in the FDNY today, not only in ethnicity, but also in sentiment. This can be seen in the immense rows of firefighters who march side by side in the city's annual St. Patrick's Day Parade, including the many non-Irish firefighters who show their solidarity with their brothers from their firehouses. Today the department is still fairly homogeneous. Of the 343 firefighters who died on September 11, 2001, 20 were Black, 20 were Hispanic, 303 were White, and all were men (Farrell, 2002). The large numbers of Irish and Italians in the department today is often attributed to the fact that many members have relatives who served in the FDNY before them.

A top-ranking chief described the lack of minority firefighters and a city campaign to recruit minorities as the likely result of the fact that most minorities do not have brothers, fathers, and uncles encouraging them to join. He said the city should go out and sell the job to build up racial diversity by emphasizing how close and enjoyable the job is.

At the time this book was written, there were 43 women in the FDNY. Despite department efforts to include more women in the ranks, it has been difficult to see this through. In some cases, female firefighters have been put through hazing rituals that could easily be misconstrued as gender marginalization. In the firehouse, as mentioned earlier, such rituals generally serve a similar purpose to a military code, in which all new firefighters are considered equal to each other until they prove their abilities to the unit. One male firefighter said:

> If a woman can get on this job and do the job, handle the weight, [pass the] same physical test I take, handle the weight through the stairs, I'll bring her. She can go right beside me, but if you get on because you're a woman, and you want to prove that women should be on the job just for numbers, other than saving a life, you're not going to one, earn my respect, and two, gain anyone's respect, because you're just there for a number.

Women in the ranks do attest to the fact that it is more difficult for firewomen to fit into "the Brotherhood." The first female firefighter to reach the rank of captain in the department is Rochelle "Rocky" Jones. At the New York State Women Firefighters Seminar Weekend in 2002, Jones, who has served more than 20 years in the department, gave a keynote speech describing the difficulties of her career. She initially took the written examination because of a bet with a few male friends from her Brooklyn neighborhood that she could pass the test within five points of their scores even without the preparation course they were taking. Recalling her days as a probie at age 24, she mentioned the thrill of receiving her own gear in 1982 and her dismay at seeing "Probationary Fireman" written inside her helmet. "That's right: 'Fireman.' I can't imagine a man wearing an insert on the front of their helmet that said 'Firewoman' for twelve months!" said Jones (Jones, 2003).

With such a strong Catholic influence in the FDNY, it is not surprising that religion also plays a key role in the culture today. The FDNY is not specifically a religious organization, but religious prayer ceremonies are held at many functions as an introduction to the events of the day. Fire chaplains within the FDNY, like firefighters, are predominantly Catholic, but chaplains also come from other faiths. Some of the most prominent fire chaplains within the department are Catholic or Protestant priests and Jewish rabbis. One Catholic firefighter spoke of the eloquence with which one rabbi chaplain speaks: "As a matter of fact, I've got him on my notification card that if I should die in the line of duty, I want him to speak at the mass, and he's a rabbi! But he's a good speaker." When firefighters begin working in the department, they are required to fill out notification cards identifying who should be called if there is an emergency and, if they die in the line of duty, how they would like funeral arrangements handled. It is almost as if the fire department has a religion of its own led by the fire chaplains.

It is uncertain when chaplains first became part of the FDNY, but in 1966, the same year CSU was founded, chaplains within the state of New York set up an official organization. According to the web site of the New York State Association of Fire Chaplains (2003), chaplains in the department:

- Are laymen or ordained persons chosen to serve the needs of the members of their departments, whether paid or volunteer
- Are persons whose skills and compassion can meet the special needs of victims of fire, accidents, and disasters
- Are available to their departments for alarms, drills, meetings, socials, memorials, and public functions
- Are available to the sick and for counseling on both professional and personal problems
- Are trained firefighters, rescue workers, qualified first aid attendants, or emergency medical technicians ready to work beside colleagues in combating fires and meeting human needs

As firefighters, chaplains aim to help people through the FDNY as one of the many ways in which they do their duty as holy men. Chaplains generally lead all the memorial services of fallen firefighters, appear regularly at fire scenes, and also show up at public ceremonies involving the FDNY to say a few words and give a blessing or a prayer. In the recovery effort at the World Trade Center in the months after 9/11, chaplains were a constant presence, ready if any remains were found to say a prayer over them, and ready if anyone needed to talk. This is another layer of support in an organization that takes care of its own. In a culture where the predominant attitude is to help and not be helped, religious support can cut through this bravado. On 9/11, Fire Chaplain Mychal Judge was among the many who perished at the World Trade Center. There is currently an effort underway to have Judge canonized with the Roman Catholic Church.

FAMILY TIES THAT BIND

It has already been noted that many of the members of the department have a family history there already. A recent book on the FDNY community, *Firehouse*, by David Halberstam, stresses this issue.

It is almost as if there is a certain DNA strand found in firefighting families . . . where the men are pulled toward the job because their fathers and uncles were firemen and had loved it, and because some of their happiest moments when they were boys had come when they visited the firehouse and these big, gruff men made a fuss over them. The job and the mission and sense of purpose that go with it have always been quietly blended into the family fabric. (Halberstam, 2002)

As described throughout this book, firefighters have two families, one in the firehouse and one at home. The firehouse family of coworkers is a Brotherhood. The family at home includes the nuclear family of the firefighter and the extended family or family of origin, which often influenced the decision to join the department.

The social status of employees of the FDNY has been another factor binding the community together. Most families are lower middle class with many children, likely due to the Catholic religion's opposition to birth control. Firefighters primarily live in the outskirts of the city in family-oriented towns on Long Island, in upstate New York, and on Staten Island. In fact, 78 of the 343 firemen who perished on September 11 lived on Staten Island, a borough known to be culturally removed from the rest of the city and one that occasionally threatens to secede from New York (Corry, 2002). Often the fathers in FDNY families are very close to their children, since their 24-hour shifts and their ability to trade mutuals with other members of the firehouse allow them to spend more time with their kids during the day, sometimes even blended into the family fabric for five consecutive days. Mothers in FDNY families often have day jobs and spend time at home outside of normal business hours. In families who lost a firefighter father, mothers have often had to take on roles that were usually held by the father. CSU found that issues of single-parenting skills were relevant for most of those families.

Firefighters generally include their families very much in the culture of their workplace. As one chief put it:

My family is actually involved in my job, my job doesn't only end here, it goes home, so it's part of the job. Since they've been babies, they've been involved in the firehouse—firehouse parties, most of my friends are on the job, firefighters who are officers—and they've been involved in my career since they were babies. That's why I've got pictures in my office. And it's not only my family. It's everybody's family. A firefighter's family is involved in the job. We take our jobs home with us, because it's not something to turn on and turn off. It's a way of life.

Growing up in a firefighter family is a unique experience. Children are brought into the firehouse and often get to know most of the firefighters who work there.

For many children, being surrounded by the extended firehouse family can be an inspiration for them to join the ranks as adults. As a second-generation firefighter whose father died at the World Trade Center said:

> I work with a lot of my father's friends who are now officers or firemen. . . . I used to ride on the fire truck when I was a little kid, just like [in the movie] *Backdraft*. And I used to be that little pain in the ass that would never stop asking questions and jumping all over the rigs for seven hours and following them around when they just want to relax and read the paper . . . and now they see that I'm on the job and I'm still the same little pain in the ass, just a little taller. But it makes them feel—because they know I've wanted this since I was a little baby—it makes them feel happy, and that I'm being taken care of by a good company.

Firefighters who have followed in their relatives' footsteps generally do not say they were directly pressured into the job, but rather that growing up in that culture gave them knowledge of how rewarding it was to do that line of work:

> I wasn't pushed to do this job. If I'd wanted to do something else, my father and mother would have been fine with it, but I think my father was happy. I mean he would have been happy if I was making a million dollars on Wall Street, but the stress of that job, I mean this job has stress, but the friendships you create, not many jobs are like this one. It's tough to describe, but you know, guys moving, guys putting on a roof, when they put up a list in the firehouse, you know there's 20 guys there. Some of them don't know what they're doing, banging nails. Some of them show up for the beverages, but you know if they're pushing two pieces of wood up to the deck, they're there, and they'll be there for the next guy. It's pretty unique.

Others admit to more familial pressure in taking the job but still stress the benefits of the friendships and rewards:

> My brother was a firefighter—typical question, typical answer. My brother was a firefighter, and I was over in Vietnam, and he wrote me a letter and said, "The fire department test is coming up in May of 1968," and I said, "I am not interested in being a firefighter." And sure enough he coaxed me into it by telling me how great the job was, and that was history. I took the test and bingo. It was my brother who actually coaxed me into becoming a firefighter.

Despite the close ties between the work of firefighters and their family lives, there are certain aspects of the job that firefighters do not so readily let their families in on. In discussing their workday with their families, firefighters generally are not as candid as they are at the firehouse. A common saying in firehouses is "what's said here stays here." At home, details of the dangers of the profession usually are kept to a minimum, and this has been something FDNY families struggled with after those dangers became more obvious on September 11, 2001. Many changes have reconfigured the structures and values of home life that families were used to prior to 9/11. In active-duty families the changes are mostly due to the more obvious inherent dangers of the job, and in families of the deceased they reflect the need to find a new normal in new circumstances.

Despite the absence of their firefighter husbands, fathers, sons, and brothers, bereaved FDNY families are still very much engaged with the fire department. Their experience of the loss of their loved ones is shared by many of the active and retired firefighters still attached to the department. One chief described the intense efforts of the firefighters to help the families as one of the most difficult struggles within the FDNY since 9/11.

> Just handling the emotions of losing 343 of our members and trying to take care of their families, firehouses have done a tremendous amount of work. And when you knew you couldn't take anybody home, I think that was probably the biggest change—that the guys have had to go on their own to take care of the families and to do that role, and it's taken a toll on a lot of people. We used to lose one person in a fire, and that firehouse would take care of that person, that family. So, they could do it. It was 25 guys taking care of one. [After 9/11,] it was a full-time job. And people in the firehouse that lost people, it really changed their lives, and if you multiply 343 by all the people that had to handle that, there were thousands of people in this job running around, taking care of families, so it's taken its toll. That's been a big change.

For centuries prior to 9/11, it was an unwritten cultural obligation for firefighters to take care of the family of a firefighter from their company who died in the line of duty. A financial precursor to the formal role of the *family liaison* described in Chapter 2 was the *firehouse matron*. In the FDNY, prior to unionization, when financial benefits to the marital family of the perished firefighter were minimal, there was a local tradition of a firehouse matron. When a line-of-duty death occurred in a specific firehouse, the members of the firehouse would voluntarily contribute a specific portion of their paycheck each payday to the widow of the perished firefighter. The widow would then perform housekeeping tasks within that firehouse. This was an embarrassment to all parties involved, both the widow and the firefighters, even though it did provide some financial security and direct connection to the members of the firehouse family for the widow and children. This was no longer necessary when firefighters became unionized and specific insurance and death benefits became available to the widows and children of perished firefighters. The personal connection for firefighters, however, was critical to the process of caring for the family of one of their own.

A few decades ago, one officer who responded to the line-of-duty death of one of his firefighters began recording helpful information about handling such circumstances, such as how to notify the family, in a book. When another line-of-duty death occurred in the department, he presented the officer of the affected firehouse with his notes. That officer added to them and passed the book down when there was another line-of-duty death. On 9/11, of course, multiple firehouses had losses, and it was difficult to continue this tradition in the same way. Copies of the book were made and distributed to firehouses that suffered losses. After things settled, any additions that could be collected were incorporated into the original book, which is still in existence. The lack of a written protocol for notifications and postdeath assistance to families had created permeable boundaries between firefighters from the firehouse of the deceased and families of the deceased. Since 9/11, the National Fallen Firefighters Foundation (NFFF) has distributed some written materials on how to deal with line-of-duty deaths, specifically a booklet called *Taking Care of Our Own: A Resource Guide,* which is particularly helpful to family liaisons. Families of both active and fallen firefighters remain a part of the greater community and feel the effects of changes in everyday life since the tragedy. The firehouses reciprocate those feelings.

HEROICS, MEDIA, AND POLITICS

Firefighters generate an air of humbleness when speaking of heroics. While on the inside they are very proud of their jobs and their trained ability to rescue people from dangerous situations and, in most cases, come out alive, they are reluctant to call themselves heroes. This may be just a case of semantics, but it seems to be also a matter of pride. Their portrayal as heroes in the media and by politicians after the events of 9/11 was taken with some reluctance. As one firefighter recalled:

> What happened 9/11, we became superstars, and no one wanted it. We went down as a company to Philadelphia, and it was overwhelming. They treated us like we were the Philadelphia Flyers. They wanted us to come down and talk to a school and receive a check. They were [driving] us around in limos [with] escorts and fire trucks and cops, blocking streets, people clapping and crying. We stayed in the Ritz Carlton. We walked in, they had every employee from the Ritz Carlton stop and line the whole atrium, and we all started crying. We were like, "This is unbelievable! Who the hell are we? We didn't do anything. There's 343 that did everything. We didn't do anything." But it was overwhelming. We didn't want it. It kind of sucked that people really realized then, after it happened, what we do. I mean, it's nice, even in this neighborhood . . . there's great people coming up to us, shaking our hands, saying thank you, you know some people understand.

The hero status did provide a boost to the firefighters' morale after 9/11 and helped them deal with the loss they suffered, but most say it became too much. It is sometimes overlooked by the public that firefighters not only experienced a sense of loss, mourning, and sadness, but also felt profound survivor guilt and despair at not being able to bring many of their brothers home.

Immediately after September 11, the Brotherhood took center stage and captured the public eye, embodying their title of "the bravest," serving literally as poster boys for the entire nation and taking on the new name of superhero, rubbing shoulders with fantasy/fiction heroes such as Spider-Man in Marvel Comics. New York City hired a marketer who had once handled Disney and Revlon products to manage the FDNY brand name. Average daily sales at the FDNY Fire Zone store in SoHo rose drastically after the World Trade Center disaster, from $600 to $25,000 in 2002 (Corry, 2002). The firehouse next to the store, which was popular among tourists even before 9/11, began leaving its doors open 24 hours for the droves of visitors stopping by to pay tribute, and other firehouses also were more open to receiving guests. The public image of firefighters went from that of what the public sometimes saw as the angry white male against affirmative action to the tragic hero characters we see on television series, such as *Third Watch* or *Rescue Me,* in movies such as *Ladder 49,* on the FDNY Calendar of Heroes, and memorialized by thousands in public ceremonies. This shift in circumstances was also felt by many FDNY families that lost someone in the tragedy. Many of them were given media attention, whether wanted or unwanted, and were under the watchful eye of the entire nation in prolonged memorial services, which were televised to allow the viewer at home to share their grief.

As time has passed, some of the publicity has become less positive toward the FDNY community. The FDNY-related headlines of late focus more on the rambunctious behavior of the Brotherhood and less on its loss. Stories of alcoholism, drug abuse, and misbehavior have been given top billing in newspapers and in some fictitious TV shows, with more of a focus on shock value. For FDNY families, the media has also shifted its attention from their grief to their scandals. This phenomenon can partly be attributed to the sensationalist nature of the media. However, it can also be explored in relation to the public nature of national tragedies. After the U.S. attack on Hiroshima, Japan, victims and their families were similarly elevated to the highest level of adoration in public consciousness, but in the years that followed, the public began to tear down the heroes and scrutinize intimate details of their lives (Lifton, 1968). In the public's observation of grief in a national tragedy, those who take center stage are often expected to remain forever innocent, almost saintly. When those figures are revealed as human, an unforgiving public can amplify their common human errors.

The paramilitary nature of the community, as well as the FDNY's position as a governmental institution, also puts it in a vulnerable position for political manipulation by a government waging war. An interesting look at politics in a similar situation is presented by Katherine Verdery and her theory of the "political lives of dead bodies" (Verdery, 1999). Verdery looks at the ways in which prominent individuals continued to influence political affairs *post mortem*. The images of national heroes, such as the fallen New York City firefighters, their families, and current active-duty firefighters, could easily be manipulated by the politics that have ensued since that event. Due to their physical absence in the world of the living, however, the influences that dead martyrs, deceased revolutionaries, and firefighters who make the supreme sacrifice have on politics do not necessarily resemble the influences that would be in play if they were living, active participants able to voice their own opinions.

In the days following the attacks on the World Trade Center, politicians captivated the attention of the nation and gave speeches aimed to emotionally move and mobilize the entire country. The deaths of 343 firefighters fueled their words. Before and after 9/11 and throughout their history, firefighters in New York City have had strong clashes with politicians and with the civilians who run the department. Politicians attending 9/11 memorial services and eulogizing firefighters they barely knew were seen by many members of the FDNY as paying lip service to promote their political agendas. While the fame of local politicians did not go unnoticed, with an event as large as September 11, national politicians also made an effort to identify with the firefighters. This continued in post-9/11 election campaigns.

The countless memorial services and constant media attention related to the 9/11 tragedy have created an atmosphere of public grief that is unprecedented in the United States and has perhaps reconfigured the mentality of the entire nation. While it is difficult to draw parallels to this case (most have compared it to the Oklahoma City bombings of April 1995, when 168 people were killed and 850 injured at the Alfred P. Murrah Federal Building), other instances of public grief that have focused around public figures can seem to resemble the attention given the New York City firefighters. At first, some of the grieving firefighters and families did not evade the media attention after 9/11 but found it comforting to be able to share the legacy of their loved ones with others. Tales of heroics were splashed across newspaper pages and filled great sections of the national and local evening news, and behind many of those individuals were widowed women, now-fatherless children, good friends, parents, and siblings. While some of the media attention helped families and friends feel like they had in some way preserved the memory of the deceased by telling his story, some of it has also been excessive. This phenomenon is described in Chapter 8. Many bereaved families have found other ways of commemorating their loved ones, such as naming streets after them, establishing foundations, or even building sports fields.

The case of the firefighters calls for a deeper exploration of the significance of collective memory and how a nation identifies with a hero or heroes. The prolonged search for remains, the people's mental images of the state of the missing, the media's constant display of public agony in waiting and subsequent mourning, and the presence of politicians at memorial ceremonies helped secure cultural legitimacy for many agendas unrelated to the lives of the fallen firefighters. One FDNY chief expressed his sentiments regarding politicians appearing at the funerals of firefighters after 9/11:

> I just think they were being politicians as opposed to really, really knowing what was going on. I think a lot of people showed up at the memorials not because it was the right thing, because they think it was the right thing to do, not because they really wanted to be there. I mean, the mayor was the mayor and he was great, but there were a lot of people who were just doing what they were doing because they thought it was the right thing to do. But they won't be around for long. We'll be here. The job will be here—the firefighter—and they'll go back to whatever they do.

In issues of collective memory, society has a visible tendency to worship fallen heroes, primarily revolutionaries. It is interesting to note then that both revolutionary national heroes and the firefighters of the FDNY aim to help out as ordinary people rather than as political elite, but have been elevated to such a status. Memory, both personal and collective, is susceptible to social processes. FDNY's fallen have continued to lead political lives after 9/11, affecting society in ways that may have seemed unimaginable in life.

THE BROTHERHOOD AND ITS LOSS

All of the aforementioned traits and attributes give witness to the complexity and specificity of the FDNY community and culture. They attest to the need for a deeper understanding of culture required of all counselors, social workers, and others trying to help post-9/11 relief efforts related to the FDNY or post-disaster responses to other unique populations. The cohesion of the Brotherhood, and of the entire community, has bewildered and fascinated New Yorkers throughout history, and while it is difficult to determine all the reasons firefighters are so close, their reliance on each other in fighting fires, their rowdy nature, familial ties in the workplace and at home, common ethnicity, religion, and most of all their passion for their profession factor in.

The sudden loss of 343 firemen and three retirees on September 11, 2001, in a department of roughly 11,400 firefighters has clearly shattered or reshaped many of the underlying codes within the culture of the FDNY, and the psychological effects are devastating. One firefighter, who had previously suffered the loss of his brother, lost seven members of his firehouse on 9/11 and said that losing those seven FDNY brothers was more difficult for him than losing his own blood-related brother. By and large, members of the community have said that the greatest change in everyday life since 9/11 is related to the psychological toll of the events. A high-ranking chief commented on the "pall" that was still present in firehouses nearly 2 years after the event:

> I think it's a little more solemn. I think that we still haven't recovered yet from the event, and I think it's going to take a long time before the pall is actually lifted. I still think that when you go into a firehouse—some are different than others—and actually you go into any firehouse that was affected either by a loss that day or a loss of somebody that passed through the firehouse, there's still a pall over those guys, and it's going to take a while before we actually lift that.

Life within the firehouse has certainly changed, but although many firefighters are still wrought with survivor guilt, they are moving forward and carrying each other. Some 7,684 members of the workforce had sought and received direct clinical services from CSU between September 11, 2001, and June 2005. Of those, 502 were retired and 7,182 were active-duty members. In 2002 alone, CSU counseled 2,849 active-duty members and 89 retirees. Counseling and psychotherapy have always carried great stigma in the department, so it was necessary to demonstrate to the ranks that these were viable options. The stigma stemmed from the work itself—rescue. Those used to being the rescuers generally want to do it on their own and are reluctant to be the ones helped. Various outreach efforts, documented in Chapter 4, helped to get this message across, including a video of testimony from well-known high-ranking firefighters on how counseling has helped them. The efforts of CSU continue to aid the many firefighters and members of the community affected by the tragedy.

The 9 months spent searching for the remains of fallen brothers at "the Pile" had a profound impact on FDNY firefighters. In all their years of firefighting, they had always brought home the remains of the fallen. While many after the event have questioned the decision to allow firefighters to look for their own in the rubble, in the aftermath of 9/11 it was a matter of course, and virtually nothing could have stopped them. Not allowing them to head up the recovery effort would have conflicted with hundreds of years of tradition and a core value in the psyche of a first responder. Theory states that after disasters people should not search for their own, but in this case culture trumps theory. The grueling 9 months spent at the World Trade Center site represented a cultural obligation for firefighters. While detail at the site was voluntary, lasting 1 month with no overtime, the sign-up sheet on the fridge of every firehouse was in plain view of all its members.

In the early days of the search, one officer stood on the rubble and declared to the others at the scene, "We won't leave until we bring every last guy back!" His words motivated the crowd, as they came from the mouth of a man who had years of experience in fires and had always found the remains of his fallen brothers. Yet he knew that in the collapse of the towers and the burning rubble even metal desks had disintegrated into dust. Firefighters are mission driven, and after 9/11 their primary mission was to recover those remains. To take away their mission would have been to deprive them of purpose at a time when they were suffering tremendous trauma and loss. Firefighters knew that digging at the site was potentially damaging to their health, but they felt they had to do it. This drive was illustrated earlier by their reluctance to reduce their shifts at the site and to leave prematurely. Remarkably, there was only one injury, a compound leg fracture, among firefighters during the recovery effort at the World Trade Center site. However, there were many lingering health problems that also resulted from their exposure to the fumes, dust, and debris.

For each firefighter, the ultimate goal of those 30 days spent at the World Trade Center site was to find a recovery. Despite the gruesome experience of finding body parts, it was generally worse for firefighters to spend their 30 days working at the site without a recovery. Finding a recovery gave them both a sense of accomplishment and a horrific memory. It is the belief of the authors of this book that firefighters worked through much of their grief and trauma at the site through the meaning of obligation to their fallen brothers. They stayed until they recovered everything they possibly could of the firefighters who perished. On the last day before the closing of the site, recovery workers swept the floor clean, removing every last particle of debris they could.

The lasting impact 9/11 will have on the FDNY community and its culture is difficult to ascertain, and the effects will only become fully evident in the passage of time.

The stigma of mental health services has been reduced, which is clearly seen by the numbers who have sought counseling. CSU succeeded so well in reaching firefighters after the event that one more senior firefighter recently commented that the young guys in his firehouse think CSU is just for 9/11, much like firefighters before 9/11 often thought CSU was just for alcohol and substance abuse. With many newcomers to the department and many hundreds having retired, the average age of members is now perceptibly lower. The event also changed many of the unwritten laws in the FDNY code of ethics, for instance in the ways the department communicates with families, in the ways individual firefighters act with their families and with each other, and in the ways firefighters themselves perceive their jobs and their lives. Confronting death not only has caused the FDNY community to rethink the way it lives, but also has required it to do so.

Some in the department are optimistic that things will return to normal but that the day will not be forgotten. Often these are high-ranking members who portray a sense of optimism to the firefighters they oversee:

> Some people still want to know why did I survive, if you were there, you think, "Well, why was it me?" So I think that's bothering people, but it's not a morale problem, it's the worst thing that ever happened to this job, it's more sad than morale, it's more emotional, but we will overcome that. That's my job.

To understand the workings of the individual in society, anthropologist Arthur Kleinman said, "When we meet up with the resistance offered by profound life experience—the death of a child or parent or spouse, the loss of a job or home, serious illness, substantial disability—we are shocked out of our common-sensical [sic] perspective on the world" (Kleinman, 1988). It could be said that not only the individual in FDNY society, but the entire community, city, and beyond was shocked out of its commonsensical perspective on the world on September 11, 2001. While in many cases therapists have been helpful, many experts have admitted that they do not yet entirely understand the impact of 9/11 on individuals. CSU has taken the approach to not medicalize or pathologize before knowing and examining particulars. Rather than immediately creating a diagnostic category for all those affected by the tragedy, a greater understanding of the details of the personal and group experiences in the FDNY can be obtained through personal narrative and may uncover the true meaning of individual suffering and aid in diagnosis and treatment.

The FDNY community, like its members, is still in a state of reinvention, and the culture is going through multiple changes. In April 2003, one officer related his understanding of this realization among the FDNY:

> Now, 19 months, and it's just starting to hit people. . . . I mean, they've been doing it all along, but the realization is setting in that this was real. I mean, people have been really busy, it's taken a long time for some people, and you still have new people going into counseling all the time. There's that—there's our machismo—and [counseling is] probably something that we would never do. But this event was nothing like we'd ever seen before, nothing like anybody had seen.

Coming to terms with the loss the FDNY suffered will perhaps take generations. The active firefighters who survived the World Trade Center will pass on their experience to the new ranks, and many of the retiring veterans will become legends in their own time.

Firefighting is considered by many to be the most dangerous job in New York City. In 2001, outside of the deaths that occurred on September 11, five firefighters died in the line of duty out of the 11,400 in the ranks at that time. To face such great danger every day, firefighters require not only great courage, but also a sense of humor, and it helps that they love their jobs.

Contrary to many misconceptions, within the FDNY there is an enormous range of education levels and professional experience. Many active-duty members hold college degrees in many professions. Among the men who died were teachers, musicians, even scientists. Firefighters themselves are aware and very proud of their skills, their traditions, and their altruism. They admit that such good qualities generally are accompanied by a wild nature:

> We're community-minded, community-based people, family people, dedicated, conscientious, besides being courageous and brave and bold, and crazy a little at some times, but to do that, that's part of the territory, to be that dedicated and that driven. Other things come with it, but it's all good stuff.—high-ranking chief

As one firefighter explained the changes in everyday life, "In the firehouse, guys aren't so worried about the minor things. . . . Guys are focused on more important things, like laughing, having fun, family, you know." Many who have experienced the death of a loved one can attest to the fact that, when an individual confronts death, life takes on a new significance. While the negative effects of the massive loss of 343 of the FDNY's own on September 11, 2001, are still very fresh in the minds and lives of the FDNY, there is optimism that the community will continue to see that loss as a reminder of the joys they find in the Brotherhood and in their jobs.

CHAPTER 4

Shaping Services to Meet Emerging Needs

Standing on the roof deck of CSU in downtown Manhattan, 1.81 miles north
of the towers burning in the background, it was not yet clear to any of us how
our lives, both personally and professionally, had changed forever.

EMPLOYEE ASSISTANCE Programs (EAPs) provide emotional and psychological services in the workplace and are shaped by the organizations
they serve. Their capacity to understand and reflect the culture of the
organization and its members greatly impacts their effectiveness. EAPs that
are an internal part of a single organization often have an advantage in this regard compared to those that operate externally and serve multiple organizations. According to some studies, internal EAPs have greater accessibility to
clients, higher visibility, and better outreach. They are considered to be better
equipped to give rapid feedback to the organization in times of difficulty (Akabas & Kurzman, 2005). At the time of the 9/11 tragedy, CSU, as the long-standing
internal EAP of FDNY, had both the knowledge and access necessary to respond rapidly and effectively to the multitude of needs presented.

CSU had always considered itself to be a nontraditional EAP, but one that
was quite reflective of the organization it served. As is true of many early EAPs,
CSU was started by a small group of firefighters who were members of Alcoholics Anonymous and desired to help others struggling with the disease. Following a typical EAP path into what is known in the field as a *broad-brush* or *full-
service program,* CSU added professionally trained staff and began to respond
not only to issues related to alcohol but to the multitude of everyday challenges
faced by its personnel, including marital stress, depression, anxiety, and other

68

mental health problems, along with those issues that were particularly prevalent in the world of first responders, namely trauma and grief. What made CSU unique was a continued mix of professional and peer staffing as well as its commitment to delivering on-site services at hundreds of locations, day or night, in contrast to limiting its intervention primarily to assessment and referral. The belief that the unique firefighter culture needed to be understood and respected in planning any response led to a level of direct service not typical of workplace practice. This was reflected in its 5-day-per-week day treatment program for alcohol/substance abuse recovery, its provision of on-site counseling for members and their families, and the response developed over the years to family and firehouse at the time of a serious line-of-duty injury or death.

Given the reluctance of FDNY members to utilize mental health services and the stigma often attached to doing so, CSU historically felt that its traditional staffing mix of professionals and peers, combined with its keen understanding of the language, mission, and family-like commitment, placed it in the best position to provide culturally sensitive and relevant services to FDNY members and families. At the time of 9/11, CSU had a staff of 12: 6 mental health professionals and 6 peers. From its single Manhattan location, the staff saw approximately 600 new clients per year with a mix of presenting problems.

While clearly the existing infrastructure CSU had in place was an enormous advantage in its response to 9/11, it would be a mistake for the reader to conclude that without such a preexisting unit such a response is not possible. In fact, it is the authors' intent to show that the principles applied by CSU can be developed and implemented not only by an internal system but by first responders and mental health practitioners joining together in thoughtful preincident planning for their community. The identification of key community players before a crisis emerges permits the development of a broad outline to be applied in any emergency. Equally important, it facilitates the beginnings of a working relationship between critical participants.

With this said, the story we can tell is that of CSU's response, the ideas that informed it, and the lessons learned from it. Looking back over the events of almost 4 years, it is now possible to connect some of the decisions made and actions taken to our earliest traditions. Often these served us well, and the discussion that follows will attempt to clarify when this was the case. In contrast, some of our past practices were better suited for a slower-paced, centralized operation, and our learning curve, slow at times and remarkably on target at others, may provide some guidance to the reader.

ASSESSMENT AND PLANNING

A vulnerability of the internal EAP is its proximity to the event, the degree to which it shares the trauma and loss of the organization and the danger of becoming contaminated and less helpful as a result. Response in the acute phase does not involve sophisticated psychological intervention. Some consider it to be more akin to administering first aid (Institute of Medicine, 2003). It involves gathering facts in the service of dispensing accurate information; providing education in the service of normalizing and depathologizing reactions; assessing needs in the service of offering physical care, emotional support, and crisis intervention. It is equally important from the earliest moments to begin to assess and plan for the long haul. Even before the outcome of the event is known, there is much that can be done and perhaps is best done by remaining apart from the actual scene.

The assessment of the immediate situation is described in detail elsewhere in this text. The story it tells illustrates the role of the EAP as an organizational consultant. The earliest focus of CSU intervention was not in the capacity of counseling individuals but rather in assisting the organization to pull together the resources necessary to respond to phone calls, organize information, and communicate with multiple constituencies. It was about helping to identify gaps and fill them. (For more about the immediate aftermath see Chapter 2.) This chapter describes the principles and ideas that informed the decisions that led to the expansion of CSU and shaped the services that developed. It addresses the mechanisms put in place at that time that continue to underlie the philosophy, design, and implementation of programs. It is our intention that this thinking, offered by us in hindsight, might be useful to the reader proactively and assist you in thinking ahead about your community and the resources that might be needed in the event of a disaster or atrocity of any magnitude. It is understood that such events cannot be predicted or forecast. However, in the post-9/11 world, where *preparedness* is an all too familiar term, we hope our experience will be of value to you.

How History Informs Service Delivery

If it is true that individuals become more of who they are in times of crisis, so, too, do organizations. CSU, much like the department it is a part of, responded to the tragedy by applying the knowledge and skills developed throughout its history to the situation at hand. As the scope of the event unfolded, it became clear that the task would be not be accomplished in a day, a week, or even a year. It would not be accomplished by 12 people operating from a single location, but rather it would require a significant expansion of all resources. The psychological impact of an event of this magnitude would be long lasting. It would endure beyond the work at the site; in fact, until that work was complete, the work of CSU would remain in its infancy. Finding ways to build on preexisting strengths and sustain them for the long haul was critical to success.

Looking back, it is clear that the core beliefs and practices of today's CSU were embedded in its early history. Core beliefs are just that, and because they are ingrained in how one thinks and operates, they do not need to be articulated or defined in the moment. They do, however, inform the decisions that are made. They are understood by all and are shared with newcomers, if not in words then in actions. Through observation and absorption, the value base of practice becomes known and continues. This bears striking resemblance to the workings of the firehouse and the role of the senior men. To be effective, expansion requires a deployment of resources that allows these core values to be consistently replicated in new locations and by new staff. Perhaps this is always the challenge of rapid organizational expansion. However, when expansion is driven by crisis, it is difficult to think beyond expediency. The implications of staff deployment, including scope of responsibility, are long lasting. They can mean the success or failure of a specific local operation. Consistency of policy and practice of a decentralized organization is difficult to establish and maintain in the best of times. It is more difficult when time for meetings, trainings, and communication is limited. These issues extend not only to the expansion of internal services but also to some degree to the development of external partnerships and collaborations as well. One aims for a consistency of quality across all services bearing the organizational name yet needs to allow for individual style, creativity, and community sensitivity. This is consistent with the tradition of each firehouse having its own name, patch, and traditions. It is part of the department but also part of the community it serves.

As CSU grew from one location to six, each of these aspects of growth needed to be managed. The greater the extent to which they are managed by those who share a historical understanding of the core beliefs and practice of the organization, the more successful they are likely to be. The implications of these issues for the development of pre-incident identification and training of service providers should be clear. At the time of a crisis, the value of being able to call upon a cadre of previously trained providers who understand mission, policy, procedure, and protocol cannot be overstated.

Defining Principles Created during the Early Years of the CSU That Continue to Shape Services

- Use a mixture of peers and professionals.
- Know when to go to the scene and when to hold back to avoid caregiver exposure.
- Go to the natural environment where the client is comfortable.
- Mandate education only; treatment *cannot* be mandated.
- Choose collaborators with a commitment to the long haul; educate them about organizational culture.
- Recognize the strengths and natural resources within the organization, group, firehouse, family, and individual.
- Create services around emerging needs.

Crisis takes us back to basics. It calls for answering some simple questions to begin to formulate a structure within which to respond. Thinking in terms of *who, what, where, when,* and *how* is a fundamental beginning step that helps to define populations, describe their hierarchy of needs, and develop services in proximity to them, which in turn promotes access. There are phases of response that are important to consider. Crisis typically creates a front-load situation: at the moment of impact it is a human response to want to help, to do something, and to apply one's skills and knowledge to the immediate situation. This response helps to counter our own natural tendency to feel helpless in the face of such overwhelming devastation. But what constitutes doing something? Is staying still and thinking things through a lesser contribution than rushing to console those most directly impacted? Does work *in the field* have a greater value than work in the office? Does the same staff provide services to the families of the deceased as to the active duty workforce?

From the earliest moments on, placing equal value on each of these tasks and creating a dialogue in which each informs the other lays the groundwork for identifying and responding to emerging needs. This process is not just recommended for the early, acute postdisaster phase, but rather continues months and years postincident. In fact, as you move further from the epicenter of the event in both time and location it can be more difficult to assess needs and identify gaps in service. The more mechanisms for dialogue and feedback that exist among all segments of the affected population, the better the possibility of developing an effective, far-reaching, and long-lasting response.

Recognizing and building on core services is essential. For CSU, these included in-house counseling, psycho-education related to stress reactions, and stress management, as well as on-site services for firefighters and families following critical incidents. Previously the primary focus had been on the delivery of office-based mental health services to the workforce. While eligible, family members had utilized these services less frequently, more often requesting referrals to local practitioners. As is typical of first responders, this was not a population that easily reached out for mental health services. Stigma about such intervention was high, as was the belief that problems are best kept to oneself and solved within the family. Concerns about confidentiality were paramount.

Previously, on-site response had occurred during an acute crisis, which historically had been both brief and contained to only a few locations per incident. A fatal fire, for example, was responded to by on-call staff being dispatched to the locations involved, most typically the firehouse and hospital. Professional staff would report to the location where family members would be present; peers, alone or with clinical staff, reported to the work locations directly involved in the event and those where the member was best known. This might be one firehouse or several depending upon the individual situation. If the member had close relatives on the job, as is often the case, that location would also be covered. The on-site response would continue so that members reporting to work for the next several tours would be seen. If new affected locations were identified, peers would report to those as well. The response at such times was thought to be comprehensive and seemed effective. However, at the time of 9/11, the situation was radically different. All FDNY locations and personnel were affected, and the disaster work would continue over many months. If services were to be utilized, a massive campaign designed to educate the entire community about the impact of trauma, the range of response, and the availability of services needed to be undertaken. Education for many thousands of people spread across hundreds of square miles was needed to reach the goal of encouraging members to view the utilization of mental health services not as a sign of weakness but as a sign of strength.

In the past, support to the family of affected members had been relatively brief depending upon the nature of the event and the needs of the family. Typically, these services were outsourced to local mental health providers once the situation was stabilized. Intervening with a family immediately after a tragedy creates an intense connection. Entering the hospital, home, and family network at a time when emotions are so raw creates a bond long remembered. Just this year a firefighter who was assigned to light duty due to an injury requested to work at CSU. He later revealed that his request was related to his memory of meeting the director of CSU when his firefighter father died years before. This fireman was eight years old when his father died yet still remembered the support provided at the time and the declaration that he could call CSU for assistance any time issues came up in the future. The CSU tradition, like the traditions of New York City firefighters, is about long-term caring and commitment.

The sensitivity and understanding shown at the time of the loss can be instrumental in the family reaching out for assistance at other times of difficulty, even many years later. Issues related to the loss of a parent can emerge over time as children move through developmental stages, reach new milestones, and confront new challenges. Families frequently would reach out to CSU at such times, preferring to receive guidance from a source that was familiar with their history without need for extensive elaboration. They sought information about the impact of early parental loss, reassurance about adequate parenting, resources for intervention, and advice for the future. These earlier experiences of brief intervention with continuing accessibility were important lessons about the significant role of CSU and FDNY in the future lives of these children. This information would have significant bearing on the development of programs for the bereaved families and the 389 dependent children who lost their fathers on 9/11. (For a discussion of services to children of the deceased, see Chapter 8.)

PLANNING AHEAD

It is important to be aware of the future implications of services offered and relationships formed. One needs to think about the long haul even as one develops and implements the initial acute response. Individuals who have experienced traumatic loss are unlikely to trust easily or respond quickly. It is important to clarify the nature and extent of available services to the degree possible at the beginning of the relationship to avoid confusion and disappointment later on. If the degree of service is unknown, that must be made explicit. For example, indicating that funding is available for 6 months of service on a once-weekly basis and that efforts to extend this are currently underway is important in the development of trust over the long haul. If services provided are intended as early intervention and temporary, that, too, should be made clear. It does not matter that such proclamations may not be remembered when termination or transfer are discussed; it is the clarification and building of trust that is most important. Control is critical, self-determination never more important. Trauma shakes one's confidence and belief system to the core; individuals feel powerless in the face of the extreme devastation they have endured and over which they have had no control. All opportunities to encourage and support the individual's capacity to regain control of their life should be fully embraced. While it was always CSU's intention to be present for the long haul, it is equally important to be direct and honest about current limitations in either funding or service availability. Though CSU had been available historically, many in the affected community had no prior knowledge or experience with us and therefore remained unaware of the authenticity of this long-term commitment. It helped to reinforce our intention often and to do so in the most clear, direct, and honest way possible.

HOW THE NATURE OF THE EVENT SHAPES THE RESPONSE

Assessing program strengths and consumer awareness of services is important in beginning to shape a direction for expansion. Equally important is the understanding of the nature of the event and how this informs the type of services that may be needed. This helps to identify training needs, provides direction for staff expansion and input into the critical decisions that must be made including what the EAP will do from inside the organization and what will be contracted out. Following this, how you choose collaborators and form partnerships has long-lasting significance.

In most situations, it is beneficial to consider the experiences of others who have previously confronted similar circumstances. In the case of 9/11, this experience was largely unavailable, although the Oklahoma City bombing was most often looked to for direction. Colleagues from Oklahoma provided both hands-on and conceptual assistance in the earliest days. However, recognizing the differences between the two events was perhaps what was most helpful in shaping services. It is useful to recognize when one is in uncharted territory: it supports the ability to creatively build upon what is available from others without feeling constrained by it. It was the ongoing nature of the recovery and the number of internal losses that most differentiated our experience from others.

Aspects of 9/11 Critical in Shaping the FDNY/CSU Response

- Longevity and ongoing nature of the recovery effort
- Scope of direct FDNY losses
- Inability to recover remains of the lost
- Public and media attention to all aspects of FDNY
- Ongoing threat of additional terrorism

Perhaps of greatest significance was the fact that this was a life-altering event for both the individual and the organization. It affected everyone in the FDNY community and would continue to do so for the foreseeable future. For years to come, it would encompass new hires by drawing a line that would determine one's status in the department as pre- or post-9/11; it would compel some to retire and others to remain; it would put firefighters on a pedestal and, by virtue of that, in the media eye, so that anything a firefighter did was news and reflected on all others.

   CSU was not immune to the lasting impact. The response required to such an event is greater than just more of the same; it is not simply 343 times one or even three line-of-duty deaths; it is exponential. The enormity of the incident and the scope of the losses would impact where service was delivered, to whom, how much, and what type. It would necessitate a shift in the acquisition of resources, both human and financial. It would call upon the development of partnerships more extensive, creative, and long term than ever before. All of this is of course known in hindsight. At the time one does not fully appreciate the extent of additional resources and creativity required. Rather, it is a time when critical decisions which have important future implications are made in a rapidly changing environment, as is recalled in the following:

   One moment you have no direct funding and find yourself seeking partners among those who do. You go to the table hoping to find a resource that will be flexible in how they offer services to your population. Will they be willing to offer separate service to firefighters? Can they appreciate the necessity of this? Will their staff be interested in learning about the culture or providing service in the firehouse? How long-term is their commitment? Suddenly you find you now have funding. You feel you should honor the commitment you just made. However, now you can invite others to the table. You can define who you want and what you would like them to do. You can hire more people, open more offices. You need to quickly set up the systems necessary to locate and manage a provider and consultation network spanning five boroughs and at least seven counties. You want to teach them what it is like to work with firefighters. You want them to care as much as you do.

WHEN LOSS IS CATASTROPHIC

Traumatic grief was not unknown to the fire department; however, both the extent and circumstances of the losses dictated a different level of response. Loss affected all segments of our population. Responding to the families of the perished presented one set of challenges, but the Brotherhood too suffered the loss of friends and colleagues as well as the additional loss of not bringing their brothers home. The boundaries of loss were not always clear: more than 70 FDNY members lost firefighters who were biological family members, and others lost civilian relatives, friends, and neighbors in addition to their firefighter friends. The number of known dead often could not be counted. The number of memorials planned, eulogies written, and services attended over months was more than in most lifetimes. How do you help people to comprehend, absorb, and process so much loss? How do you help them answer the complicated, direct, and painful questions of their children? How do you help those who can't stop the tears or those who can't cry at all? How do you respond when asked how a just God could allow such deaths to occur? How do you prepare yourself to listen? An extensive array of services was needed. They would be offered both individually and in groups by CSU staff and external colleagues.

   The issues of grief and loss were compounded by the search for remains, which was slow, decisions about memorial services, which were complex, and media attention, which was endless. These issues evolved over months, then years. The impact on families was enormous. As time continued, those who had a recovery felt fortunate compared with those who had no identifiable remains to bury. At first the expectation of a recovery was so great it kept families at home waiting for the call and unwilling to be far away if burial arrangements needed to be made. Later the idea that a call still might come began to fade. Life continued. Decisions concerning what to do with additional remains had to be made. Children matured and asked probing questions as they began to grapple with the idea that a body was not recovered: *but where did he go?* The grief was often overwhelming; the unanswerable questions were endless. Each anniversary and media exposé would reawaken that which was unsettled yet set aside. *Should I review the coroner's file? What about Father's Day? Should my child read names at this year's anniversary memorial? Why won't the media leave us alone?* And then there was the money, *blood money,* as it often was called. Aware of feeling fortunate to have one less thing to worry about, it was simultaneously a blessing and a curse.

The needs of 343 families were complicated and varied. Each firefighter, officer, and paramedic was an individual, each family unique, each situation special. At the same time, the potential for community support, one family to another that was immediately visible at the family meetings organized by the city in the earliest days after the attacks, was great. Recognizing and building on this by bringing the bereaved together in homogeneous groups has been one of the greatest sources of comfort and support to many family members and has sustained them over the long haul. (For more on bereavement groups see Chapter 7.) Connecting with and caring for one another has at times been the first step toward reconnecting with life. All of the issues outlined could be discussed with one another in a way that was not possible in any other forum, and as a result empathy and sensitivity to the unique circumstances of each began to evolve. Those who received notification of remains felt concerned about disclosing this news to those who had none. They later brought comfort by sharing how little difference it really made. Those with grown children felt lonely; those with young children, overwhelmed. Each came to appreciate the similarities and differences and reached out to one another with a level of caring and concern that helped each of them to recognize that the capacity to care still remained. Later the work would be to reevaluate and reestablish ties with friends and family outside of the bereaved community as yet another step toward reintegrating with life.

WHEN MISSION IS ONGOING

Anyone working with first responders, be they firefighters, police, or military, must understand the importance to them of staying on mission. With the exception of the military, mission is most often relatively brief. In contrast, the mission of 9/11 for FDNY continued for 9 long months—hardly acute and certainly different from the typical FDNY mission. Of course initially the exact time frame for this work was unknown and estimates frequently anticipated an even longer recovery period. In this regard the situation was much more akin to military trauma: ongoing, uncertain, and complicated by the loss of brothers and the related survivor guilt.

Services offered during an ongoing mission must, by necessity, be offered on site. They are different than traditional mental health services offered in the office. Those who choose to deliver them must understand that first respon-

ders expect to remain in a dangerous situation to accomplish their mission. They must respect and support resiliency. It is important to recognize that stepping away from the mission, even for a time, is a complicated psychological decision that is best left to the individual member. The belief that *no man be left behind* fueled the anger, guilt, self blame, resolve, and resiliency that kept firefighters digging at the site hour after hour, day after day, month after month.
. Interventions offered on site are different not only in location but in how they are conducted and what they are intended to do. They must provide triage and education that allow responders to choose their own time to seek help. This is different from traditional in-office psychotherapy; it is not about uncovering the unconscious but rather understanding what is often all too conscious. It is putting a name to one's experience, normalizing reactions to trauma, and reducing assumptions that exposure automatically equals PTSD or the opposite, that first responders by virtue of training are immune. These actions are consistent with crisis counseling, which can begin on site with the offering of education, guidance, and support and may or may not continue in the office.

For 9 months CSU ran two operations, one office-based and one field-based. The importance of opening offices in closer proximity to where members lived was related to the limited time firefighters spent at home and the need to support them in staying away from the hot zone (Manhattan) when they finally did go home. It also allowed more opportunity to reach the families who were feeling increasingly isolated and in need of information, support, and services for themselves and their children.

The field operation included both services at WTC and in firehouses. (For more on services provided in firehouses see Chapter 5.) While the most intense firehouse services were provided in the 63 units that suffered the direct loss of a member on 9/11, approximately 300 locations were visited as resources permitted. It was beneficial to maintain a fluid boundary between field and office. CSU's main office in lower Manhattan at times served as respite from the pile for both members and peers who visited regularly during those months to offer support and education about services. Proximity also allowed clinical staff to visit the site becoming more familiar to the members and decreasing the stigma associated with talking with a mental health professional. It facilitated teams of clinicians and peers meeting with all work crews at the site as they began and ended their 30-day rotations. (For more on these interventions see Chapter 7.)

In our experience, the offering of services on site, which supported members remaining on mission, was an important first step in providing access to a broader range of services. Allowing members to take time out when they felt it was needed and having the organizational authority to do so permitted an intensification of intervention at the desired time. We believe it was important to respect the members' self-assessment and support their need to remain focused. Rarely was someone seen as unable to work. More frequently firefighters needed support and permission to take a break from the work that they considered their moral obligation to perform. This was important in gradually correcting the myth that coming forward for services would ground you. In fact neither the fear of the organization—*if counseling got involved no one would work*—nor the fear of the members—*if you went to counseling you would be told to not work*—proved true. Most members wanted and were able to continue to work. Most benefited at specific times, from taking a break from work. Being able to facilitate this and combine it with a period of more intensive therapeutic intervention was found to be the best combination. Still, one needed to understand the different levels of intervention. A break from working at the site and attending memorials was just that—a temporary break. Therapeutic intervention, even twice a week in the office (as was the norm during such breaks), was different when offered at that time than later when the work was done and the mission ended. Only then could the trauma and loss be approached, examined, and experienced in a deeper, more direct way. It was later, after the department-wide memorial was held in Madison Square Garden on October 12, 2002, that many firefighters were able to give themselves permission to step back and feel all that they had been holding in abeyance.

LISTENING AND RESPONDING TO EMERGING NEEDS

Field-based programs provide good examples of the overlap between outreach and service delivery. Contact with members at work locations provided not only opportunities to offer information but also to listen to the concerns of the workforce. Listening is an underrated skill and one that is far more complex than generally acknowledged. Sending peers or even clinicians to work locations to *listen* and *bring back what they hear* is easier said than done. One hears many things in the firehouse, not all of which bears repetition. Some of what one hears can immediately be put into action, such as when hearing that members are unclear about how to access the services that are available to them and their families. Other things are reported and ultimately find their way into a number of different program offerings. For example, for a long time the prevailing affect in the field was anger. The listening stories brought back to CSU were for the most part not useful as most often the anger was either undirected or misdirected. However, listening beneath the anger facilitated an educational approach where the relationship between anger, trauma, and loss could be better understood. This was helpful to both the individual experiencing the anger and also those who were often the unfortunate target of it. Later in the process, after the mission was complete, we were able to take this information a step further and offer anger-management groups to those still grappling with this problem.

Providing education about stress reactions and acute stress disorder and distinguishing these from PTSD, the main focus of media attention, was very important in allaying anxiety and supporting resiliency. The media often played a role in pointing out a direction for CSU attention. This took many forms and worked in many directions. Often the media would highlight a subject of interest and be the impetus for important and interesting discussion as when they reported on the impact of 9/11 on school children throughout the New York area. What was the implication of this for the children of FDNY? How should we address these heightened concerns? At other times, as when the media predicted extremely high rates of PTSD among firefighters or gave statistics relating suicide and trauma survival, they made our work more difficult. Placing the reactions of members and their families in the context of normal human reactions to abnormal events was beneficial to all. Giving basic information about sleep disturbance, escalating anger, isolation, and other typical reactions seemed to be helpful to most people. Educating and normalizing began the work of destigmatizing services by putting a face on mental health services in general and CSU in particular. It helped members to distinguish between distress and dysfunction for themselves and for those they cared about.

At the same time that questions, complaints, worries, and fears expressed during site visits were brought back to CSU by the peers, additional clinical staff were hired in what had grown to be six locations, and the number of CSU clients increased dramatically. Clinical supervision and meetings created a mechanism to track emerging needs. Outreach, program development, and service delivery are integral and overlapping parts of a system, each component of which informs the other (Figure 4.1). To the degree that these systems work well, program development is seamless. It is an activity cycle that can

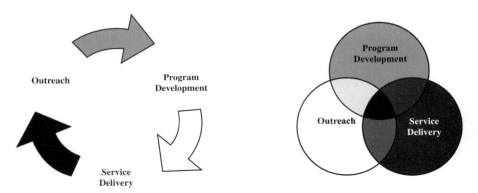

Figure 4.1 Relationship and overlap between outreach, program development, and service delivery.

begin at any point. Peers are trained to listen for emerging needs during out-reach visits. Clinicians are trained to listen and, through collective listening, identify patterns of emerging needs. Program development staff tracks the in-formation and develops services designed to manage the gaps. Whether ini-tially identified by peer or clinician, it was the dialogue between the two groups that solidified impressions, prioritized needs, developed services, and spread the word about them.

Both peers and professionals were encouraged to follow their interests. In this way, those who felt most passionate about an issue became the spokesper-son and in this way helped any number of initiatives to develop. It was in this context that the needs of new populations would emerge: the marshals who worked mainly at the morgue; the liaisons who assisted the families of the de-ceased; the chauffeurs who returned from the towers with no one they had driven there; the pipers, eulogy writers, and others who planned memorial af-ter memorial; the families at home who felt first neglected and eventually an-gry or depressed; the many children who cried each time their father left for work. Each of these groups emerged with needs, some of which overlapped one another and some so unique as to require a new and innovative pro-grammatic response. All were entitled to individual clinical services, and the constant outreach mechanism helped them to be aware of these services and, we believe, more inclined to access them.

GETTING THE WORD OUT: THE IMPORTANCE OF MULTIPLE METHODS OF OUTREACH

Months of peers and clinicians becoming a known presence at the site and at firehouses did a lot to destigmatize and demystify mental health services and to increase the credibility of CSU. Developing a variety of materials that could be utilized by outreach, workers helped to get the message across. Partner-ships with members of the media assisted in the creation of specialized train-ing materials, including professional quality videos featuring members of FDNY stressing the importance and acceptability of accessing CSU and other mental health services. Gradually education was extended to the department's training facility, where access to all members via mandated training schedules was made possible. The distinction between mandated training and mandated treatment is vital. CSU remained true to a long-standing philosophical belief that mandating treatment was not effective. However, training and education are part of the department's culture and are accepted by FDNY personnel. Through organizational collaboration, it was possible to offer education to thousands of members of the workforce by designing curriculum that cov-ered a broad range of information about trauma, grief, substance abuse, issues related to family life, and available treatment options. Adding these classes to training modules already mandated by fire operations not only ensured maximum exposure but also sent an important destigmatizing message about mental health services and the organizational priority placed on self-care.

The importance of outreach at worksite locations cannot be stressed enough. It needs to continue for the duration of the operation. While the use of in-office services is likely to increase during this early time, this should not be a signal to reduce on-site services but rather a sign that on-site services are having the desired impact. It is important that office-based services be available to meet the demand without long delays. The effectiveness of first responders is measured in the timeliness of their response, and they are likely to judge others in the same way. The availability of alternative treatment resources was also important for those who for reasons of geography, availability, or specialized need were unable to come to one of the six CSU offices. This also provided an option for those whose concerns about receiving help within the department simply could not be overcome. This was not a time to argue about auspice or create roadblocks to recovery. The focus was more importantly and appropriately on the quality of services made available and the ease of access. It necessitated the development of a large cadre of collaborators throughout the geographic areas in which members lived.

Outreach to other segments of the population was somewhat more complicated. The most difficult group to reach was the family members of the active-duty workforce. Disinclined to bring materials home from the job, it gradually became clear that family members often were unaware that firefighters were receiving information on the job and that they too had access to services. Efforts to increase this flow of information included web site postings, invitations to host meetings for spouses of individual firehouses, and community-based offerings closer to home. Although none of these offerings reached the level of success that we desired, some were more successful than others. (For an example of service to active duty members and spouses see Chapter 9.) In the long run and despite the expense involved, mailings to the entire workforce in a format easily identifiable as targeted for the family is perhaps the most effective strategy.

STRENGTHENING THE CSU IDENTITY

FDNY is a large bureaucracy with many different departments. Mailings bearing the FDNY shield can be about a vast array of subjects of varying importance. It is likely that some are read avidly, others tossed aside. As CSU went about the task of developing outreach materials and mechanisms, it seemed that developing a CSU logo that would make its literature immediately identifiable and distinct from the other FDNY mailings would be an effective strategy in forging a separate identity. This was felt to be a useful strategy with the active-duty workforce, some of whom historically had difficulty seeing CSU as separate from HQ or the medical office. This had serious implications related to the perception of confidentiality, which could be helped by underscoring the separateness of CSU.

The need for a distinct identity was somewhat different among the families of the deceased, who in the months following 9/11 were receiving piles of mail from FDNY and others at a time when they scarcely had the energy to open any of it. In January 2002 CSU developed *the LINK*, a bimonthly newsletter addressing bereavement issues, and mailed it to the homes of all known family members of the 343 deceased. *The LINK* was and continues to be the single most effective mechanism for communication, outreach, and community-building within this group. Read avidly when little else had meaning, *the LINK* helped family members from all areas feel connected to a larger community. Especially to those who for reasons of geography or inclination participated in little else, *the LINK* became a kind of barometer for how they were doing as they tracked their experience in relation to the issues described and discussed in each issue. Unlike material related to grief and bereavement offered on many web sites and in books, *the LINK brought it home*. It was here that issues of the collective grief of the department, the endless wait for remains, the announcement of FDNY-only bereavement groups, and related information could be found.

Over time another way in which CSU developed its distinct identity was in utilizing the theme of *connections* in naming targeted programs. Originating with Couples Connection, programs that followed included Stay Connected (retirees), Kids Connection (children who lost fathers), Extended Family Connections, and Community Connections (active-duty members and their families). Those familiar with any one of our programs are more likely to recognize the name of others as part of CSU and as a result either participate themselves or recommend others in need of the particular service. While not initially planned, this was an additional, though not essential, strategy for program development.

ESTABLISHING PROVIDER NETWORKS

In an ideal world resource networks would be developed through an organized process of introduction and mutual assessment followed by a trial period of evaluation and adjustment. Growth would be controlled, and both the desired size of the network and the mechanisms for ongoing communication would be established at the outset. In contrast, it has been our experience that establishing effective networks is by no means uncomplicated even in relatively normal times and even more so in the aftermath of a terrorist attack. Our post-9/11 experience bore little resemblance to the ideal situation previously described. Instead resources came from multiple directions at once, often having already established contact with clients, and each having different desires for collaboration. It is for this reason that the authors urge the development of resource networks within communities before an incident occurs.

There were different issues in the development of networks for specific services, such as child bereavement or firehouse clinicians, compared to the network of individual private practitioners working with FDNY personnel and their families.

INDEPENDENT PRACTITIONERS

Psychotherapists in private practice were the most difficult to establish effective collaboration with. This was mostly because of the network size, geographic spread, and the nature of the membership—private, independent practitioners. They understandably did not see themselves joining in collaboration; they simply were responding to the needs of a new patient. It was difficult to balance a desire to be inclusive, not exclusionary, against the need to limit the network to a size where quality control could be maintained. We had no interest in becoming a managed care network, yet we were in a similar position with clients who chose to receive treatment external to our own offices. Since funding was most often provided incrementally, it was extremely difficult to be clear about the limits of available services when those limits were fluid. This necessitated the establishment of regular intervals of communication where progress could be discussed and available resources evaluated. Most often we communicated quarterly with the more than 200 private practitioners who were working with our clients at any given time. There was a large volume of paper work, and tracking systems that needed to be set up and maintained to make this system work. At times several people were involved since there were both clinical and billing functions to monitor. These were new functions, initially the technology to support them was not in place and the learning curve was steep.

It helps to recognize that it is impossible to fully control the development of such a network. Clients will invariably find their own resources, and when the professionals located by them are qualified, it is important to support this. Not all will welcome the necessary collaboration, some will change over time. Often as practitioners began to see multiple members of our community, the desire for a greater understanding of the culture and the specifics of the FDNY's 9/11 experience led to an increased and/or improved collaboration. To the degree possible, this type of information was transmitted in the quarterly phone contacts that were required as part of the quality assurance process that facilitated contact between CSU and private providers and allowed specific clinical information to be discussed with client consent. While this fell short of the imagined network meetings or collaborative models possible in some of the other more contained projects, over time networks were built, collaboration occurred, and relationships developed with people whom one never met face to face or did so only after years of telephone contact. What helped most was a spirit of collaboration and mutual respect. The interface between the private practitioner and CSU, while not typical, was consistent with the type of case management frequently practiced in EAP work. However, not all the private practitioners were accustomed to, or comfortable with, that role. When CSU was mistakenly viewed as the managed care or insurance entity, the discussions reflected this tension, were less collaborative, and more focused on requests for additional sessions. We tried whenever possible to convey our desire to maximize the benefits available to all of our constituents. Clinical discussions were not supervision but were a form of professional consultation that worked best when there was a shared appreciation for both the individual situation known to the clinician and the aggregate data that CSU brought to the table.

Establishing a Network of Private Practitioners

- Consult with an expert to set up your system.
- Identify needed expertise and create a user-friendly database for ready access.
- Establish clear limits based on time frames, not clinical information.
- Establish a single point of entry into the system; this avoids splitting and reduces the potential for internal conflict.
- Meet regularly to identify systemic problems and address them immediately.
- Set up an e-mail link with providers to communicate nonconfidential material quickly and efficiently.
- Identify the team players and use them when referrals are requested.

SPECIAL PROJECTS

Special projects afforded opportunities for a different level of collaboration. Different models developed based on the particular program and the reason for collaboration. Some partnerships were forged primarily to expand resources while others brought expertise that CSU did not possess. For example, our expertise was more in working with adults than with children. While gradually we were able to add this skill to our clinical staff in those offices where children were likely to be seen, the unique and immediate needs of the families of the deceased necessitated a different response. Within this group the concerns expressed were not only for the present but for the future as well. Initially, requests for service were less about the particular behavior of one child and more often the unanswerable questions about the impact of the event on all of the children in a particular family. Listening to these families it became clear that the ideal program would bring services not only to the community but, when possible, directly to the home. Not only would this address the difficulty of managing to keep numerous appointments in various locations at a time when organizing was exceedingly difficult, but equally important, services in the home provided a family focus that supported the surviving parent as the person in charge and the reactions of children as normal rather than pathological and in need of treatment. The services provided needed to be comprehensive and incorporate, or relate to, multiple disciplines in order to plan for the broad range of problems that might emerge. When required, referrals needed to be coordinated with CSU but also individually handled by walking the client through the process when necessary. All of these factors were considered in developing the close collaboration and partnership formed with the Columbia University Family Assessment Program described in Chapter 8.

Each of these models looked and operated somewhat differently. In all cases CSU served as a consultant to outside providers regarding organizational issues, imparting a consistent philosophy of treatment, and information about the availability of other services. While less than perfect, for the most part partnerships emerged and evolved, members received much needed help, and providers learned more about our community and its needs.

Partnership Collaboration Models

- Program interventions are developed, designed, and implemented by CSU, which contracts and oversees independent practitioners for service delivery (Chapter 5).
- Program interventions are developed, designed, and implemented by an outside entity while CSU facilitates outreach and provides training on FDNY culture; each collaborates on identifying and responding to emerging needs (Chapter 8).
- Program interventions are developed in partnership between CSU and a selected consultant who collaborates on all aspects of program design and implementation (Chapter 9).

As providers became known and strengths identified, individual practitioners were pulled in to collaborate on particular programs, including the development and delivery of psycho-educational offerings, such as the Couples Connection program described in Chapter 9. Other collaborations emerged to assist with training for peers and professionals, the development of audiovisual materials, and the creation of communication tools. *The LINK* was one example of a partnership and collaboration built over time. It was our experience that the attention and consistency needed to produce a high-quality newsletter could not have been handled internally at the time it was most needed. The initial investment made in working collaboratively with the authors of the newsletter more than paid off as their understanding of the issues involved gradually increased along with their sensitivity to the population and understanding of the culture. After brainstorming meetings were held, the newsletter authors were able to contact appropriate people for input. CSU continued to review copy for final approval. Perhaps such a newsletter sent to the homes of all employees in the early months could have facilitated community building and healing for the families of the surviving workforce.

One of the most typical errors made by service providers approaching CSU to offer service was the informality of the approach and the failure to provide clarity as to what and why one would be an asset. The exceptions to this introduced themselves with a clear written presentation of credentials, past experience, and plan for collaboration. They requested a meeting or conversation without pushing it. They waited and respected the response offered without attempting multiple entry points into the organization which most often led to confusion, duplication, and frustration for all parties. Knowing the added value that a potential collaborator brought to CSU facilitated decision making regardless of outcome. Some of the best examples of collaboration are discussed in detail in other sections of this volume. These chapters illustrate very different collaboration models, each unique to the specific type of service provided.

Building Partnerships: Dos and Don'ts for Consultants

- Do wait to be invited in.
- Don't assume there is nothing in place.
- Do be clear on what you can offer and why you think it is of value.
- Do respect boundaries; don't do end runs around the appropriate people because you are impatient or think you know better what is needed.
- Do create a feedback loop with the designated representative and use that person consistently to make your needs and observations known.
- Do see yourself as a representative of the organization.
- Do anticipate termination.

BUILDING A STAFF: BOTH PEER AND PROFESSIONAL

As stated earlier, firefighter peers had always been a part of the CSU staffing pattern. In addition to those who were assigned full time to the unit, there were a large number trained over the years to assist in responding to an individual incident. Since these critical incident field responses were brief, the need for a substantial number of peers to work over a sustained period of time had not previously existed. As fire service personnel from all over the county helped with the acute response, CSU began to recruit and train additional FDNY peers. (For more on visiting peer help see Chapter 2.) There were compelling reasons for the majority of these peers to come from the ranks of retirees. They wanted to help; they were unable to officially dig at the site; they allowed those who were authorized to work on the recovery to do so. There were always a few full-duty firefighters who, in addition to their firehouse tours, worked additional hours at CSU.

The importance of peers cannot be overstated. The development of a team that is reflective of the composition of the workforce is important. For example, while all firefighters can assist with access and credibility, those known to members both personally and by reputation are an even greater asset. Those working in, or retired from, a particular geographic location or specialized unit can enter as a family member and, knowing the family, are able to quickly and keenly assess what is needed. Peers provide outreach in a number of ways. On a weekly basis peers visit approximately 30 different FDNY locations giving information and listening to members' needs and concerns. This provides a constant feedback loop between field and office. In addition, peers have the advantage of outreach in a more personal manner than is often appropriate for the professional. When an officer or member expresses concern about a particular member, peers are often in the best position to reach out, assess, educate, and when possible and appropriate, refer. Often, given a diverse and well-known peer team, a specific peer can be hand picked for such an assignment; "Joe used to work with that guy's brother" is a frequent response when assigning such work to peers. As relationships between peers and clinicians develop, this too helps in solidifying referrals. Once a peer has gotten involved and worked hard to encourage a reluctant member to seek help, he wants to refer that member to someone he knows, feels comfortable with, and believes the member will connect with. The more opportunities for peers and clinicians to come together and share ideas and experiences the more confidence they will convey when making referrals.

To be successful, peers need effective and varied outreach materials as well as training to support the development of new skills. All peers have the ability to comfortably enter a firehouse and bring a measure of credibility with them; understanding the role and finding comfort in it, however, is far more difficult. It is often easier for peers to disseminate information than to listen to members' concerns and bring them back for consideration. It is difficult for most to shift from a *fix it* to a *listen to it* mentality. These issues of role transition are an important aspect of peer training. While content is important, in our experience process is even more important. There is a caution when training peers about trauma, grief, family issues, substance abuse, and so on, that relates to the old adage of *a little knowledge can be a dangerous thing*. Unless the role of the peer and the boundaries of that role are clear, such information is potentially more harmful than helpful. In contrast, a peer who is trained to listen not lecture, to facilitate a group discussion by helping others to participate, and to encourage appropriate use of resources is invaluable. Understanding mental health services, such as being able to articulate why therapy is useful or what it is, can go a long way to helping members schedule that appointment they have been avoiding. Often it was through self-disclosure that help-seeking behavior spread:

- A conversation at the kitchen table where a well-regarded senior man suddenly talked about his experience at CSU
- A videotape brought to the house with well-respected members of the department talking about seeking help after 9/11
- Peers acknowledging personal experience with counselors

Still, it is important for peers to increase their knowledge of the mental health issues they are most frequently asked about. No one likes to feel ignorant or uninformed in the face of requests for information. These are intelligent men with a natural and healthy curiosity that grows as they continue to do this work. It is important to nurture this interest and continue to involve peers in professional development opportunities lest they become stagnant and disenchanted with the work. In fact, several peers have gone on to more professional training with the intention of becoming mental health professionals in the future.

Developing a professional staff brings about some different challenges. While many professional resumes—often unsolicited—arrived at CSU, not every trained clinician is equipped to respond to the level of trauma and grief the situation demanded. In addition, while a significant part of the job is the office-based clinical hour, there is a larger context which is equally important. This is not the same as private practice. Participation in the development and delivery of groups, psycho-educational programs, and community building would at times be called for. An appreciation of the mission of EAP work, where both the individual and the organization are the client, is critical. The temporary nature of funding was an additional obstacle that had to be overcome in attracting and retaining a clinical staff. New staff needed a crash course in fire department culture and the psychology of first responders. This is in addition to providing all clinical staff with access to training in current trauma and traumatic grief intervention strategies. Training does not end there: it needs to keep pace with emerging needs and be supported by opportunities for both individual and group supervision.

CARE FOR THE CAREGIVERS

All counseling services are contingent on the health of the counselor. Education and training in professional disciplines emphasize this core value. Much has been written about the need for self-care for mental health practitioners in general and more specifically for those whose work is focused around trauma and grief. The impact of listening empathically to a population relating horrifying stories of witnessing death, handling bodies, survivor guilt and self-recrimination, traumatic exposure, and sudden, unanticipated loss has been said to transform the therapist (Pearlman, 1999). While different terms have been used to describe the phenomenon, vicarious traumatization, secondary traumatic stress, and compassion fatigue all describe the occupational hazard faced by the trauma counselor who, in seeking to help the survivor, bears witness to their pain hour after hour, day after day, client after client (McCann & Pearlman, 1990; Figley, 1995). Also relevant is the less frequently mentioned concept of *vicarious bereavement*, which is described by Rando as the experience of grief and mourning following the deaths of people not known personally to the mourner. Situations of group survivorship where empathy, sympathy, and identification are present enhance the likelihood that vicarious bereavement may occur (Rando, 1999).

Discussions about self-care frequently suggest a balanced workload where trauma clients are interspersed with others, thus reducing exposure to such difficult material. But how does one apply this concept in the aftermath of a disaster where all potential clients have been exposed to the traumatic event and suffered traumatic loss? This was the situation for those working exclusively for FDNY, where some clients had been caught in the collapse, virtually all had been exposed to traumatic sights and smells while digging at the site or working at the morgue, and in addition, all had suffered the loss of many of their closest family or friends. What is the additional risk when the therapist has been exposed as well?

The impact on the mental health practitioner of being so closely connected to a very public event should not be minimized. As has been mentioned many times in this text, there was a fascination with all things connected to FDNY from which CSU and its staff was not exempt. Suddenly everyone was interested in what you did and how you could bear to do it. The reactions to this can be difficult and different for each individual. One implication is that work can intrude even at those times that one wishes to be away from it. This was the experience for most of the counselors who worked directly with CSU; the closer the affiliation perhaps the more acutely it was felt. From inside CSU it at times felt that those more peripheral to the work sought the identification more, wearing it at times as a label of inclusion to mark their involvement in this historic event and to feel that one was making a contribution. One CSU clinician tells the following story:

I was sitting in the audience at a trauma workshop . . . enjoying both the opportunity to learn more about the work I was doing and the break from doing it. It's the typical Q&A that follows such a program, some questions of interest, some not so much, some long-winded comments that seem more about having something to say than an actual point of intellectual curiosity or clarification. I am taken aback when someone identifies themselves as working with firefighters. The person is unknown to me; their comment, which may apply to the one or two firefighters they are treating, is not consistent with any pattern that we are seeing with the hundreds being treated at CSU. What do I do? If I identify myself will I appear to do so just to wear the FDNY label? Am I certain that this is not the case? It is not my intention to debate the point being made, but to clarify the observation; question the generalization. I care deeply about how firefighters are described in the aftermath of this tragedy. Will this be understood? Is this the place to do this? Do I identify myself, knowing that as soon as that occurs many questions follow from both well-meaning and interested colleagues as well as those simply wanting a glimpse to the inside? Being in the room for the day as just an interested, anonymous practitioner has been part of self-care, yet not being recognized as in the thick of it can also be disappointing. How similar to the fiancée who says she enjoyed no one knowing her story and then hated that no one recognized her pain!

The parallel process is a concept often written about in the psychotherapy literature. It describes the similarity that may occur between what is happening with the patient and the therapist. The initial reference was to the experience of the clinician in supervision as being similar or parallel to the experience the clinician was having with the particular patient being discussed. It has since been stretched to describe other such similarities. The intrusion of 9/11 into one's life when it was not expected, welcome, or appropriate is one example of the way in which the experience of the clinician at times paralleled, albeit with less intensity, that of their clients. Experiences such as the following were not without benefit in sensitizing the clinician to the experience of the client.

I remember watching a movie on videotape, nothing particularly memorable or important, just something to escape into, relax after a hard week. The tape begins as usual with some trailers of new releases. Suddenly there it is . . . *The Guys* . . . a film about writing obituaries for the fallen firefighters. I think, if such a moment is unnerving to me, what must it be like for my clients? There I am, back at work.

THE REWARDS OF THE WORK

While the work is difficult, it is simultaneously rewarding. Intervening early in the aftermath of trauma frequently results in a relatively rapid exacerbation of symptoms. When asked about their experience, most staff spontaneously talk about the rewarding nature of working with a population that is relatively healthy, well-resourced, and appreciative of help. Both internal staff and outside consultants have frequently commented that firefighters and their families are an extremely likeable and interesting group of people to work with. This general characteristic of the population is perhaps one part of the equation that contributes to staff wellness; the other part is the context in which the work is done.

The firehouse has a lot to teach us about creating a supportive work environment that encourages teamwork. In many ways CSU parallels the firehouse where meals are cooked and shared, humor and camaraderie are encouraged, and mutual aid is apparent. Creativity is fostered by an open-door policy that encourages all members to share ideas freely and to become more involved in the programs and projects that most interest them. In this way teamwork is fostered as both peers and clinicians have taken leadership roles in the development of programs for retirees, children of the deceased, family liaisons, military vets, and others. Still, in times of extreme stress more is needed.

The Need for Self-Care

Our experience affirms the necessity of incorporating self-care into the work life of both professional and peer counselors. There are differences in the specifics of the self-care programs for each of these groups; however, the similarities form a clear pattern of how the organization can assist and support the self-care of its employees. Based on the previous experience of CSU, it was determined that, to the degree possible, self-care for both groups of staff would be built into regular work routines and delivery of services within the unit. The major program components included training and education, clinical supervision, social outlets, support for individual counseling, and the availability of alternative wellness resources (Figure 4.2).

Education and Training

The leadership of CSU agreed that it was critical to establish a baseline of knowledge for both professional and peer counselors employed by CSU. While different, there were many areas of overlap, and when appropriate, it was helpful to plan joint educational seminars in areas of common interest as a means to encourage interaction among people who needed to build trust in one another. Because of its New York City location, CSU staff had access to experts in their respective fields. One of the gratifying experiences in the aftermath of 9/11 was that many of these experts were willing to share their knowledge with a group of professional and peer counselors committed to assisting the members of the FDNY. Educational seminars were planned for the workday whenever possible. This demonstrated CSU's commitment to ongo-

Figure 4.2 Components of a self-care system.

ing education and, in the early months of the response, allowed staff with heavy clinical schedules the opportunity to share work time with professional colleagues.

Guidelines for Education

Professional	*Peer*
• Incorporate into work schedules as possible.	• Incorporate into work schedules as possible.
• Assess knowledge gaps via personal interactions and survey tools and schedule training accordingly.	• Important skill sets include: listening and presentation skills, group facilitation, case finding, referral, and follow-up.
• Utilize external experts who add to knowledge base while encouraging dialogue among participants.	• Collaboration with a recognized teaching institute assures teaching of basic and advanced skills.
• Encourage individual counselors to pursue specialized areas of interest (e.g., group or marital counseling).	• Utilize in-house clinical experts on specific educational topics to increase interactions and build trust between peer and professional staff.

Professional and Peer Supervision

Individual clinical supervision is a mainstay of professional practice. Good supervision provides the support necessary to critically examine both the treatment of the client and the impact on the professional. It helps to structure the work and support service delivery by providing consistent guidelines for clinicians and peers. It is the place where education is reinforced, learning needs are further assessed, and skills continue to be developed. Equally important, if implemented well it provides a safe space in which the clinician or the peer can talk about the many difficult challenges involved in the work they do.

Clinical supervision for professional staff should be offered weekly, preferably by knowledgeable in-house supervisors. If this is not available, it should be contracted for externally. Group supervision can be useful, and when facilitated by an external consultant it can provide both additional training as well as opportunities to discuss important issues triggered by the work including issues of countertransference, secondary traumatization, and self-care.

Providing supervision for peers presents a different challenge. Unlike professional counselors, most peers are new to the process and unaccustomed to having their work examined in this way. It is helpful to organize peer supervision in a less formal format and in a more familiar setting. In the case of firefighter peer counselors, this means meeting in groups around the kitchen table. Each day begins with peer counselors gathering at the kitchen table to report their previous activities, plan the day, and seek peer validation of their approach to the complex issues presented in the firehouse during their visits. At times, professional counselors having their coffee will be drawn in to these informal sessions. As trust develops between these groups, their opinion may be increasingly sought out.

In addition to the many informal group gatherings that occur in the life of peer counselors, we believe it is also important to offer a formal group supervision meeting facilitated by a profession counselor, preferably external to the system. These meetings serve to reinforce educational offerings, create opportunities for needs assessment, communicate agency goals, and more formally identify peers who become overwhelmed by the task of their work and may need to take a break from it. It is equally important to identify a specific peer team leader from within the organization who is there to support individual peers as needed. It is particularly helpful to have this person available to resolve questions as quickly as possible that occur while peers are in the field. Accurate information available in a timely manner will quell destructive rumors, which can occur frequently in a workplace in crisis, and in addition, lends credibility not only to the peer's interest in helping but to his or her ability to do so.

ADDITIONAL SUPPORTS

Along with the more formal structures of education and supervision previously described, other types of self-care activities are not only supported but encouraged. Providing time and space for social interactions, either a lunchtime meal that encourages professionals and peers to interact in a nonthreatening way or the occasional off-site dinner that includes the partners of staff and allows them to gain a new level of insight into the work of the counselor, is suggested. These activities demonstrate leadership's support of staff and also provide additional opportunities for staff from all sites to interact more fully.

It is also important to encourage the utilization of counseling and other healing services, such as the auricular acupuncture that is provided on site to clients and utilized simultaneously by staff. Sponsoring these and other programs, such as yoga, massage, and natural healing services when possible, makes them easily accessible and clearly conveys support for self-care as opposed to giving only lip service to the idea. When full support for such services is not possible, the message can be conveyed by encouraging staff to join together to contract for specific services and, as appropriate, making space available for their use. As an alternative, contracting for discounted group rates at local facilities is also a possibility.

No matter how busy the schedule, utilization of earned vacation times should be encouraged as well as time spent away from work with family. Whenever possible staff should be genuinely thanked for their work and external acknowledgements of an exceptional job should be shared with all staff.

In a traumatic crisis situation, a burden is placed on those professional and peer counselors who provide direct services to clients. The leadership of an agency needs to accept some responsibility to promote self-care for each worker. Ultimately, each worker needs to be provided with the tools of self-care; however, each worker must be responsible to utilize these tools. The payoff for the agency is a healthy workforce with a low turnover rate. For the worker, payoff comes with the satisfaction of providing services to a unique population while enjoying the support of valued coworkers.

KEEPING THE MACHINERY GOING: FUNDING AND RESOURCE DEVELOPMENT

Learning to deal with the multiple entities involved in post disaster funding can be complicated, frustrating, and difficult. This can be especially true for those whose work did not require fund development prior to the disaster. It is helpful to recognize that, while you may not be an expert in funding mechanisms, you are the expert when it comes to defining the needs of your community. While it may be tempting to avoid this arena believing that funding will find its way to those in need, this can prove to be a mistake. It is important to identify someone who can familiarize themselves with the often multiple funding streams that become available quickly in the aftermath of a disaster and then be directly involved in making specific requests to them. This person can be a fund development expert who is familiar with the ins and outs of government grants and private philanthropy or someone within the organization with the necessary skills who can devote their time and energy to this important task. It is often difficult for someone with a skill set that lends itself to client intervention to step back and deal with funding requirements. It can feel like one is doing less. Support and recognition for the importance and frustration of this work is helpful. When it comes to making a direct funding appeal it is recommended that those who know the population best be directly involved as they most often can articulate the background, needs, and importance in the most compelling way.

When there is a preexisting internal EAP or mental health unit, it is logical and we believe advantageous to secure postdisaster funding directly from the source and then be in the position to directly control the resources available to your community. Not getting to the table immediately can unfortunately mean that the money is directed to other community organizations leaving you in the position to have to outsource all services. This is a viable choice, however, we believe it is one that you should choose rather than have chosen for you. Multiple sources of funding are likely to evolve and are helpful to provide funding for the broad range of services that may be desirable. Postdisaster funding is always time limited and necessitates looking ahead for the next layer of funding even as the current one is just underway. It is the ongoing assessment and educated projection of client need that determines the level and duration of funding required.

THOUGHTS FOR THE FUTURE

It is important to remember that hindsight is 20–20, and many of the ideas presented are offered to the reader from that perspective. There are always two threads to attend to: one related to the ongoing assessment and delivery of the services that are needed and the other to the people required to provide them. At the time of a catastrophic event it is necessary to move into action, often with little time to plan, organize, or identify the principles that will guide one's actions. While there will always be a great deal that cannot be predicted about such events and the response they will call for, it is our belief that there is a certain amount of preincident planning that will be helpful regardless of the specific situation that occurs. This is true for both emergency service administrators and mental health professionals. It begins with the development of partnerships between the two groups. Emergency service systems that already have an EAP in place have a natural point from which to begin to talk about the range of services that might be needed in the event of a major incident. They can review the current state of preincident education and determine its level of adequacy. They can begin the work of ensuring a place for mental health services in the organizational response to a major event. For those systems without EAP services, likely the majority of first responders, we recommend partnering with local providers, membership organizations, agencies, or independent practitioners in your community. This is the time to teach interested mental health professionals about the needs of first responders and to select those who work well within your system. Mental health professionals with a particular interest in this area can approach local emergency service systems on their own suggesting a method of mutual exploration. This is the value of preincident contact; it allows a period of mutual inquiry to see if a partnership can be beneficial. There is much to be learned on both sides of the cultural gap that often divides these two professional communities. A level of comfort and knowledge about the cultural norms and customs of each can go a long way in making a postincident response more successful.

CHAPTER 5

Providing Help in the Workplace: The Firehouse Clinician Project

T HE GREATEST moment for a first responder is to be the first one to get to a person in dire need and then save them. Despite the dangers, first responders do it because it is the right thing to do, and it sets in stone the purpose of a life on the job. It is a sign of courage, luck, and respect. It is the stuff of stories around the kitchen table. It is a yardstick that measures two dimensions of their daily existence—bravery and cowardice.

How does one judge bravery and cowardice? Certainly, people who have had to face such tough choices will judge themselves along some continuum that reaches from these two opposite poles and is deeply ingrained in personal self-evaluation. The act of self-evaluation for them, as it is for us, causes the deepest levels of pride and shame. The degree of pride or shame they feel is determined by characteristics of the demand, the crisis, and the dangers of the situation. When life-and-death choices have to be made, the consequences of those actions to self-concept, what they will see when they look at themselves in the mirror, and who they will be as reflected back in the faces of those they love and respect, are as far-reaching to their individual lives as 9/11 has been to the world.

THE MINDSET OF FDNY FIREFIGHTERS

Emergency responders, by definition, do not know what they are going to face before they get to the site of an emergency. Initial information provided by dispatchers is limited. Firefighters and officers, relying on their own experience, will dictate the response on the scene. All the rehearsals for possible emergencies cannot predict the exact best response for the next crisis. How first responders act is determined by some mix of the limited information they have been given, the specialized training they may have, the years on the job and quality of their experience, the tradition of their company, and the context of the crisis.

Firefighters are often asked how they can approach an emergency and dangerous situation when everyone else's instinct is to run. The answer that they tell you is the one I have found most accurate: they like action in general, and they are trained to respond in the way that they do, the way that makes others say they are brave. What they and those who ask do not fully appreciate is that responding to an emergency or dangerous situation has consequences that last beyond the moment. Surviving danger often means keeping the experience as a memory that will continue to influence long after.

The stories that follow are true.

John's Story

The context is the day of the WTC collapse. Not much was known about the overall condition of the site and the surrounding buildings that were still standing. But these men were well schooled in the traditions that honor rescuing people. They were highly experienced in facing dangerous situations. They knew they were going to go where no one should have gone. But for the hope of finding someone, saving a life, they could see that the structures should have been sealed off, taken down, and certainly not entered by even the most skilled rescuer. Even a probie would have known that.

Still, the chiefs hoped that people were still alive but trapped, because there was word of cell phone calls. They had to send in any available crew to try for a rescue, knowing that more firefighters could be lost. Had the chiefs allowed themselves the luxury, they would have been punishing themselves for not having been better prepared after the 1993 bombing that tried to take down the towers by setting off a truckload of bombs in the underground parking lot. This time, all they could do was to give the order to send their men into a zone where regulations and second guessers might give them even more regrets for the rest of their lives.

The first team went in and could not find anyone, but how far into the building could they actually go? The structure was on fire and unstable, truly dangerous. As far as they could see, for as much as they could explore, no one was there.

A second team was called. Still, the dust had not settled, the ground was shifting and fires raged on. The structure continued to weaken. They, too, got as far as they could, risked more than they should, and came back empty. Nobody alive or dead. They retreated.

Little could be done at that time to gain control of the situation. Surrounding buildings were on fire, dark with smoke, structurally unstable, and near collapse.

The chief asked again. This time, the company was a Special Operations company. Their training is more intense, more specialized. Their attitude is in their title—special. A veteran on the job with extra training in urban search and rescue was paired with someone with much less experience on the job. A team of five made their way in and pushed farther than the other teams, passed the lobby, through corridors, and up steps, in the dark and smoke, checking each floor. They looked for the most likely place from where people could escape, the place everyone knows to avoid in a fire, much less the magnitude of the collapse of the towers. They searched each floor until they found the elevator. And that is where the intact bodies were discovered. A cell phone lay nearby. An elevator stuck near the fourth floor, its box crushed closed, trapped its passengers.

A single survivor was pulled from the entire wreckage of the World Trade Center. It wasn't because people didn't try. Many tested the odds against safety and pushed against the dangers to find someone. Finding anyone was simply impossible. Adding to the grief and tragedy, it is an episode that may never leave the hearts of those first responders.

What is the effect of the experience on that team of Special Operations men who located the deceased?

Along the dimension of bravery and cowardice, how will the firefighters who found the dead civilians in the elevator think of themselves? What is the effect of second guessing oneself, questioning the skill and bravery of brother firefighters and officers? Will they think of themselves as brave heroes or cowardly failures? How will they think of the firefighters who could not get to the fourth floor? As therapists, our job is to cure by not making judgments. John's job is to save lives by making judgments. How do we help John?

THE INTERVENTION: PLACING CLINICIANS IN FIREHOUSES

A firehouse clinician is a professional mental health worker assigned by the FDNY CSU to a specific firehouse. The group targeted for intervention is everyone directly and indirectly associated with the firehouse. Obviously, this includes all the firefighters and officers permanently or temporarily assigned to the house. In a firehouse with one company, that might include 28 firefighters. Perhaps not as obvious, the target population includes the immediate and extended families of those firefighters, and the families of the dead. Less apparent, the mental health worker becomes available to all the people who may be part of the life of a firehouse and who may touch the lives of the firefighters.

That group includes retirees with special ties to that particular firehouse and people from the community who spend time around the firehouse. The only characteristic individuals from the community seem to share is that they are well known to the firefighters and are somehow important in the lives of the firefighters and the firehouse. For example, there was Tim, the middle-aged community activist with his own set of problems, who was always in various stages of recovery, and young adult Wardell, who dreamed of becoming a firefighter and took pictures of them at fires.

Genesis of the Project

Prior to 9/11, there was no such title as firehouse clinician. The model was invented out of necessity by Malachy Corrigan, coauthor of this text and current FDNY CSU director, and by the subsequent, collective efforts of CSU. When there was a fatal fire, Malachy would go to the firehouse. Neither the emergency mental health needs of firefighters nor systemic issues of the department could be filled by one mental health worker or the relatively small staff that grew over the years of his tenure. While Mal was the only one 20 years ago, others at the CSU learned to work within the FDNY and firehouses in a manner similar to his example. The changes that swept through post-9/11 took CSU along. Thus, his 20+ years of experience prior to 9/11 and the collective experience of the CSU became the source of knowledge and instruction for the 42 firehouse clinicians who responded after 9/11.

A search of the literature of placing mental health clinicians in firehouses reveals no publications. No articles have been found that describe using mental health personnel in this manner. Although disaster response has included psychological and social services for decades, as far as could be learned, actually assigning a clinician to a firehouse had never been attempted.

The concept of placing mental health workers within an affected community is not new. Miller (2002, p. 288) recognized that "Because many mass terror victims cannot or will not present themselves to traditional mental health services, psychological care must be organized around outreach programs in the community." The new part is thinking of a fire department and firehouse as a community for the purposes of designing an intervention. It may be one of the lasting contributions of this effort. Think of the people connected by mission, employment, proximity, and values. Community is measured not only by the traditional factors of neighborhood, economics, religion, or race. Community can also be defined by identity, shared experience, and loss.

As it evolved, the Firehouse Clinician Project was not as carefully thought out as one might have hoped for, but considering this was developing in an ongoing disaster, it could only be guided by the preexisting practices of the FDNY. It is important to remember that it was not and could not be implemented systematically, like adapting other interventions. A number of groups and forces combined in the turmoil of the 9/11 recovery to create a role for firehouse clinicians.

The response to 9/11 came in all varieties and from everywhere. In general, people closest to a disaster site are the most affected, both in terms of loss and in terms of needing to act. People who lost loved family, friends, and colleagues were more affected than those who did not. Those closest in proximity to an impact site were more affected than those who were farther away. In general, New Yorkers and the metropolitan communities were more affected than communities at a greater distance from the impact sites. The composition of affected communities inevitably forges the response of that community. Virtually everyone everywhere wanted to give something to the recovery effort. Construction workers brought their machines and tools. The finest restaurants brought gourmet foods, and neighborhood bodegas delivered homemade and off-the-shelf foods. Citizens with nothing but their blood lined up at blood banks. New York City's psychotherapists, psychologists, and social workers wanted to give mental health services. Historically, psychotherapy has always thrived in the free and intellectually open environment of New York City. For this reason, there are probably more mental health professionals in the New York City metropolitan area, per capita, than anywhere else in the world. They, too, wanted to help. Psychotherapists appeared at the WTC site and firehouses believing that they, too, could give what they had, and it would be needed as much as anything else.

In a traumatized city, there were thousands of traumatized psychotherapists reacting just like everyone else, needing to give whatever they could. However, the intention to give does not always translate into being helpful. Construction workers got into conflicts with each other. People gave too much of one supply and not enough of another. Blood banks overflowed with unneeded blood. And, psychotherapists sometimes insisted on helping those who did not want or need or were not ready for a mental health intervention.

One e-mail I received in my role as a disaster response county coordinator for the New York State Psychological Association typified the reaction of some clinicians. It read, "Dr. Greene, can you get me over the police barricades at the Armory? Those people need our help." The Armory was a location where relatives were posting flyers for the lost and where other kinds of information and services were being coordinated.

Some independent mental health clinicians showed up at the WTC wanting nothing more than to provide an ear to the grief stricken. Still others went directly to firehouses to offer counsel and comfort. What those clinicians did not realize was that they were actually burdening the firefighters, who were overwhelmed by their grief and their desire to find the bodies of their fallen brothers. The traditions of the firehouse always dictate being polite and caring to the community, and most of the men tried to both work tirelessly at the recovery effort and accommodate those who appeared at the firehouse.

Other mental health professionals with organizational savvy and clout approached the CSU and Medical Unit to offer clinical services. Like the other elements of the department, these units were also overwhelmed with recovery work and providing services to those showing signs of a traumatic response. They, too, wanted to be polite to their community. However, many clinicians were already acting on their own, outside of the system and family of the department. To manage the situation of clinicians wanting to help and to prevent rogue clinicians from the unmonitored, burdensome practice of going into the firehouse without authorization, the Counseling Services Unit worked with these outside clinicians to develop a systematic method to fulfill two goals. First, many more people needed social and emotional assistance than the limited staff of the Counseling Services Unit could possibly respond to quickly; utilizing outside clinicians to fill this need provided a good solution. Second, the inappropriate but well-intended helping of some of New York's mental health community could be shaped into a positive force rather than a disorganizing one. Organizing representatives from social work and psychology could satisfy both goals. This project became the Firehouse Clinicians Project. The Counseling Services Unit assigned outside social workers and psychologists to all the firehouses that suffered a direct loss. The officers and men of the firehouse were officially informed that a mental health worker was going to be coming to the firehouse. This gave a civilian mental health worker the authority to expect some level of cooperation to enter the house and address the firefighters. It also afforded the Counseling Services Unit of the FDNY the authority to screen, educate, and exert some control over the mental health professionals who previously had been burdening the firehouses and system.

THE POPULATION: DEFINING WHO NEEDED SERVICES

The firehouse clinicians served a target population that was as varied as the array of New York City communities. The potential population for services could be as unique as the individual characteristics of that particular firehouse, plus its own families and community people who became attached to that house. Firehouse clinicians had to have an appreciation of the communities in which the firefighters lived and where they worked within various parts of the city itself, an area that was geographically dispersed hundreds of miles in all directions around New York City. Firehouse clinicians had to serve a population of firefighters who were shaped by the function of the firehouse within the FDNY. Firefighting companies differ in their professional responsibilities. For example, engine and ladder companies, or special operations, each have special tasks and responsibilities at the events they respond to. Companies have different levels of training and attitudes to optimize their response during an event. Thus, the target population for the firehouse clinician could also be characterized by the mission and mental expectations of the company and its firefighters. A clinician might reasonably anticipate that the firefighters of a house known to be aggressive at a scene might have more aggressive people assigned to it, or firefighters that have experienced a wider range of events. For example, special operations companies, like squads and rescue companies, which might be sent to fight a more dangerous part of a fire and have a different manner of accomplishing a mission, could have characteristic attitudes that bind them. Their pride in their mission may be reflected in their mental expectations of the clinician.

Firehouses and firefighting companies are 24-hour, 7-day-a-week operations. To fill the manpower needs, firehouses have permanently assigned firefighters and officers as well as temporary ones who fill in for those who are on medical leave, on vacation, or on assignment elsewhere. The firehouse clinician has to provide services to all groups, firefighters and officers, those temporarily assigned, and those permanently placed in the firehouse. These individuals have different schedules and rotations through the 24/7 life of the firehouse. Firehouse clinicians have to find ways to service everyone. Periodically, over the months that the firehouse clinicians were deployed, that developed into being available at whatever hour the clinician's services might be necessary. It was not the original intention of the CSU that this be a 24/7 assignment or that the target population be more than FDNY members and their families. It is also not one of the enduring lessons of the CSU that mental health workers be asked to visit firehouses all the time. This, like all experiences, needs to be tempered by the demands of the situation.

It would be a mistake to restrict the description of the target population to terms of traditional demographics. Certainly, firefighters are predominantly male, with characteristic racial and religious affiliations that are important elements in their cultural norms, as described previously in this text. However, one must be careful to avoid typical professional advice on working with blue-collar first responders. Stereotyping may be a human flaw and potentially functional in times of stress, but it is destructive to being helpful. Stereotyping may improve the speed at which we can assess people and situations by providing assumptions and filling in blanks when we don't have the time or opportunity to collect the facts. In an emergency situation or any stressful one, stereotyping—making a quick assessment—may help people make better guesses. But, in many situations, making assumptions about people is a great error. Stereotyping can often lead to perceiving people not for who they are, but as images of our own misplaced prejudices. Sitting in a comfortable therapist's chair and in one's own office, a private environment, one can sort through biases and take the time to get to know the other person. Mental health workers may be just as prone to stereotyping as anyone else when they are outside of their therapy offices. Making false assumptions—stereotyping—may be even more likely at the site of a disaster or in a firehouse, out of the controlled environment of an office and in the middle of a highly charged scene. One's attitudes and reactions cannot be masked or explored like they can in the more predictable setting of a psychotherapy office. Further, demographics do not reveal the compelling influence of the workplace culture, which is so powerfully exerted in the firehouse. No doubt, this is true among other groups, not only among firefighters and first responders.

Men are commonly considered to be less alive to emotional expression. The stereotypic macho types, like firefighters, are often thought of as even less attuned to feelings, relatively uneducated, and unsophisticated. Biases like these are just as destructive in the field situation as they are in the office. More important, these stereotypes do not apply. Most firefighters are at least as able to process emotions as the general population and probably better than many because they have more opportunity to talk and get to know their coworkers, whom they also live with in the 24-hour lifestyle of the firehouse.

THE SITE: FIVE BOROUGHS OF FIREHOUSES

Clinicians were assigned by the CSU to firehouses that lost a current member on 9/11 and served the firefighting units that were stationed in those houses. The criteria to be eligible for deploying a firehouse clinician to a particular site or population was simple, but in practice became influenced by a number of factors. Some companies wanted a clinician and all available services, while others were passively open to the idea of having a mental health clinician join the firehouse but did not actually request someone to help. Other firehouses needed prodding to address apparent or anticipated mental health issues.

In the initial phase of the project, 62 firehouses were covered by 42 clinicians. Most clinicians were assigned to one house, and a few clinicians covered several companies and houses. Each clinician was paired with a peer counselor, an experienced officer who introduced the mental health worker to the house and remained available for consultation throughout. The scope of the project grew to affect thousands of lives. Firefighters, families, retired firefighters, and people in the community could connect to the FDNY services through a personal connection in their firehouse, their second home and second family. Thousands of people could be reached by the FDNY in a very personal way through a mental health worker who knew them and came to them. These same thousands of people could also be heard by the FDNY as the clinicians brought personal but anonymous concerns back to the FDNY.

THEORETICAL ORIENTATION

Mental health clinicians in general tend to identify themselves with a particular theoretical school for doing psychotherapeutic work. Some align themselves with the psychoanalytic model; others might call themselves behaviorists, cognitive-behavioralists, or any of the dozens of theoretical identities. Little empirical data exist to show how theoretical bias relates to the effectiveness of on-site services. In fact, it is not at all clear how to evaluate on-site mental health services; forming an opinion about appropriate theoretical assumptions for on-site mental health workers is certainly open to debate and interpretation. However, based on our experience, the theoretical identity of the mental health worker is less important than the interventions of that clinician. Psychologists, social workers, and counselors need to maintain an awareness that they are working with people who are at work, always ready mentally and physically to step into their boots and onto the rig.

Providing mental health services in this context means facilitating the normal human response to trauma and grief; it does not mean treating all of the target groups with psychotherapy or a modified version of psychotherapy. Mental health services in this context may mean talking in ways that psychotherapists talk, but more likely it means providing a range of activities that are likely to have therapeutic value. Thus, it is less guided by theoretical orientation than by the practicalities of the situation, experience in relevant conflicts, confidence and optimism in one's innate abilities, and universal human compassion.

GENERALIZING LESSONS

Generalizing the lessons learned from one disaster to another is more than an inexact science. Potentially, it can have unintentionally poor consequences for the next target population. For example, it can often be useful to have a large meeting of those immediately impacted by a disaster. This meeting can be used to dispel rumors and give individuals opportunities to connect and vent. Calling a large meeting at a firehouse in the early stages of the 9/11 disaster would have been counterproductive. It would have added work to the firefighter's already impossible schedules of clearing the site, attending funerals, caring for families of the lost, and caring for their own family. Just because some groups are tasked to respond first does not make all first responders sufficiently similar for the purpose of offering mental health assistance on site. Thus, taking lessons and techniques from one disaster experience and applying them to another must be practiced with great caution. For another event in a different context, a large house meeting might be most effective. In this instance, the views of the captain and senior firefighters helped determine that meeting with only those on duty would be best.

One fire department cannot be assumed to be sufficiently like another for the purposes of replicating the Firehouse Clinician Project. There are too many potential differences in the culture of the departments and differences in the catastrophic events. Nor is it advisable to generalize indiscriminately from one firehouse to another within the same department or even from one firehouse clinician to another. A systematic program to deploy firehouse clinicians is just one tool for responding to a potential mental health crisis. In the post-9/11 world of New York City's fire department, and all the variables that implies, attaching clinicians to firehouses made sense.

It might be useful to think about the mental health interventions as tools to help first responders. Mental health professionals have to choose a psychosocial intervention method from an array of techniques like firefighters have to choose physical tools from a truck to resolve an emergency situation. Firehouse clinicians are consultants that are like having an array of tools at your disposal. The more tools carried by firefighters, the better the odds they will have the right ones to help. The more tools or techniques mental health workers know about, and the more they know about using those tools effectively, the better chance they have for helping. If there is one lesson, then it may be that there are many means for supporting first responders; that mental health clinicians can play a part in that support; and that training, experience with trauma, and knowledge of the population and culture can be used creatively to find the new normal.

INTERVENTION GOAL

The first goal of the firehouse clinician, like on-site mental health responders in general, is to make mental health services available more easily by making them more accessible. Some people in or out of traumatic situations simply will not go for help when they need it. The probability of helping increases when the modes of service delivery increase. That probability can be increased for all of the target populations by placing another source of help in closer proximity to those who might need the service. Some people prefer going to a private office to discuss private matters. Others would never consider visiting a mental health professional's office but would talk to someone about intimate experiences while at work. Families, separated from the worksite and reluctant or ignorant of helpful resources, also can be reached via the worksite through the firefighter. Strategically placing professionals at the local job site, in this case the firehouse, created an opportunity for the target groups to gain from the knowledge of mental health professionals without stigmatizing their activities and concerns.

The second goal is to provide services that actually meet the needs of those who access the services. An on-site clinician, who has been accepted by the affected population and has sufficient knowledge of the array of services and skills to meet the needs of that group, can match the people, needs, and services. The effectiveness of those services is more difficult to gauge. Measuring the effectiveness of all mental health services in all settings is generally elusive, and in the midst of a disaster, is even more difficult to operationalize. However, two classes of measuring goal effectiveness would be useful to keep in mind. First might be objective data such as the number and type of contacts made by each on-site clinician and referrals made to traditional centers for help, but reliable tracking of this data is extremely difficult. A second source of effectiveness would be the level of satisfaction reported by the target population. Simply, do the firefighters want the clinicians to be present? FDNY CSU surveys showed that only 3 of the 62 firehouses did not want the clinicians to continue.

Firehouse Clinician Goals

- Make mental health services accessible.
- Match available services to the needs of the firehouse.
- Identify individuals having extreme reactions or who are feeling very depressed or isolated.

It is unrealistic to think that reliable data can be collected in the early phases of the response to a disaster. Too much is happening. There will be more time and need later on to have the data that should guide decisions as the response progresses. In the early stages, however, effectiveness data can be obtained from the clinicians themselves if they are trained to be alert to the signs of effectiveness.

One firehouse clinician reported that in the early days of her meetings at the firehouse, people would leave the room or turn up the television while she was trying to make a presentation. These were not-so-subtle signs of problems with the intervention or with the clinician. In contrast, some firehouse clinicians reported being invited to be a guest at the meal, signaling that at least the clinician had not done something to offend and would be accorded this courtesy. Why was one clinician accepted and the other rejected? There are many factors that determine acceptance and rejection in any situation, and this setting is not different in that respect. Age, sex, religion, interpersonal skill, training, relevant experience, timing, nature of the clinicians introduction to the group, and nature of the firehouse itself surely are among the factors that can add or detract from the success of the clinician's mission. However, these variables are within the awareness of every good clinician and cannot be ignored. Over time, the clinician who seemed to be rejected was able to form a strong bond with the firehouse, while the one who had been invited to the meal was eventually rejected. One clinician's sensitive persistence permitted the firefighters to get to know her and appreciate what she could offer. The other clinician also became known to the firefighters, and they discovered that her talents did not come across well in a firehouse.

Perhaps the best indication that the firehouse was open to having a firehouse clinician was its willingness to engage the clinician. Engagement can take many forms ranging from friendliness to confrontational. One firehouse clinician recalled:

> It was nearly time to go for the meal; that is, it was time to prepare lunch, and the television was on. A news program was reporting on a liberal versus conservative conflict when the firefighter at the refrigerator started making loud comments about liberals. I had the distinct feeling that I was being baited. I did not take the bait but recognized that this veteran firefighter wanted some interaction with me. Later, we got to talking, and he needed a referral for his depressed daughter.

In a way unique to each firehouse, successful clinicians were made to feel part of the firehouse, included not only in meals, but events for the entire company that took place both in the firehouse and elsewhere.

Goals may be more specific to the nature of the firehouse or to individuals within the company. The firehouse may need general information on Posttraumatic Stress Disorder (PTSD) or loss, while individuals may have questions about medications and the reemergence of problems that they suffered from earlier in their lives. Topping the list of clinician goals is suicide prevention. Although it rarely happens, no one can dismiss the danger, especially because the chances for suicide increase after trauma. Suicide prevention by education, awareness, and making services easily available is a necessity. However, it would be foolhardy to believe that suicide attempts and completions can always be prevented. By placing suicide prevention on the list of goals, clinicians can take the necessary steps to reduce its likelihood and increase the chances that someone within the target population would also be alert to those warning signs. The overarching goal of this intervention was to improve accessibility to services and not to get everyone into treatment. Talking explicitly about suicide normalizes the feelings of concern, teaches everyone the warning signs, and provides a safe route to access help.

Some have described the role of the on-site mental health worker as delivering *psychological first aid*. While several definitions may be found for this term, it usually refers to the initial help administered to a victim immediately after trauma that improves an individual's ability to function within a relatively short period of time or prevents the later development of psychiatric disorders. The firehouse clinician is also not present to give crisis intervention treatment.

It seems unnecessary to describe the activity of an on-site mental health worker as administering anything to a patient, much less a treatment that is analogous to physical medicine. On-site mental health workers are not like physicians or nurses who follow a medical model or administer medication or bandages. Rather, the goal of an on-site mental health worker like the firehouse clinician is to be helpful and support resiliency, the definition for which can only be developed by the individuals who comprise the life of the firehouse. This might be termed a biopsychosocial model. Successful firehouse clinicians support the resiliency of the firehouse, firefighters, families, and communities. Sometimes, the experience a mental health worker has with seriously disturbed people can be used for triage, to identify a person having an extreme reaction, becoming nonfunctional, and showing signs of a serious mental problem. However, the frequency of this sort of activity is relatively low.

Traditionally, mental health workers provide psychological treatment, or psychotherapy, to cure mental illness, a psychopathology. Traditional theory says that by curing the pathology, the person gets well and their functioning improves. On-site mental health workers, firehouse clinicians in this case, do not administer psychological treatment to relieve a pathology that somehow results in better psychological functioning. A model of intervention that treats an illness must assume that its targets, in this case firefighters, are ill. Most people who experience trauma are not and do not become ill. The distinction is important because thinking of the task as doing something like a treatment procedure to the firehouse, such as providing psychological first aid or crisis intervention, can subtly suggest to the firefighters that they must be ill and must be treated to cure their psychopathology. It is wrong to suggest that first responders have to have been made ill by a trauma and must reach an illusory goal of curing their psychopathology. In fact, in practice, assumptions by the on-site mental health professional that they have to universally diagnose and give psychological first aid and crisis intervention to the sick and injured first responder are counterproductive.

The firehouse clinician is on-site for an undefined, potentially extended period, not just the initial period when psychological first aid may be relevant. Dispatching a firehouse clinician also requires a longer time commitment to providing this service than is implied by procedures called *psychological first aid* or *crisis intervention*. Thinking of the work as joining with an existing culture that has its own strengths and weaknesses is a better model for assisting first responders. With the help of the skilled clinician, target groups are able to define their own goals that will comprise recovery, and they are more likely to achieve those goals. This model is positive and flexible, and it builds on existing strengths without ignoring potential problems and without suggesting that first responders have to be cured of an illness.

SELECTING AND TRAINING FIREHOUSE CLINICIANS

Hindsight. Not everybody who wants to go on site has the skills. Otherwise solid professionals can do and say things that are not appropriate outside of an office setting. A license to provide mental health services is not a sufficient qualification, although it may be a legal necessity. Advanced training in one or more of the prevailing models of on-site trauma intervention is also not necessarily useful and fitting to all cultures because, while on-site help may be the treatment of choice, it must be uniquely modified for that environment, at that time, and for that particular disaster. The optimal way to select on-site clinicians is to know who they are going to be prior to the event. On-site mental health workers should be screened and given some level of training before they are ever needed. On-site workers and potential target populations will work better together when they are familiar with each other. Like all preventive measures, it is most efficient. No uniformed organization made this their standard of practice before 9/11 and probably very few have made this effort even in the post-9/11 world. Professional mental health organizations were probably more advanced in being prepared to respond to the mental health needs of mass populations after a disaster.

The mental health clinicians used for 9/11 came to the CSU from a variety of sources and with all levels of expertise but had substantial ignorance of firefighter culture. As the CSU developed the plan to bring mental health professionals to the firehouses, other professionals approached the FDNY to join the effort. All were screened by the CSU staff. The guiding principles for selecting suitable clinicians came from their experience working with firefighters, their knowledge of the unique FDNY culture, and their strong mental health expertise. They understood without needing a crash course that the central characteristic of firehouses and firefighters is that they have group-based functions and interpersonal dynamics. Consequently, the CSU staff believed that professionals with experience facilitating groups plus professional experience with disaster and trauma would be most qualified. That assessment proved accurate.

Organizations whose functioning depends on the mental well-being of their teams in the midst of disasters should learn from this and implement appropriate education and training for their people. Ignoring the psychological well-being of their people will surely detract from the effort, make everything else more difficult, and add to the long-term risks. It is always easier to talk to someone and accept their assistance when a good relationship has been established. Selecting on-site helpers for firehouses or with any emergency response personnel is better made in advance when training and education can be mandated. Finding appropriate mental clinicians after a disaster makes the on-site part of the job more difficult. Consistent with the successful aspect of the CSU philosophy, education and training can be mandated but psychotherapy and other similar treatments cannot. Referrals for treatment may be required in some circumstances, but a successful outcome cannot be mandated.

INITIAL TRAINING TO BE A FIREHOUSE CLINICIAN

Even several months after 9/11 there wasn't a great deal of time to have very much formal training for the 42 mental health clinicians who were going to be assigned to the firehouses. A number of mental health professionals were asked to come to the CSU and were given a morning's worth of information. A knowledgeable captain, Frank Leto, CSU Director Malachy Corrigan, and Assistant Director Dianne Kane talked to us about the culture of the New York City firefighter, what we might do in a firehouse and the obstacles we were likely to encounter. Their advice: be helpful (whatever that might mean), don't get in the way, and have lunch with them if invited. An invitation to eat at their table might be a sign of acceptance, our most valued initial goal. Only later did we realize that being invited to eat at the kitchen table could merely be a sign of politeness, a courtesy offered to everyone by men dazed by the events, attention, and impossible workloads.

THE BEST ADVICE

> The most important piece of advice I had about working at the firehouse with firefighters was offered by three people at three different times. Their intention was to both interview me and prepare me for the job. They all said, "You are going into somebody's home, not just their place of business." Without that perspective, my job would have been infinitely more difficult. It told me that I could not be a psychotherapist because psychotherapy is rarely practiced in someone's home, and when it is, the limits are strictly delineated to emergency care or behavioral therapy, neither of which applied in this situation. I was forced out of previous models of providing help and needed to develop a different way to think of myself in that situation.

When we are invited into somebody's home, we act accordingly. We do not take on the persona of our employment role. We are guests and have expectations of our hosts that we do not have with our clients who come into our offices. We behave differently towards a host than we do with clients. At the same time, the firehouse is where the firehouse clinician works and must maintain the same ethical and therapeutic guidelines that exist in any professional setting. The potential for role confusion and therapeutic error is significant. Whenever psychotherapeutic services leave the known rules of the office, the chance for unknown, unpredictable, and confounding variables increases. Consequently, both the risks and the rewards for the mental health worker and for the target population are high.

It is recommended here that on-site mental health workers think of themselves as a resource for the target groups. A resource can be giving without stigmatizing the other. A resource can be flexible to the needs of a situation. A resource does not have to be an expert about events in which there are no experts and give the right answer to questions for which there are no right answers. A resource can collaborate with target groups to find solutions. A resource can comfortably be a guest and can make a host feel comfortable in being a good host.

> As a resource, I had knowledge that I could offer and they could draw on. I could give them information or explain the experiences that are common to those who have endured traumas, what the clinical world calls symptoms. In this way, the potentially abnormal could become normalized. I was an available person to vent to, in the firehouse but not quite of the firehouse, and not connected to a formal medical office and a fear that damaging information would end up in their medical record. The men appreciated the reassurance about confidentiality and would later thank me for providing resources, if not therapeutic support.

Phase One: Pairing the Firehouse Clinician with a Firefighter

Each firehouse clinician was paired with an experienced, respected officer who worked as a peer counselor for the CSU. This provided the clinicians with their own resource, someone knowledgeable about the cultural subtleties of the fire department and the particular firehouse. Associating the program and the clinician with a respected "brother" gave both some initial credibility. It also offered the firefighter/peer counselor easy access to professional expertise. One firehouse clinician said:

> One Friday afternoon, I got a call from the firefighter who had been assigned to connect me to the firehouse, the officer who introduced me at my first visit. He was worried about a firefighter from another house who had been on a drinking binge, was depressed after continuously working at the Pile for weeks. The firefighter's wife was scared for her husband, her children, and herself. The officer wondered about suicide and homicide. I discussed with him the kinds of information I would want in a clinical situation, and could help him clarify why he continued to be worried even after the firefighter had reassured the officer that no additional intervention was needed. When the officer talked about the dangers, continued use of alcohol, significant depression, labile emotions, access to a weapon, history of violence, he knew that he

had to get that firefighter to safety. Reluctantly, like a first-year intern, he acknowledged that safety might mean having him hospitalized against his will.

THE FIRST VISIT TO THE FIREHOUSE

As the project unfolded, a pattern emerged. The CSU peer and the firehouse clinician would meet prior to their first visit to the firehouse to become acquainted, review the plan for the first meeting, and to exchange contact information. Professional mental health workers can be as misperceived by firefighters as mental health workers can misperceive firefighters. Just as firefighters can be mischaracterized as being people who drink too much and who run into buildings that are on fire because no one else would, professionals can be stereotyped as nerdy, bookish, snobbish liberals who have ridiculous attitudes about everyday issues. The potential divide between these groups first had to be overcome by the officer and the clinician. One firehouse clinician said:

> The second piece of advice the officer gave me was "don't be a nerd." It didn't matter that I grew up on many of the same streets of Brooklyn as some of the firefighters. That was a long time ago and our roles had changed. I had to accept the possibility that I might be seen with a bias, and that I might have to work to change that perspective.
>   The officer arranged to meet me at the firehouse at an hour he knew we would be welcomed, after the morning tasks were completed but before lunch so that we would not interfere with their routine. He did most of the talking about the program but also about everything he had in common with the firefighters, people and events.

There are two goals of the first meeting. One is to become acquainted with the people, to learn some names, make initial contact, shake hands, learn about the company, and let the firefighters be exposed to having a mental health worker in their home. The second goal is to set up a time for a second meeting or times for a series of visits that would be convenient for the company. It is important to remember that everyone has a routine in their home and at their job. The visiting mental health worker, indeed, any visitor or guest, can be disruptive to that routine and a burden to the hosts. Demonstrating respect for the job by considering that their work comes before yours is paramount.

On the clinician's second visit to the firehouse, the first one without a peer counselor, the following conversation took place.

Senior firefighter:

> "Did you hear? Last night they think they found parts of our guys. It was under the ramp. Maybe a finger bone and some of the hand. It was pointing to

one of our guys and he stopped everything to get it. The tools look like ours. Would you like some coffee?"

We sat at the kitchen table, a round piece of wood with the names of past house members carved under clear and highly polished polyurethane.

SENIOR FIREFIGHTER: Do you know who was lost?
CLINICIAN: No.
SENIOR FIREFIGHTER: Would you like to know about them?
CLINICIAN: Sure.

Pictures came off the walls, and the storytelling began. Their lost brothers were best friends, good fathers, great firefighters, loved brothers. Ordinary men.

They showed me a map of the towers and recounted their reconstruction of the collapse, where their brothers were when they died, and how it happened. Crushed, pulverized, never knew what hit them, that was how they explained it. They showed me a twisted tool with the firehouse number welded on and a mangled helmet with its front piece sufficiently intact to identify the owner's firehouse. In a basement storeroom, they saved buckets of dust with white chips scooped from the ruins, the potential remains of the men possibly mixed in. Someone would have to go through it by hand, carefully inspecting for bone fragments that could be sent to the lab for identification.

They had lots of questions for me and about me.

Unlike individual clients who visit my office, this group had many more questions about my skills and experience. That may have been because firefighters generally evaluate other firefighters based more on their experiences than on their titles. If a firefighter comes from a firehouse that is active and has a reputation for having the right traditions and doing the right things, respect is offered freely. I was an unknown, and they needed to evaluate me. Meetings at the firehouse from the first solo visit until they became comfortable with me were more like job interviews than mental health sessions. They wanted to know about my experience. Did this mask and reflect their concerns for my competency, their safety, issues of confidentiality and trust? Did they wonder if I could listen to the horrors they were routinely suffering without them then having to take care of me, as sometimes happened with others when they shared their stories?

No one actually said they were going to interview me, but that is what happened. In my opinion, people can tolerate and forgive a lack of experience, foolishness, and being outright wrong but not be so generous with dishonesty. Sometimes in an office visit for psychotherapy, some questions may not be explicitly answered out of concern for how the answers might affect subsequent treatment. In this on-site experience, openness and honesty are the better choices.

The questions below are the ones the firefighters shot at me, and this is how I answered them:

Had I treated FDNY firefighters before?
No.
Any other firefighters anywhere?
Only a few from other departments outside of the city.
What kind of experience did I have that would be relevant to them? After all, something like this had never occurred. What could I offer?
I have had years of on-site responding to disasters, suicides, assaults, rapes, and accidents. Maybe some of that would be relevant. Plus, years of practicing psychotherapy and other details that would have been on a résumé.
Could I answer their questions about medications?
Not my area of expertise, but I had some knowledge.
Had I been to "The Pile"?
No.
Why not?
I would have been in the way. I had no business there.
Could I be on the side of the firefighters?
I would be honest about my opinions.
Could I obey the rule that what gets said in the firehouse stays in the firehouse?
Yes, but there are limits to confidentiality like dangerousness to self or others and abuse of a child or an elderly person. I am mandated always to act to protect life. No compromising on that rule.

While my meeting with the crew on duty at that time went well, there were other crews with different men who were not there at that time. They would come in on another shift, and I would have to find a way to gain the trust, if not respect, of each group. In this way, I was functioning as a group therapist but working with a group I would not meet as a whole except in rare circumstances like a house meeting or activity like a picnic, holiday dinner, or dance.

THE CHALLENGES OF THE EARLY MONTHS

During the post-9/11 months, the firefighters were still working long hours in nearly unbearable conditions, and many had little time or patience for a mental health worker. As a group, they would tend not to be open to an outsider, however cordial they might appear publicly. Added to that natural and necessary reluctance to accept my presence, they were angry that they had not been contacted earlier and more forcefully by those who professed caring for them. They felt that all the authorities, including CSU, barely reached out, perhaps sending a retired peer counselor with no mental health service experience or ability. In their eyes, the union only came around when checks from donors were involved. Politicians didn't visit the house because, as it seemed to these men, they were too far from WTC to attract media cameras. Many firefighters were simply expressing all of their emotions as anger. Anyone could be the focus of that anger, deserving or not.

Another challenge of the early months was helping the firefighters deal with the attention they received from sources that generally ignored them. The influence of the media and actions of politicians touch the individual experience of first responders and can contribute to the ongoing damage of the event or help in withstanding its stress. For one firehouse, the lack of attention made them feel worse. When attention was given, it was in front of cameras, which made the intent of the attention suspect. When officials appear with the press, or in connection to financial issues, the inherent suspicion between civil service employees and authorities hurts because it supports the feeling that the individuals are not cared about and that their grief and fear are not a priority. One of the most useful actions authorities take is saying thank you to those who have put themselves at risk. Authorities who make a show of saying "thank you" in front of the press or when money is involved do not appear to first responders to be showing thanks. The true intentions of these authorities may be good at these times, but they may also appear to these groups at certain times as belonging to one of the many groups who exploit them and become the object of the disdain for modest firefighters. This type of media and political attention perpetuates the psychological damage first responders suffer from trauma.

It should be remembered that most firefighters, and probably other first responders to 9/11, would not have considered themselves victims because they were not dead or physically injured. Like combat soldiers, they feel the true heroes and victims are the dead. For many firefighters, if the buildings did not fall on them and kill them, then they were not heroes or victims. To suggest by manner or word that they were victims of the event could trigger the guilt that accompanies surviving, a reaction that can persist for months, years, or permanently. But the mental health worker might be better off thinking that first responders to an horrific event are or will be victims in the sense that they are being exposed to experiences that are likely to become emotionally toxic. Laurence Miller, PhD, an independent practitioner who has responded to trauma-inducing events, offers useful suggestions gleaned from his work and from others on how to deal with victims that can be adapted to going on site with first responders (Clark, 1988; Miller & Schlesinger, 2000).

Introduce yourself by name.   You want them to recognize you and you want to get to know them, so remember names. Firefighters shake hands. I was taught how to shake hands by my high school football coach. His mitt was huge and powerful. If you wanted to measure up with him, and what aspiring football player would not want the respect of the coach, you had to be aggressive, stick your paw into his, and meet his strength. I got to know each and every person's right hand and could look into their eyes. It helped me remember their names and nicknames.

Pay attention to the subtleties of language.   In the early days, no one was dead. Firefighters were lost or missing. It took months before most would say what everyone knew, that their brothers were dead. Respect can be demonstrated by sensitivity to language.

Be ready to state what you can do.   From the start, a mental health worker can be expected to be asked what they, mental health services, can do. Can they make anyone feel better? The truth is obvious and isn't the design of these kinds of questions. The subtext is honesty and safety. Are you going to tell them the truth? Are you going to offer more empty promises that everything will be okay? Do you know what they are going through? The better response is to find out what they might need and what they might consider helpful. Help for themselves is expressed as help for their children, wives, or for the families of the deceased.

Each day, it is better to ask "How are you today?" rather than simply the more generic "How are you?"   Asking how someone is today permits someone to be better by comparison without having to deal with what it means to be globally okay. Being okay in general implies getting over something that is not yet even comprehended, a prerequisite for later stages of recovery. Trying to make an on-site intervention useful by prematurely asking if the person is alright communicates a mental health worker's lack of sensitivity or experience with trauma.

Don't put pressure on memories.   Finally, it is my treatment philosophy and others' never to push, pull, or probe for a memory of a traumatic experience. This is as true at the initial meetings, when one is just trying to establish a relationship, as it is throughout the intervention process. Clients tell us when they are ready to let these memories and feelings spill out. It is our job to convey an open attitude, make the conditions optimum for the person's emotional safety, and communicate our acceptance, willingness, and ability to listen when they do choose to share their stories. Some psychotherapeutic approaches might call this supporting the defenses and giving permission to talk about traumatic memory. From an on-site encounter with a mental health worker, clients may choose to consult for medications, EMDR, psychotherapy, or any sort of opportunity to deal with their issues. It is not the role of the firehouse clinician to provide psychotherapy treatment in the firehouse. One need not respond to people at the firehouse as a psychotherapist would respond in an office to be therapeutic.

Be mindful that the alarm can go off at any moment and the firefighters have to be ready to go to work.   Talking about emotions and traumatic experiences often takes time, energy, and focus that can be distracting. First responders do not have the luxury of letting that distraction get in the way of the work they may be called to accomplish. It is not appropriate to open up emotional floodgates that cannot be immediately closed as the firefighters are called to a job. When first responders are on call, titrated emotional containment can be more therapeutic than expressiveness. Weakening a person's defensive structure while they are engaged in an important task is likely to detract from their ability to perform.

ICE BREAKERS

Group therapists and facilitators are famous for finding structured activities to encourage group interaction and discussion. Initially, it was believed that structured exercises would be needed to get the firefighters to open up. Indeed, some firehouse clinicians had success with such techniques as asking people to write down questions on pieces of paper so that the clinicians could publicly address the issue without identifying the questioner. However, this was not the universal experience and one that was not continuously used by anyone. Often, ice breakers were not needed or could be dispensed with fairly quickly.

One of the myths about men, especially firefighters, is that they do not talk about their feelings. Nothing could be further from the truth. Firefighters talk a great deal about their experiences and process traumatic feelings in their own ways. The traditions of the New York firefighters have evolved to create a more natural context in which men can express themselves. As Addis and Mahalik nicely document, men may be less likely to seek professional help within society in general but will be more likely to seek help when the context supports a masculine role.

One of the historic patterns of the firehouse is to go back to the house after a bad fire to talk about it. There, the men dissect each step of the event: the first call to the box, what they witnessed on the ride to the location, who did what, what could have been done differently, or how similar fires were handled in the past. Experienced firefighters would make sure that junior firefighters were included in the mix. The veterans would watch out for adverse emotional reactions among the junior men. Thus, cultural traditions and rituals dictate processing emotions back at the firehouse, within the safety a culture that enforced confidentiality and away from uninformed, potentially judgmental outsiders. If the mental health worker can be included in this process, then to the extent that we can respect the firefighter culture and that our knowledge base is useful, we can help the firefighters.

Informational Materials and Handouts

Following the long standing practice of the Counseling Services Unit that education and training can be mandated but treatment cannot, informational materials were extremely useful. A handout is easy to distribute or can be left in the kitchen and available to everyone on all shifts at any time. People can read handouts at their pleasure, think about the information, bring them home, and percolate with questions that can be asked in private. Handouts are so easy to create that they can be customized to address unique issues in a non-threatening manner.

A symptom list of PTSD could stimulate conversation about which of the symptoms each person at the table felt the most, how medications worked, and how long symptoms might be tolerated before treatment was recommended. Handouts were offered for dealing with their children and the children of the widows. One of the more useful handouts was a parent-child activity book, "Helping America Cope: A Guide to Help Parents and Children Cope with the September 11th Terrorist Attacks." Paid for by The September 11th Fund and adapted specifically for FDNY, it put into the hands of the firefighters something concrete they could bring home to help comfort and reassure their wives and children. As a handout, it opened discussions about recognizing feelings and managing anger. It gave them age appropriate words to say to their kids that might explain events. By talking about helping others, we can sometimes help ourselves.

REVAMPING PROFESSIONAL BOUNDARIES

Psychotherapists have a lot to say about boundaries and treatment. Boundaries generally refer to the frame of treatment. Therapists make the point that they are professionals who are different than clients, and that the boundary separating the differences must be maintained. Our lives are separate from our practices. Therapists are schooled not to reveal very much or nothing at all about their personal life. There is supposed to be a boundary between the information that reveals the real person who is the therapist and life of the client. Therapists don't generally go to a client's place of business or join with them and their wives and children at work-related events. Therapists usually don't get invited by clients to dine with them, and in general most in practice would not only decline the offer but possibly even interpret an unconscious motivation behind the invitation. Many psychoanalysts would not even shake hands with a client. Traditionally, in most forms of therapy, the client visits the office of the therapist, where the therapist is most comfortable, and talks about the world from the client's perspective. Most therapists see their job to work within that frame to facilitate insight; they are a source of knowledge to help explain the client's problem so as to promote understanding and probably behavior change. Therapists, especially psychodynamic ones, use interpretations, a reformulation of the client's words and actions that occur within the boundaries, to reduce psychopathological symptoms. That is, by interpreting or explaining the feelings, thoughts, or behaviors of the client to the client in psychological terms, the issues troubling the client can be resolved.

Effective on-site mental health workers don't do that. They must have a different view of boundaries and what it means to be helpful. For the on-site worker, helpful may be best defined as doing whatever the people and situation determines will be helpful. Circular as this definition may be, it shows that helpful must be defined in the terms of the client and not necessarily by theory or preset criteria. One day that may mean becoming the audience for favorite firehouse stories or sharing stories of fishing trips. On another day, that may be finding a referral for a wayward teenager or answering a question like "What do I say to the widow when I go to the funeral?" One rather slight female firehouse mental health clinician said,

> My firehouse wanted me to wear their equipment to see what it was like for them. They were right. Just wearing 60 or 100 pounds of gear wore me out, and then they reminded me that I would need to put on the oxygen mask and carry a heavy tool. I didn't like it, but I could understand why they thought women wouldn't be good on the job. I think they gained some respect for me, too.

Another mental health worker might have launched into a discussion about sexist attitudes, job qualifications, and job structure in the fire department and in society. Surely, these men could relate to those topics, and it might have been therapeutic. Perhaps another context would have suggested that such a conversation or confrontation would be most useful and therapeutic. But, this was not the time or place for that, at least in the judgment of that firehouse clinician. For her, it was about mutual understanding and acceptance. It was one of her visits to that firehouse that proved to be helpful and instructive. With her improved relationship, respect, and connection, other conversations would be possible. Without it, little more might have been possible and all the resources she could offer useless. Most therapists don't think in terms of interacting with clients in this way so as to improve the connection and therapeutic alliance.

Several firehouse clinicians had been invited to ride with the men on the fire engine and some accepted the invitation. Where should the line between helper and helpee be drawn? On-site mental health workers should never forget that they are not first responders and should not endanger themselves, their clients, or the public. But, the safety of the boundary line between the mental health worker and the client that exists in the office does not apply in the same way to the on-site situation.

The need to be professional remains, but the meaning of professional behavior suggests that we first do no harm, then we do what has to be done to educate and also be a resource for any needs that arise. Protection against the therapeutic complications of boundary violations can be sustained by close contact with other mental health workers and supervisors. Because boundaries are so different, it is often difficult for the firehouse clinician to see the firefighters from their firehouse in private therapy while still visiting that house. The urge of the firehouse clinician may strongly favor seeing those firefighters because of the intense bonding that occurs. In firefighter culture, the desire and tradition favors helping your own, a pressure that is less likely to develop in an office-based setting. CSU supervisors anecdotally report that it is better to limit this in most cases and refer back to the CSU or a different outside therapist.

GROUP DYNAMICS: PERSONALITIES AND RELATIONSHIPS IN THE FIREHOUSE

Becoming accepted by the firehouse means that the firefighters will be more than polite to you. It means that they will talk to you, laugh with you, sometimes make jokes about you, test you, ask you for help, and invite you to meals. I don't know if riding on the truck is a sign of that acceptance, but how a clinician feels about the house and how he or she feels that they are perceived is surely one important sign. When firefighters volunteer to you the stories that make them uncertain, that surely is another sign. Gaining a better level of acceptance also means that you can offer more resources to fulfill needs that may not be spoken about. Showing oneself to be trustworthy can be achieved by as many actions as there are reactions.

Firehouses are at one level merely a group of men with an internal group structure that any group might have. As noted in the chapters on firehouse culture, the interpersonal structure of the firehouse is a function of rank, captain, lieutenants, and seniority measured in years on the job. In addition, firefighter culture demands respect for those who have been at good firehouses, busy firehouses with admirable traditions.

Acceptance by a respected firefighter can carry significant weight with the other men, making acceptance by everyone much more likely. Similarly, lack of acceptance dooms the on-site mental health worker's mission.

The officer in one house had previous, positive contact with a mental health professional much earlier in his life. That experience made him more willing to accept a mental health worker in his second home, the firehouse. That officer gave that firehouse clinician a chance to prove his worth, and consequently, so did his men.

Another firefighter had a reputation for being *the house mother.* The crew respectfully and appreciatively joked that he liked to take care of everybody and did lots of extra things around the house. That firehouse clinician let himself be taken care of by the house mother and tested by that firefighter, winning his trust in the process.

Some firefighters, like some people, are simply more welcoming than others. Those welcoming firefighters can help an outsider, a mental health worker, get to know those more reluctant to open up. This, too, improves the opportunities for the mental health worker to gain acceptance and become a useful resource.

UNDERSTANDING THERAPEUTIC RELATIONSHIPS: TRANSFERENCE

Even though the role of the mental health worker is not as the conventionally defined psychotherapist, the usefulness of thinking about relationships as transferential and how that can be employed in formulating interventions is an important consideration. Ralph Greenson's classic text on psychoanalysis defines transference as "The main characteristic [of transference] is the experience of feelings to a person which do not befit that person and which actually apply to another. Essentially, a person in the present is reacted to as though he were a person in the past. Transference is a repetition, a new edition of an old object relationship. . . . The person reacting with transference feelings is in the main unaware of the distortion" (Greenson, 1967).

With all the talk that went on at the kitchen table, in groups at other places, or in more intimate, individual conversations, there were ample themes that suggested transferential experiences. References to parents and authority easily could have been understood as reflecting ways this firehouse clinician could be a transferential object, a person in the present being reacted to as though he were a person from the past, a parent for example. Perhaps this is true for highly structured groups in general, say from the military, other organized groups of first responders, or paramilitary groups. Many traditional treatment modalities encourage understanding clients from this point of view. In addition, these traditional treatments recommend using that reference point to explain the client's symptoms, feelings, thoughts, and behaviors. They might advise the mental health worker to use the therapeutic intervention of interpretation, the psychological explanation of the issue, to reduce the client's symptoms. Perhaps that treatment method makes sense within the confines and treatment boundaries of the office setting. However, firehouse clinicians do not operate within those boundaries. Firehouse clinicians are in some ways part of the group, not distant observers like office-based workers. They cannot utilize the same perspective on interpersonal relationships. In any event, no useful purpose is served by trying to make sense of the first responder experience based on transference. Even worse, interpreting transferential aspects of their relationships only heightens anxiety, and that does not help ease the pain and uncertainty of trauma.

PARKING LOT THERAPY

Here is a situation often repeated with firehouse clinicians: As the clinician would be leaving the firehouse, someone might say, "Let me get the door for you, doc," and they might accompany that clinician to his or her car. With no one else around, the firefighter could begin asking questions and opening up personal concerns in a way that would not occur in the kitchen. The depth of the conversation could be as significant as any in office sessions. Its potential productivity could be far greater than from a mandated session, or one delayed by months or years of hesitation. Usually, the conversation led to greater intimacy and referral to a professional within or external to the department. Sometimes it was the start of bringing a new service to the firehouse, such as more activity books that could help them talk about the event with their children. Sometimes it was a good place to ask questions pertaining to their own personal nightmares.

If the mental health worker is uncomfortable and rigid about the boundaries and feels that therapeutic conversations can only occur within the privacy of an office, such conversations and opportunities as parking lot therapy may be missed. Many have observed and recorded that mental health workers and others often provide help simply by bearing witness to the suffering of these first responders. But, before one can bear witness, one has to be present with the person when they are able to express themselves. Apparently, a parking lot can be a favored location. The absence of even the minimal formality of a closed room, like a kitchen, or perhaps the inherent open feeling of an outdoor parking lot seems to ease some into sharing their unexpressed concerns. Would these individuals have sought help by going to a clinic office at some other time? Would that have been a better alternative? The evidence suggests that earlier opportunities for education and other resources is best and supports an unconventional approach like parking lot therapy.

MEETING EVERYONE, DIFFERENT TIMES, SHIFTS

The hours of the firehouse clinician are not 9 to 5. The workday revolves around the hours of the firefighters, 24/7. To meet everyone, the hours working at the house have to vary over each day and week or weekend. To maximize the advantages created when services are brought to where people work, rather than having them come to a facility, it is useful to go to the firehouse at different times. Some people talk best in the evening when the daily routine is over. The night brings out different fears. Ruminative thoughts that are so common among the traumatized often seem most intense at night. Conversations can occur at these times with people who might not otherwise be so inclined. Late one night and over the course of unpredictable, unscheduled moments in the firehouse, I pieced together the following:

> Al had seen more than his share of bad scenes and was at "The Pile" more than most, doing more than anyone should have. He suffered from a reoccurring vision of cutting a person's body with a saw so as to extract it from the wreckage. The smell in the air at the Pile could be stimulated by the odor of sharp cheeses.
>
> Another memory had again forced its way into his mind a week earlier and was making him nervous. It was triggered after his wife asked him if he could figure out why their son's room smelled so bad. Al looked under the bed and found a week-old Halloween pumpkin, saved there by their son to preserve that fun day. When Al reached in to remove the soggy, smelly mess, he flashed on what he had done at the Pile: lifted someone's mashed head from the ground into a bag. I learned about how poor Al's general health had become, how often he thought about how his father had died, that he seemed to resemble and identify with his father, and that he had a host of illnesses that he was not attending to well enough. The following week, he saw his physician. By being around the firehouse at rotating times over months, I could talk with him when he was most emotionally available and informally encourage him to improve how he took care of himself. I learned that he began to follow his doctor's advice more closely.

Being on site at different times and therefore available to meet everyone when they might be more ready to talk can contribute to the effort to make services more accessible. In this case, it probably contributed to that firefighter going to his doctor and following good medical advice. On-site availability gave him and the mental health support process the opportunity to deal relatively simply with a common result of trauma, flashbacks, and poor self-care. Would mandating him to an office for traditional treatment have enabled him to discuss his flashbacks and fears or promoted better self-care?

PREPARING TO BE A FIREHOUSE CLINICIAN

Mental health workers are trained to try to understand basic, true human nature. They study the basest human desires and the loftiest goals of human potential. Therapists learn to listen to the abused and the abuser, to daily struggles, challenges, and defeats. However, little effort is made to expose mental health workers to the brutal horror of mashed human bodies and the experience of fear of those who choose to go to the rescue of another. Ask a therapist what might go through the mind of an abused child, and as awful as that might be, therapists can probably conjure up a real or realistic story. Try asking a therapist to discuss what it is like for someone to put their own life at risk and you will probably not hear anything more than what a layperson might offer. The mental health workers who support first responders need to be able to listen to the experience of fear and understand how to respond in a helpful manner. Even now, years after that event and years of people in combat, a database search of the professional literature brings no references to the trauma of first responders or, similarly, the trauma of soldiers, who also suffer from the trauma that bravery demands. Research has focused on traumas inflicted by being the victim, traumatized by the actions of another rather than the trauma of making dangerous choices that might define bravery. On-site mental health clinicians need to learn how to listen to people who have experienced both the terrible consequences of other people's nefarious deeds as well as the excruciating conflicts that their own bravery subjects them to.

LISTENING TO FEAR AND BRAVERY

Some people call the sudden, intrusive return of memories of horrific events *flashbacks*. Immediate reality recedes and the memory of the trauma becomes the center of attention and predominates the current reality, if only for a few long seconds or minutes of distraction. Flashbacks are a potential component of traumatic experience. They can be created by being victimized and by choosing to act bravely.

The following story is true; only the facts that could lead to discovering this firefighter's identity have been altered.

Bill is a bright, skilled, decent man. He had been a firefighter for about 4 years and married for 6. When he is reminded of 9/11, and sometimes without an identifiable trigger to that period of his life, the following thoughts take his attention. Some images of the WTC rubble inescapably drag his memory of 9/11 into my mind as well.

BILL'S MEMORY OF 9/11

The sweet smell of a baby, its total weight gently pressing onto his shoulder with every rock of the chair, the dim light of early morning, the Mrs. asleep, exhausted by a previous day's child care. The three-year-old is romping through the living room, a dad's watchful eye anticipating the danger of tangled feet and an unpredictable fall onto an everyday, seemingly benign object.

But the smell in his nostrils was not sweet. It was putrefying. The weight on his shoulder was not a baby but a gas-powered saw. There was no rocking chair, only the shudder of shifting hulks of concrete and metal. The light was dim because he was three stories below the surface and daylight could barely make its way through the debris. Nearby was not the body of his wife but a corpse. This firefighter was flashing between mental images of home and the harsh sensations of the reality surrounding him. Missing from the picture in his mind of a living room filled by a growing three-year-old and a watchful dad, was the dad. This firefighter wondered how his family would fare without him if he was killed under a pile of rubble as he searched for survivors from the collapsed World Trade Center Towers.

He knew the dangers of crawling through tons of unstable wreckage better than anyone. His second job was as an ironworker. Going under the Pile violated every rule for safety and prudence. The chance for serious injury or death was high, and he had everything to live for. That had to be balanced against the possibility of finding someone alive, rescuing anyone. Or he could recover a body or body part and surface with a measure of closure for the grief stricken, the only remaining comfort for the grieving.

Before him was the dead body of a man wedged under tons of steel, concrete, and office furniture. Should he return to the surface knowing that he had searched and not found anyone alive? The body could not be dislodged from the debris and brought back up whole. Would it be better to wait until the cranes and bulldozers pulled apart the mix of wreckage and bodies for sorting through later in safety?

Brave people put themselves in dangerous situations where soul-searching conflicts appear like trap doors to hell. Thinking more of a dead man's grieving family than his own family's potential grief, this firefighter took the saw off his shoulder and removed a body part that could be identified by DNA analysis.

Bill voluntarily placed himself in a dangerous situation and had to make a decision. No matter what his choice, there were going to be profound implications to his mental state, for his self-image, and quite possibly for the lives of his wife and children.

Being in that situation changed that man. In a related manner, listening to those types of stories affects mental health workers. The impact of empathizing with the story teller, for the mental health worker, can be more influential than many of the feelings for the stories that are typically told in psychotherapy. Unfortunately, most therapists think that their training and skills are sufficiently similar for them to deal with the emotional impact they generally report after talking to the traumatized. In fact, the force of stories of traumatic events is often much greater than the forces they experience everyday. The on-site mental health worker needs to appreciate the potentially far-reaching impact this work is likely to have on their life and the life of their family. With this fore knowledge, they can decide if they are willing, able, and trained to listen to stories of the horrific and gruesome and what it is really like to become the hero.

Among the most difficult experiences for any person to endure is touching human remains. What must it be like to work amid the torn parts of people, to smell days-old flesh, all the while at high risk for violent death? The mind is seared by the experience; it becomes unforgettable and the memory unavoidable. Historically, the most effective salve for this disturbance is telling the story to others who can hear it without burdening the storyteller with additional worries. For many, though not all, telling and retelling the story of the trauma is in itself one way to gain a sense of mastery over the event. Many say that it helps to tell the story to someone who will not be harmed by the telling, who can listen without overreacting and without the teller having to take care of the listener. In some ways this is why firefighters do not talk to their own families and friends about tragic events. They don't want to worry family and friends. They talk to each other, and sometimes they might talk to others, even a mental health professional, if the conditions are right.

Retelling the story of trauma or grief as a preferred treatment is not a recommendation or a contraindication. It is simply a fact that some will talk about the experience, some won't, and some will retell it even to the point of retraumatization. The point is that some will tell their story to a mental health worker. That mental health worker needs to know what to do for that client and for themselves.

Many experts on trauma talk about the impact of listening to stories of trauma. Charles Figley coined a term for the syndrome that sometimes appears in listeners and among helping professionals: *compassion fatigue*. Others have called it *secondary trauma* or *vicarious trauma*, and some have even classified it as *negative countertransference*. In the broadest definition of countertransference, that all feelings of the mental health worker in response to a client represent countertransference, listening to rescue and recovery stories is sure to cause strong feelings and countertransference in the listener, whether mental health worker or not. In fact, first responders can talk about experiences that are so bad such stories are prohibited from the news media and are rarely found even in the literature of mental health professionals. When they are reported, the stories are sanitized. The graphic nature of the experience is reduced to the language of professionals, not the emotional, simple, and descriptive language of an average person who has been horrified. Who wouldn't have a strong reaction when listening to a person nervously talk about "scooping up pieces of a guy's brains . . . and the stinking air that I had to suck up"? In these situations, negative countertransference refers to the feelings and actions of the mental health worker who is reacting to the firefighter, that makes matters worse for the client, who in this case is a first responder.

However, it is also a mistake to suggest that an appropriate countertransference reaction means that the mental health worker is unaffected by listening to such experiences. Is it normal or healthy to remain unchanged by the knowledge of what it means to be a first responder, or soldier, or victim, or unfortunate bystander? At some point, perhaps different for everyone, the mental health worker listening to the stories of trauma and responding with affect appropriate to the situation can exhaust the listener's emotional resources. Compassion fatigue is an apt description. Analogous to physical fatigue, it is counteracted by good self-care, rest, relaxation, the love of others, getting away from the grind, and a kind of self-reflection that leads to a transcendent perspective.

Everyone who wants to work with first responders and others who have had traumatizing experiences should understand that the act of listening empathically to the traumatic is likely going to transform them. The transformation is very different from the changes that working in the mental health field in general might initiate. The terms secondary or vicarious trauma correctly suggest that the listener is being conditioned to have a feeling of trauma similar to the affected client. In the language of behavioral psychology, it is much like a secondary reinforcer that derives its strength from being chained to a primary reinforcer. Some degree of vicarious trauma for the mental health worker may be inevitable but, like the traumatized person, may not be pathological. For an on-site mental health worker like the firehouse clinician, vicarious trauma may be another example of any first responder's reaction, a normal reaction to an abnormal event.

Vicarious trauma, or compassion fatigue, affects the whole life of the clinician. It is the kind of experience that one walks around with, that colors the entire day and all of its activities. Thus, its impact is seen in one's perspective toward both work and home life. The changes to emotional state and cognitive outlook are palpable by spouses and children. This work affects family life, and that ought to be considered when doing this kind of work. If the family of the on-site mental health worker does not support this activity, then it may not be the best use of that clinician's skills or the right thing to do for the family.

Simply being part of a mental health response to a public event alters the reactions of others who know the work that you do. Their reactions may be well intentioned but not always helpful. On-site clinicians need to be prepared for that. One psychologist with significant on-site experience said:

> With every on-site response I have taken part in that was also an event that was well known to the public, I found I was treated differently by family, friends, and acquaintances. One beautiful, clear, and sunny spring of 2002, I attended the wedding of a cousin. It was one of those rare times when everyone is together for a good occasion and can catch up on each other's lives. Rather than our continuing to talk about our now grown-up children and the good old days, the conversation turned quiet and serious. Perhaps one of my kids mentioned that I was working with firefighters, and I was both questioned about my experience and complimented for my service. Everyone's reaction was understandable and appreciated, but it was not helpful to me at that time.

To some degree, everyone who works at an event that receives public attention and touches the emotions of the public is seen differently. But the mindset of the general mental health worker is not prepared to deal with this. They have to make their relationships to clients completely secret. Clinicians are highly trained to keep a strict boundary between information learned in psychotherapy and everyone else. They are not accustomed to having everyone know who they work with, what the likely topics of conversation might be, and certainly not accustomed to receiving the degree of attention and social praise for their work on an event like 9/11. Responding to a public event, especially being embedded in the on-site response to a disaster, leads to this new challenge. The solution is relatively simple. To move a conversation along, it is usually sufficient to thank people for their kind words or make general, sympathetic remarks about tragedy. In rare instances with persistent questioners, a polite reminder that mental clinicians are prohibited from talking about their work is enough.

PREREQUISITE SKILLS FOR ON-SITE MENTAL HEALTH WORKERS

The clinician's general mental health expertise can be life saving. On-site mental health workers need to be able to accomplish two central tasks: support individuals and the group as a whole, and recognize when somebody has needs that exceed the natural resiliency of their first responder peer group system. On-site clinicians can add to the support of first responders by developing resources to acquire and deliver information and concrete services. With firefighters, clinicians can encourage the kind of talking, tolerance, and understanding that have a long and established pattern within the FDNY. With the special knowledge mental health workers have from their training and practices, they can also spot individuals who are not coping well or may be developing the symptoms of problems that brother firefighters might miss or not want to report. Remember, sometimes close-knit groups try to protect their own from the judgments of outsiders and not admit to themselves how serious certain problems can become. The intervention may be a simple preventative one like suggesting a day off. On-site providers in general, and firehouse clinicians in particular, being part of the house but also not part of the house, can help by alerting the officers and senior firefighters that someone needs more help and that outside resources have to be found. On-site mental health clinicians need to be able to cross freely between the boundaries of house insider and outsider and be a psychological diagnostician rather than group facilitator.

The images associated with unexpected death are always going to be difficult. Every firefighter remembers their first experience witnessing death and especially the death of a child. Clinicians who work with the traumatized certainly will hear about these images and experiences because they are the most traumatizing. On-site workers in particular will be exposed to the most immediate and raw accounts because they are close to the scene in time and location. For this reason, it is best if these clinicians have some experience with death, the circumstances associated with trauma, the psychological consequences of making decisions in the midst of disasters, and the images of destruction that disasters perpetrate on the human body.

On-site disaster response is also about the challenge to living after death and destruction. Those not dead are survivors and often suffer from a constellation of feelings called survivor guilt. Samson and Opp (1989) presented a definition of guilt among war veterans that applies generally to survivor guilt among first responders. They say the veteran's guilt is "a sense of regret over loss (experienced in the context of relative helplessness), accompanied by a theory of attribution that establishes a sense of personal responsibility and generates powerfully self-condemning thoughts." Conventional treatments that have therapists addressing the emotions and thoughts that comprise and perpetuate a survivor's self-condemnation are not sufficiently effective, they and others would admit. Instead, Samson and Opp have found that other combat veterans talking in groups can be beneficial. This is another good reason why placing a mental health worker on site, in the firehouse, can help the veteran firefighters talk to each other in a helpful, healing manner. On-site clinicians need to know all about survivor guilt.

A story often told after 9/11 was how communities made heroes of surviving firefighters and the paradoxical effect it had on them. They were given parades, asked to make speeches, and presented awards. Sadly, these honors frequently precipitated the feeling that they did not deserve the luck that put them off duty or away from falling debris or kept them from being killed in the collapse of the towers, let alone to be honored. One firefighter said during a parking lot therapy session that the only way he could be present at any event that honored a deceased firefighter was to say out loud the names of those who died from his firehouse.

Another area of knowledge especially useful to on-site clinicians is death notification, because there are useful and harmful procedures and words for this task. Appreciating the processes and practices surrounding death and grief can be helpful, even if not noticed, while ignorance in these matters can be harmful and remembered forever.

FLEXIBILITY IN THEORY AND PRACTICE

On-site mental health workers, like first responders to emergencies, never quite know what challenges await them. All the training in the world may not be enough preparation. In the end, all that will matter will be reflected in outcome measures: how much suffering and disability prevented, or how many suicides completed. Clinicians who need to work strictly within theoretical guidelines, and perceive modifications to standard psychotherapy practices as ethically wrong, may have much more difficulty with this model of applied psychology because they may have to adapt quickly to situations that their theories do not address.

On-site mental health workers of all the various professional disciplines need to be flexible about their professional role and identity. One firehouse clinician took over an office in a firehouse and asked the officer to mandate appointments for everyone assigned to the house. That request was poorly received both by the officer and the firehouse. Another captain commented that if their firehouse clinician had tried that approach at his house, he "would have thrown the clinician out." One could conclude from the anecdote that if mental health workers see themselves as medical practitioners always delivering the same office-based service but in a make-shift, on-site office, then similar poor outcomes can be expected. Sometimes a casual conversation while making coffee or answering a telephone is more helpful than 50 minutes of office-based psychotherapy.

RELATING TO FIREFIGHTERS

Surprisingly, firefighters and mental health professionals share many characteristics, and appreciating those similarities can make the mission easier to accomplish. Both psychotherapists and firefighters tend to love their jobs. It is a common feeling among those who help others for a living. Being a helper can be very satisfying. While they both have been known to brag that they would do their work for free, in reality, both groups feel underpaid. Mental health workers and firefighters do not miss the fact that human misfortune keeps them employed. Neither wants to profit from tragedy, and both groups want to be there to help and work hard to be ready when that call comes.

RELATIONSHIP OF COUNSELING SERVICE UNIT TO THE FIREHOUSE CLINICIANS

One of the challenges to on-site mental health workers is the relative infrequency of contact with supervisors and colleagues. Without even the casual contact that is inevitable in a clinic setting, the clinician is more prone to their own stress reactions, deviations from normal practices, and compassion fatigue. Pre-planning for these challenges improves the program and may prevent problems.

Initially, contact with CSU was through an individual interview that was as much an interview as it was an introduction to the language, structure, and culture of the fire department. The interview was followed by a group meeting in which the lead staff at the FDNY was introduced, basic culture of the FDNY explained, and procedures outlined. Most importantly, firehouse clinicians were welcomed and given a direct connection to experienced officers and highly trained counselors. Names, faces, and phone numbers made a strong connection between the on-site task and clinical support. They were encouraged to call with questions.

Later in the program, CSU invited the firehouse clinicians to monthly group meetings. There, they could share their experiences, learn about forms and procedures, and develop a sense of camaraderie. Although each one worked in isolation at their firehouse, a sense of being connected to others who faced the same challenges was apparent. CSU facilitated firehouse clinicians to share their experiences in how they could stimulate discussions among firefighters in firehouses. One clinician brought donuts to the firehouse. Another found it better to bring a box of cookies that could be passed around the kitchen table. Whoever took a cookie had to talk. It turned into a Gestalt therapy–style group. Another firehouse clinician talked about how she brought a 5-pound bag of pistachio nuts to pass around as she led a discussion. The humor of bringing nuts to the nuts was not lost on the firefighters or on the group of firehouse clinicians. The monthly meetings provided an opportunity to laugh, too.

One of the most important experiences for any helper, but especially ones who respond to disasters, is the simple act of being thanked. They do not require ribbons or parades, and money is not their motivation. They appreciate someone saying thank you. The FDNY Counseling Service Unit never forgot to express its thanks. They said it often and sincerely. They seemed to thank one's effort, if not their success. They were free with their availability, expertise, and appreciation. This made the job easier, more satisfying, less stressful, and ultimately, easier to bring to closure at termination.

On-site mental health workers can add to their self-care routines by getting feedback and thanks from the authority they report to and making that authority aware of any personal need to hear their thanks. While asking or recognizing the need to be thanked, if not appreciated openly, may not come naturally to the clinician, it may be useful to assess one's own feeling when this message is delivered. Typically, therapists are taught that wanting a patient's appreciation is a negative sign that indicates a problem in the therapeutic relationship. That may be true in the typical office setting, but it was not generally true in the field and under existing conditions. Rather, denying the need for appreciation at appropriate times could well increase the likelihood of complications to the on-site worker's relationship to the first responders.

TERMINATION COUNTERTRANSFERENCE: THE TIME TO LEAVE THE FIREHOUSE

There comes a time when the clinician should stop coming to *the job*. The job and its mission remain, but the people, the place, and the events change. It is an inevitable and desirable development, but it can be met with mixed emotions by both the firehouse and the clinician. Ending therapeutic relationships, called the termination phase, has been well studied and practiced. From a traditional setting, clients and therapists need to say good-bye, review the work of the therapy, and plan for continued progress. Like all good-byes, it has the potential to be an emotional and important experience. However, termination from an on-site relationship can be much more difficult. Remember, the boundaries of the treatment relationship were less defined and more fluid than in the typical office or clinic setting. The firehouse clinician is more of a real, spontaneous person compared to the more measured stance in a traditional setting. The bond formed between the on-site mental health worker and first responders has a more real life quality and is less controlled than the typical office-based relationship. One of the consequences of modifying therapeutic distance is found at termination in the feelings of the firehouse clinician.

Many firehouse clinicians felt the termination phase was the most difficult. They had become close to the firefighters, identified with their plight, and appreciated some of the unique characteristics of the world they live in. Personally, I found it difficult to leave a culture in which people are valued by their ability to "do the right thing," as they might say, and return to a culture where that attribute is not nearly as prized or supported.

FIREHOUSE CLINICIANS POST-9/11

The unanimous feeling among the firehouse clinicians was that it was beneficial for both the firefighters and themselves. Some had firehouses that were welcoming, which created a much better result. Other clinicians had to confront less welcoming and even hostile firehouses, and their experience was far more trying. Still, they too reported similar benefits to firefighters. Supportive resources were utilized by the affected population more often and more satisfactorily when those resources were made available closer to the scene. Once the clinician overcame the major hurdle, acceptance by the firehouse, resources could be delivered, and both firefighters and clinicians felt better, making long-term benefits possible. It also made the termination experience both more difficult and more satisfying because the attachment was stronger. Some houses were angry when the clinicians terminated. Those houses seemed to interpret the removal of the clinician much like they regarded the loss of any FDNY support. To some, it meant their needs were being ignored again. Others interpreted the end of visits by firehouse clinicians to mean that they were moving on, that life could return to normal.

For several of the firehouse clinicians, the connection to the firehouse and the FDNY continued. In some cases, the firefighters were able to call the clinician and have an easy entry into psychotherapy for themselves, their marriage, a child, or other family. Most firefighters who responded to an informal survey reported that they valued having a clinician assigned to their house and that feeling was reflected in the satisfaction of the firehouse clinicians. They all believed the program was useful and valued their personal experiences. The connection between the clinician and the firehouse continued after the program ended. Firefighters invited many of the clinicians back to the firehouse to events like retirement parties and Christmas parties. Those relationships are still evolving even years after the firehouse clinician project formally ended.

CHAPTER 6

Modifying Psychotherapy for Individuals

INDIVIDUAL PSYCHOTHERAPY WITH FIREFIGHTERS

Individual psychotherapy is not an innovative treatment. When most people think of mental health treatments, they probably think of a therapist and a client sitting down and talking one on one. We would hope that this text helps to dispel that singular image of a mental health intervention, especially for trauma and for those suffering the emotional consequences of responding to a disaster. Helpful mental health interventions can take creative, innovative forms. Individual psychotherapy is a reliable tool that has its own time and purpose, and it can become innovative when modified for unique circumstances.

Many excellent texts are available for learning about individual psychological treatments for first responders, trauma, and all the associated diagnostic categories like Acute Stress Disorder, Posttraumatic Stress Disorder, and traumatic and complicated grief. That body of literature will not be reviewed here. Rather, the issues related to the individual psychotherapy modality of treatment that were present in many cases among firefighters before and after 9/11 can be highlighted and instructive. Generalizing from these observations on individual treatment for firefighters and first responders from 9/11 to another disaster may be useful. But the caveats on generalizing from one disaster to another, or individual psychotherapy after 9/11 to another event, must be applied with caution. Therapists will have to be innovative as they respond to the circumstances and clients.

PRETREATMENT CONDITIONS

In a typical pre-9/11 year, CSU might have completed intakes on 600 individuals. The nature of their complaints varied but frequently were related to trauma, alcohol use, and family issues. Treatment could be provided by the handful of CSU staff. Other sources for psychological treatment and medication were available to firefighters by accessing a psychotherapist or psychiatrist via health insurance. There are no statistics to show the frequency via private means or measurements of the attitudes towards psychotherapy in general. Similarly, the relative use of individual treatment versus other treatments is not tabulated. However, it is reasonable to guess from anecdotal knowledge that talking to a psychotherapist was not a preferred mode of coping and probably not something that would have been readily shared with anyone beyond closest friends. Certainly, routine coping by using resources provided by a mental health professional had not been a standard practice for first responders.

In times of unusual stress, organizations and individuals have their own styles and rituals for adjustment. A generation ago, after a fatal fire, traditions would have had the firefighters buy a couple of cases of beer and talk informally. In this way, they were able to vent, learn, share, and in their own way attempt to recover if not heal. However, for the generation of active-duty firefighters working just prior to 9/11, using alcohol to assist helping oneself was not only understood to be ineffective and self-destructive but was actively discouraged and could result in punishment. Still, talking to a psychotherapist was not generally encouraged or even acceptable to many.

Attitudes towards mental health services changed enormously after 9/11. Going to some form of psychotherapy was actually encouraged by fellow firefighters. Generally these suggestions to firefighters by brother firefighters were well intentioned and not an expression of firehouse hazing. Even if this advice was not accepted, it represents a near complete reversal of attitudes toward mental health services and the FDNY CSU in particular. The change in attitude evolved over time. Often increased use of CSU was related to meaningful events, ceremonies, or anniversaries. Accessing psychotherapy services often coincided with what each person considered or marked as the after-9/11 period. It was not simply a matter of time. "After 9/11" meant as much emotional distance and what happened to that individual from 9/11 on as it did the simple measure of days, weeks, and months post-9/11.

The number of intakes at CSU had reached just over 200 by October 2001. Monthly intakes continued to fluctuate in the range of 100–250 until peaking at over 300 in June 2002, coinciding with the closing of the World Trade Center site. The next peak occurred in September 2002 at the time of the first

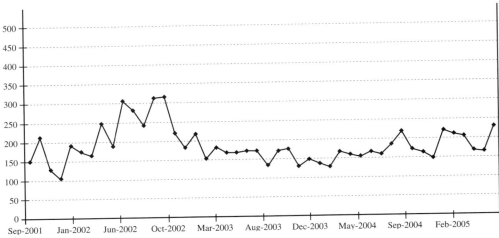

Figure 6.1 Total new intakes treated by FDNY CSU month
by month (Sept. 2001 to June 2005).

anniversary. These figures are more than triple the average pre-9/11 rate, which has not reoccurred in the nearly 5 years since. In contrast, intakes for all CSU locations have continued in the range of 125–235 per month since just after the first anniversary (Figure 6.1). From September 11, 2001, through June 30, 2005, CSU saw an average of 188 new clients per month at its offices, and in addition each month, referred an average of 47 additional individuals to a community provider.

Initially, the job and the emotions rallied everyone into action. With so many friends and coworkers suddenly dead or missing, with fires and emergencies calling, and the threat of greater catastrophe, both real and imagined—overwhelming shock, grief, and adrenaline ran high. One mental health director recalled that her memory of that period was that the typical work was slow and many felt the need for normal jobs. It may have been that people needed to be busy because there was an emergency and the country was on alert. None of the dedicated firefighters wanted to leave the job at the World Trade Center site before it was finished. There were those who felt that individual therapy would have taken them from the recovery effort and would have caused more stress than it relieved. For some, coping with the immediate crisis would postpone private concerns. Individual therapy could be a choice at another time. For a few, the signal to stop working came from a physical injury or limitation. Others needed individual attention sooner. Some, overwhelmed by exhaustion and grief and reaching the end of their endurance, had to be induced to stay away. Unfortunately, many went well beyond their limit, adding to their personal trauma.

Leaving the site generally did not mean the beginning of the after-9/11 experience. Marking the time when an event ends becomes important because it is one of the criteria required to diagnose a person with a posttraumatic disorder. Fixing that moment in time when the trauma has ended was not simple in this event. The end of the trauma and the start of the time for meeting the diagnostic criteria could have come at any time from the initial event through the closing of the site 9 months later. That time could have been when someone's remains were revealed or by attending a funeral. As has been discussed more thoroughly elsewhere in this text, the most common mark signaling the end of the trauma came with closing the Pit, but the peak time of CSU intakes came 3 months later after the first 9/11 anniversary. Ongoing events reminded them that there was nothing more they could do other than deal with their own grief and trauma. There was a widespread feeling of losing control over one's life path, a common experience in disasters. As time progressed and reminders of 9/11 accumulated, the need for mental health services expanded. Thus, the calls for individual treatment followed the same pattern as the need for all the interventions. They increased and continued over time triggered by events well after 9/11.

Not only did firefighters use the individual treatment option more often over time, but some also could be more open about past trips to therapists for themselves, their marriages, or their children. The acceptance of mental health services was apparent in the increased frequency of CSU use and in the openness about having used these services. There is a difference in providing individual treatment to individuals who are reluctant clients compared to willing ones. It is reasonable to assume that shift occurred post-9/11 because of the approach used by CSU to make services available and the effectiveness of the treatments themselves.

THE PARAMETERS OF INDIVIDUAL TREATMENT

What is the goal of individual treatment for a firefighter or anyone who has been traumatized by a disaster? Is the goal of individual treatment the same for the effects of 9/11 trauma as for any trauma, large-scale event, or disaster? Is there anything different about treating a firefighter for trauma from 9/11 compared to anyone else suffering from another major disaster or individually traumatic event? How might a firefighter be traumatized from this giant event versus the trauma of witnessing the sudden loss of one life? What characterizes good treatment versus bad? What does *helping* or *curing* mean in the context of terrorism and war? These were some of the larger questions that mental health counselors would have to address over time as people progressed through treatment.

THE CONTEXT

The nature of a disaster and the response by the society is intimately involved in the private relationship between therapist and client in the crucible of individual therapy. The nature of the 9/11 disaster was ambiguous at first. Clients and therapists did not quite know how to understand or label themselves. They were at once like victims of a crime and soldiers in a war, and at the same time firefighters, first responders, and recovery workers. They felt like they were on the front lines yet also at home with their families. In a society that mythologizes firefighters in children's' books, they regularly live with the contradictory image promulgated by disdainful politicians and the public's suspicious views. Post 9/11, politicians and the public treated them like celebrity heroes. At the same time firefighters had to function without a satisfactory work contract from the New York City government. Society's mixture of views was confusing and could be observed by mental health workers at the level of individual therapeutic interactions.

Shortly before 9/11 one firefighter had moved into a new home a long distance from the boroughs of New York City. Like many who live on modest civil service incomes, he and his wife purchased a fixer-upper that necessitated a substantial commute to the job. His best friend, who was killed by the 9/11 terrorists, was someone he had counted on to help with the needed home repairs. So, while he worked to find his friend's remains, his residence still demanded repairs and the garbage still needed taking out. While he was glorified by ceremonies and plaques at dedications for his friend, inside he could not find a way to think about himself that made sense. He and his wife still had the same needs for each other but even greater difficulty meeting each other's needs. Moving into a new home is stressful enough, but now they had to negotiate their needs in the context of greater demands on their time and emotions. He worked even longer hours and recognized that she felt uncomfortable making demands on him as he was prominently in the middle of a context of war, terrorism, heroism, and grief. At the same time, being with her was most important for him. The expectations of society influenced their relationship, and psychotherapy was one place to understand those issues.

In the case of this firefighter for this event, psychotherapy touched on the influence of a huge societal event to the most personal and important events of daily life. The context of individual therapy related to 9/11 firefighters included international terrorism, firefighting and recovery, a war and a response taking place at home, and talking about it with a therapist who was probably also a New Yorker and one of those potential victims the firefighter-client was protecting. This context is not one that the teachers of psychotherapy prepare their students to address.

As has been observed by many disaster workers, every disaster tends to be different and each requires a different intervention tailored to its dimensions. Individual psychotherapy for firefighters needs to take into consideration the unique context for their intervention as well and to modify technique to suit that context. A more extensive discussion of context may or may not be part of the typical psychotherapy session, but it commonly was during the response to 9/11. For those who continue in treatment, it remains part of the conversation. It is not a resistance to treatment, but is an acknowledgment of the world in which they live.

In general, developing an understanding of the context of a disaster means to understand the situation and the impact of the event and situation on oneself as a person and on the clients. Taking a combined approach to understanding—a macro-view from the point of view of the community, a view as an individual who, like the clients, is also affected, and a view from the perspective of the client—is part of the task for all therapists. It is most important to remember that there are many ways and settings in which extensive damage to property and massive human suffering can be created. Nature and people provide innumerable ways to increase human suffering. Nevertheless, the same geological forces that cause earthquakes in Italy, Iran, or Los Angeles, will shape a unique intervention. For Americans, a car bomb in Baghdad is not going to trigger the same response as one in Mobile, Alabama. Of course, there are many other kinds of differences between disasters—for example, manmade versus natural disasters, domestic versus international, and so on—and these too will impact the psychotherapy relationship, process, and treatment. Every difference in the event will have consequences that make the intervention unique and influence the special relationship between individual therapist and individual client.

Additionally, disasters are always about the destruction of property, life, and social order, and the creation of powerful emotions. The comfort and assumed stability of the social organization always becomes highlighted when it has been interrupted by disaster. Appreciating the social order and relationships that connect the individual to their family, firehouse, and community both pre- and postevent often needs to be included as part of the individual therapy experience. As Miller (2002) aptly states, "Faith in the social order is restored by other people's availability."

THE INDIVIDUAL

Individual psychotherapy is always customized for that particular client, of course, and it is the unique strength of the modality. It is also true that individuals who have been traumatized also share common features in how they experience life after the trauma. While disasters vary by cause, time, place, resources, and more, psychological responses to disasters are more similar to each other than they are different. When an event is horrific and overwhelms any person's ability to cope, the mind usually reacts in predictable ways. It has been observed throughout history that people who have witnessed the horrific consistently demonstrate differences compared to their pre-trauma state. Currently, those observations are encapsulated in the psychiatric diagnoses of Acute Stress Disorder and Posttraumatic Stress Disorder (PTSD). Simply, that means that after a trauma, people do not necessarily experience life as they did before. They often report being numb to feelings and disconnected from themselves and others. Their thoughts are often interrupted by intense, consuming memories of the terrible events. At other times, they may suffer from poor recall. Their emotional and physical sense of self is altered. Fundamental beliefs about themselves and the world, both conscious and unconscious, are questioned. Sometimes, their previously most sacred beliefs feel false, and this can create profound uncertainty about the very meaning of life. People who have experienced trauma can have episodes when they do not think very clearly, exercise bad judgment, and make poor decisions when previously they would not have acted that way. They can feel highly and unpredictably anxious and manifest it by general hypervigilance and irritability that is all too apparent to those around them.

Firefighters and other first responders seem more practiced than others at coping with these traumatic experiences. However, there is no single way peculiar to firefighters for coping with trauma. The ability to tolerate and reconstitute oneself after trauma can be developed from religion, becoming fatalistic, using psychological defense mechanisms, and many other ways. However, if anyone is going to remain a first responder, he or she has to find ways to manage traumatic experiences. After all, the world of the first responder is all about getting to an emergency situation where there is likely to be life-threatening or horrific events. It is a way of life and has to include the horrific as a relatively mundane part of it because seeing terrible things can be relatively commonplace. This does not mean that they are unaffected by what they have to do sometimes.

It is not that firefighters do not talk about the bad things that happen. They are simply not accustomed to talking about what they go through to an outsider or inside an individual psychotherapy office. Firefighters, if not good storytellers themselves, have heard many well-told stories. They may mistakenly think they do not need to talk about bad things and instead want to protect others from the images. Firefighters are more likely to experience the personal consequences of trauma and disaster by complaining about their own their irritability that makes their wives and children unhappy than to say that they are personally unhappy. But, if the setting is right for the individual, every firefighter can recall with chilling clarity the first time he pulled the lifeless body of a child from wreckage. Death, horror, the agony of fearful, no-win choices, and the reactions that are often labeled psychiatric symptoms by outsiders, are ever present, even if not verbalized. And that was never more so than post-9/11.

The readiness of the client for psychotherapy, where they are likely to talk about events that would previously have been restricted to other firefighters, and the psychotherapist's timing to make therapeutic interventions addressing these issues is a matter of great debate. We take the position that, for most people, there will come a time for talking, that sometimes a mental health professional can be the best person to talk to, and that the skill of the therapist, including judging readiness for talking and intervening, can make a critical difference.

CHOOSING INDIVIDUAL PSYCHOTHERAPY

One of the factors that maximizes the effectiveness of the mental health system's response to disasters and trauma is when it can match the characteristics and needs of individuals to suitable treatments. Sometimes an individual can be best helped by the special features inherent in seeing a therapist individually. That can mean sitting down with one mental health professional away from the site of the disaster and in a treatment office. A one-on-one conversation in a private room designed for talking, bound by rules of confidentiality, and with each person playing the role of helper or helpee defines individual psychotherapy. A single person, the therapist, making himself or herself emotionally available at a specific time and place, plus available on an as-needed basis, just like the commitment of any psychotherapy, can significantly add to restoring the feeling that order is returning and chaos is receding, perhaps the most important benefit of any treatment for trauma.

Two considerations may address most concerns for selecting individual treatment versus other modalities. First, self-selection is often the best way to match person to treatment variables. If both individual and other options are equally available, the client is probably going to be able to choose the better one as often, if not more often, than any selection tool or criteria. A second determining factor may be shame. Regardless of the cause of the shame, a firefighter, probably like anyone else, may be more likely to find the individual setting more conducive to discussing these feelings and the events that triggered them.

TREATMENT CONSIDERATIONS

It is our opinion that psychological treatment is not necessary for everyone who has been exposed to a disaster. Some experts have recommended that trauma and grief counseling should be mandated for everyone all the time.

Fortunately, beliefs in cookie-cutter, mandatory approaches are more popular among media pundits than among professionals. To be fair, some professionals sincerely believe that universally mandated trauma and bereavement counseling is best. That, however, has not been validated by CSU's experiences. Still, there are people and circumstances when traditional, individual psychotherapy is preferred and useful. The special techniques of the therapist can make individual treatment experience worthwhile for those who need the privacy and concentrated relationship that only individual psychotherapy provides. The private nature of the individual session is an excellent venue to open up about the specific, troubling symptoms that motivate people to seek help from a professional. Like most people who seek consultation, firefighters usually have tried to resolve their problems on their own. Individual therapy or other treatments including medication can be encouraged as a way to reduce unnecessary suffering, the underlying philosophy of making all treatments readily available.

If language is the foundational unit of psychotherapy, then context is the place where that foundation is laid and takes meaning. Both the use of the client's language and the ability to navigate the client's context are necessary for all of psychotherapies, regardless of theoretical orientation or target population. All groups have their own, unique nuances in using language and creating context. First responders are no different. New York City firefighters and their families live in a context that is complete with its own language and culture. In this way, they are set apart from the general population and even from other first responders. Psychotherapy is not likely to be useful unless the mental health worker takes the time to learn the language of firefighters and appreciate the context in which they and their families live. For counselors employed by CSU and already experienced in the FDNY culture, this was already part of their lexicon. However, using outside therapists presented challenges for CSU, first responders, as well as the therapists.

Recent trends in psychotherapy place culture in the forefront of factors that ought to be assessed and included in treatment plans in general. The chapter in this text describing the New York City firefighters' culture is a useful reference for therapists doing individual psychotherapy with this population. The context of the firefighter has a logic formed from its history and tradition. Their language is precisely defined by their experience. Prior to 9/11, words like *pile* and *pit* were bland parts of the English language. Today, they are immortalized in the language history of firefighters as *the Pile* and *the Pit*. Surely, most disaster workers will not have the storied history of FDNY, but every group of responders will bring their culture with them, and their experience and sensibility about themselves is likely to be an important consideration in the psychotherapeutic process.

In addition to language and context, mental health workers need to appreciate the characteristic psychological and situational forces that shape the client. Firefighters in general are subject to special situational demands. Firefighters in New York City also have to respond to the special nature of this remarkable city. On 9/11, those demands changed some of these firefighters' mission and, along with it, changed the context.

Firefighters have always had to think about fire, death, and dying in ways that others do not. Ask a civilian to talk about fire and you might hear that fire is the gift of the gods. But, for firefighters, it is uniquely experienced as the archfoe. Most people do not think about dying from fire. But for those in the business of fighting fires, it must be addressed. In the firehouse, their other home, the alarm will sound and it will be time for battle. The firefighter's life is always engulfed by the danger of the job. Sometimes it can be ignored or maybe forgotten, but fire is never far and, more likely, it is psychologically close to threatening life and family with loss, disability, and despair. Despite the primal fears and the frequent injuries associated with their employment, firefighters with the FDNY prior to 9/11 had always said with total sincerity about their work, "It's the best job in the world."

After 9/11, verbalizing the same enthusiasm for the job carried more complicated implications and ambivalence. Suffering so many losses and witnessing so much horror as they despairingly searched for lost brothers and civilians, and later recovering merely parts of bodies, took its toll. Post-9/11 threats of attacks on their homes with modern weapons of mass destruction changed the job. The situation firefighters now live in is more than fighting fires and cleaning up dangerous materials. From the early days and months after 9/11, there was renewed emphasis on nerve gas, smallpox, and dirty, radioactive bombs. The context had changed, and the job had changed. The culture was threatened and potentially changed, too.

Psychotherapists always have to listen, learn, and respect the language of the client, especially when they come from a different culture or context. This is also true when providing mental health services to the groups who are the first to respond to disasters. The psychotherapist offering individual therapy needs to be sensitive to the firefighters' culture and the continuous transformation of the context and language of that culture.

TREATMENT GOALS

Psychological treatment goals for the traumatized are often about helping to restore a person to their pretrauma level of functioning. If a traumatic event caused a person to feel less connected to the people in his or her life, less active in a number of social events, and created more marital discord than before, then a commonly accepted goal might be for that individual to return to pretrauma functioning in those spheres. Sometimes the losses to people and property make a return to pretrauma functioning impossible. Too much has been lost or changed. An alternate method of determining goals for treatment is to accept some criteria for a reasonably healthy lifestyle and helping the client reach those criteria. Using this model, posttrauma functioning might even exceed pretrauma levels as one reaches for a recovery that can compensate for what was lost.

Treatment goals for trauma are usually different than for other problems. After trauma, one does not simply go on as if life is the same. Life isn't the same. Something has happened to change how life is perceived and comprehended. Something about life's fragility is known that was not known before the incident. You cannot un-know something. You know the potential for trauma is only a hair's breadth away, and that everything you rely on can change instantly. The everyday, mundane order of life, the people we love, our physical being, can be destroyed without warning. Psychological treatment does not change the rules of life. It can help someone talk and think more productively about the event, perhaps reduce the potentially debilitating effects, and support transcendence, a manner of developing some emotional, intellectual, and spiritual comprehension of their experience. Rarely does someone who has experienced major trauma say that their posttrauma life is just the same as their pretrauma one.

This is not to suggest that everyone who experiences trauma will suffer PTSD or will need some corrective emotional experience. We believe that is a false assertion. We believe we are simply stating the obvious when we say that posttrauma life is different in important ways from the pretrauma life. Traumatic events and disasters have a profound effect on the individual psyche and the society. Life changes, and we all must adapt to these profound changes. It is better understood today than pre-9/11 that most people do not suffer PTSD and related disorders. We are reminded how ordinary people rise to meet challenges and that first responders are an especially resilient group. The therapist working with individuals may find it useful to remain mindful of the strengths of that person, such as their inherent ability to cope, and recognize those efforts that are probably underway before the person enters the private psychotherapy session.

Once people recognized that they could be safe and that there was going to be a future after 9/11, they wondered if they could ever be normal again. Soon, there was talk about finding a "new normal." Life was not ever going to be like it was, but someday life was going to resemble what they used to take for granted. Life would go on as each person found their new normal in their own way at their own pace.

One of the more common goals characterizing successful psychotherapy with firefighters was finding the new normal. If there was such a thing as an initial cure for the trauma of 9/11, it was finding the new normal. Within that experience, emotions could return, attachments to others would be possible, terrible experiences talked about, and previously enjoyed pursuits could again be part of life. But the old way of life, pretrauma and pre-9/11 global functioning, was generally not a realistic option. Many aspects of pre-9/11 functioning had to be regained, but other and possibly new and healthier coping skills had to be developed.

CSU produced a booklet about finding the new normal, and those words embodied the experience about where each person's psychological state was in relation to the recovery process. "Finding 9/12" became a phrase that implied recovery without forgetting those lost and accepting the possibility, if not inevitability, of the resilience to move on.

The psychological health associated with successful psychotherapy also means being able to see the world mostly as it is. A healthy person can perceive and understand relationships, family, work life, and leisure reasonably accurately. A major part of life is vocational, and this is especially true for firefighters whose personal lives and work lives are so closely interwoven. In the pre-9/11 world, the rate of change was slow. The firehouse, the people, and doing the job of responding to calls, even though they were unpredictable emergencies, were relatively the same everyday. In the post-9/11 world, change was blindingly fast. The job changed almost instantly, and rapid change continued for many months, turning into years of change. The people working on the job were not the same ones as pre 9/11. Many were dead, others were on new assignments, promoted, or retired. The job itself included many new and potentially more deadly challenges in fighting terrorism. In the months after 9/11, the thoughts were about anticipating the next bombing, identifying some exotic, highly infectious disease, and having to contain deadly toxins and radioactive substances. The nature of change is that it creates stress, and change was everywhere. The change in the job, the prolonged period of change, and the rate of the changes were what brought many to treatment. However, having stress under these circumstances is not abnormal and not a psychiatric disorder. Treatment, whether individually or in groups, via education or any other means, was about informing and normalizing that reality, not about analyzing personal histories that may or may not relate to distortions in perceiving and understanding. Conceptualized treatment as curing a mental illness and resolving an underlying psychopathology to restore psychological health was not useful.

Recognizing that behaviors, feelings, and thoughts that might seem excessive, inappropriate, and subjectively distressing are symptoms of trauma and grief rather than underlying psychopathology is not a new discovery. The earliest citation found in our searches revealed that Lindemann (1944) made this same observation with grief reactions, and, as noted by James and Gilliland in their textbook (2005), Caplan (1964) applied this to traumatized people.

The treatment of traumatized people often brings out an old controversy among mental health professionals. Some believe the ultimate path to recovery rests with analytically understanding one's personal history, intrapsychic dynamics, and unconscious conflicts that are worsened by the trauma. An opposing group believes that this analytic approach to a traumatized person not only is not helpful but is counterproductive and potentially harmful. This group believes that recovery is facilitated by strengthening social supports, basic knowledge of how people respond to abnormal events, limited cognitive restructuring, and improved environmental and economic resources. It is a controversy that was apparent after World War II when the Veterans Administration had to help many injured soldiers. While with what was then called the Veterans Administration Mental Hygiene Service, Luchins (1948) noted a similar dispute. His solution divided the population into two groups. For one group, he identified personal inadequacies as the primary cause of ongoing symptoms of traumatization. Certainly, at that historical point in the development of psychological treatments, having a personal inadequacy would suggest an individual psychoanalytic treatment approach. The other group comprised "those whose main cause of conflict lay in objective circumstances over which they had little control." For this cohort, Luchins suggested better treatment outcomes were obtained when the therapist attempts "to discover what roles social field conditions have played and *are playing* in the development of this particular personality constellation, and how he can best utilize social forces to produce changes in the personality in the direction of better mental health." That is, therapists need to appreciate the additional concrete, real issues that confront the traumatized person and provide resources rather than treating them as being inadequate to the tasks of life after trauma.

In our experience with individual treatment, regardless of the severity of the personal issues that predate the identified trauma, supporting and strengthening the client's social network and educating the person that it is normal to respond to abnormal events with abnormal reactions yield better outcomes. Surely, in the early postevent stages, people can have severe personal problems and be fully resilient. The severity of preexisting personal problems may not be a good predictor for who is best served by individual treatment, regardless of the theoretical orientations inherent in cognitive restructuring or psychodynamic therapy. Individual therapy needs to be part of the treatment options that aim to improve understanding and restore meaningfulness. For some, constructing meaning and insight may facilitate relief from symptoms.

IMPLICATIONS FOR PSYCHOTHERAPY TECHNIQUE

It is through the specific techniques of psychotherapy that this form of intervention can aid the redevelopment of social order, interpersonal connection, and sense of control about life. Rapport is always thought to be the first necessary step in psychotherapy, and for trauma treatment it is even more important. In our view, when therapy is indicated, one curative element is the therapist's emotional availability, knowledge, and commitment demonstrated in the consistency of private appointments that supports an individual's drive to overcome the crisis. This is not an endorsement for one theory over another but a statement of belief based on experience that individual psychotherapy can be useful. Certainly, the time at which this modality is introduced to the person makes an important, even critical difference, as do other variables like the characteristics and training of the therapist and the unique characteristics of the client.

TIME IN RELATION TO TREATMENT AND PROCESS

Timing in both the start of individual therapy and offering of specific interventions or comments to clients always requires careful consideration. In the early phases of responding to disasters, providing individual therapy was not useless or counterproductive, as some have suggested. First responders want to and need to do their work, but there were firefighters who came to CSU early on and still worked. Apparently, the best time for individual therapy for first responders is like the best time to provide individual treatment for all other problems, when the client decides it is needed. Both attending treatment and recovery work can serve therapeutic goals. Why interfere with that? Of course, the person who self-refers and wants to be taken off line is a different situation. They need to be temporarily relieved from duty and evaluated for continued fitness. However, we can see no justification and many contraindications for mandating individual consultations. The role of education, both pre- and postevent, is a more important consideration. In this way, responders can know when they might need a consultation and when to refer a coworker. The treatment of self-referred clients usually differs from other-referred ones.

The time from the traumatic event to the start of psychotherapy is often a consideration for the therapist as a treatment plan is developed and specific verbal and nonverbal interventions are introduced. However, at what point in time is the traumatic event over? As discussed elsewhere in this text, the trauma on 9/11 was not the only traumatic event, and it did not signal the beginning of when to expect the appearance of trauma symptoms. For some it was many months, even years, later. The client's internal construction of time and the end of the event should be considered as one weighs interventions that are modified based on time from that event.

Firefighter clients do not generally start posttrauma therapy by saying, "Here is how I was traumatized. This is what I saw. This is what I did." They are more likely to say, "The guys told me I was messed up and that I should talk to a shrink," or "I don't like that I have been yelling at my kids." In this way, individual psychotherapy for this group is not different from other groups. One can easily explore the chief complaint, build rapport, and remain alert for the signs of acute stress, Posttraumatic Stress Disorder, traumatic or complicated grief, and any classification of psychological problems. Some therapists believe they ought to ask the client about the most emotional, traumatic experiences directly and at the first meeting. Listening to traumatic stories can be like watching a train collision. You can't take your eyes off of it. Therapists need to be careful not to confuse their own motivations to talk or not talk about the disaster with the client's readiness to talk. Theories can be used to provide a rationale for asking or withholding questions that the client is or is not ready for. Clients signal their readiness to talk about topics. If unsure if the signal is there, ask and be prepared to respect the answer. Readiness to talk can be immediate, can come years after an event, or never.

The fact is that many people would rather not talk to therapists about their traumas because they do not expect much help from the conversation. Firefighters often find it best to talk to others who have been through what they themselves have been through. It is not a psychological resistance to psychotherapy as some theories might suggest, and it is not necessarily that the therapist is behaving incompetently. It can sometimes mean that those people have found more help from others who made it through a similarly terrible time. That terrible, traumatizing experience sometimes appears to change certain people in ways that only those who have been similarly traumatized may be able to comprehend. On the other hand, it would be foolish to suggest that in general talking does not help or that anyone, given the current state of scientific knowledge, can predict who will benefit from talking and who will not any better than the clients themselves. This should not be confused with traumatic avoidance. Sometimes, traumatized people avoid talking about the trauma, and that avoidance is a problem that is related to other problems they are having in their lives. In that case, helping a person to talk is part of the resolution of the other, identifiable problems. Such clients generally present with a problem and are seeking a solution. That motivation can be addressed and lead to talking about the trauma in a way that helps rather than retraumatizes. The progression of talking about the trauma still must go on at a pace that matches the client's readiness. Talking about the trauma helps for some but not for others. Time from the event is one factor that influences readiness and benefits that can be obtained from exploring those feelings.

APPOINTMENT TIMES

Firefighters work in shifts that stretch around the clock. Like most clients, they prefer to arrange for individual sessions conveniently before and after work. However, they often don't have any choice about overtime. They cannot predict when emergencies start and end or when the job mandates they work overtime. Therapists who can be flexible with their schedules, such as holding appointment hours for late morning and late afternoon, support the feeling that someone can be consistently there for them to counter the isolation and loss of certainty that follows disasters. Some therapies regard changes to the schedule of appointments as a resistance to treatment. This is not necessarily the case for firefighters.

INTERVENTIONS

Firefighters come from varied backgrounds, and like any group, some have survived severe childhood experiences. That does not necessarily mean that their purpose in treatment is to repair or overcome those experiences. Skills developed in childhood to cope with those challenges may also be integral to their functioning. Instead, they may simply not know what they want, and a good enough invitation may help them to talk about many issues. Through talking and the other supports in their lives, they may feel, connect, and believe that there will be a new normal and redevelop a sense of control. Interpreting the unconscious may inhibit that process. Individual psychotherapy may also lead people to talk about childhood patterns, but first responders may not be opening up like this so they can unlock some developmental lesion. Rather, it may be their way to explain their thinking as they try to be fully understood.

Normalizing, depathologizing, and validating are useful interventions at any stage of treatment and in any format, individual or group. It is in fact quite remarkable how simply explaining that it is not uncommon to experience any of the trauma-associated complaints can reduce a so-called symptom and relax an agitated person. Anyone unfamiliar with typical reactions that can be suffered after trauma can be puzzled and frustrated if they feel "spaced out," forgetful, or numb and not know why these experiences are occurring. Timely and sensitive explanations that such experiences are normal and not signs of pathology, as well as validating that they are quite distressing, can put a person at greater ease and promote the return to a sense of well-being. Of course, it is essential that the therapist be sufficiently versed in what constitutes an abnormal event and the range of human reactions to abnormal events, and also can identify them during the therapy to deliver sensitive, well-timed feedback. In this, experience working therapeutically with firefighters may be especially valuable. Firefighters, having been exposed to numerous experiences throughout their careers that would qualify as being traumatic, are often both surprised and ashamed at having these normal reactions.

BOUNDARIES

Trauma suffered in a major disaster, one that is both large scale and highly public, changes the therapist's approach to the traumatized client in ways that do not occur when the trauma is suffered in private, away from the public spotlight. Someone who has suffered spousal abuse, for example, may be able to hide that experience from the therapist. The therapist might not know that the abuse instigated the individual session. Someone who has been in a major and public disaster rarely needs to tell the therapist about that event having happened because the therapist already knows. The information is public. The client may choose not to talk about the event, but the client cannot prevent the therapist from knowing something about it before the client chooses to reveal it. For this additional reason, initiating a discussion of the details of the event must have clear signals that the client feels it is time to talk about it. Timing the private discussion of the public trauma is one way therapists demonstrate a respect for interpersonal boundaries and that the client has control over their life.

An important part of individual therapy for these firefighters has been about providing an invitation to talk. That invitation has to include safety, confidentiality, and the assurance that their story is not going to make you into yet another person they have to take care of. Many firefighters have told similar stories about people who seem appropriately interested in helping them and who ask about the rescue attempt and recovery experiences. When these firefighters started to open up, they found the other person's emotionality inhibited them from speaking freely. Sometimes, their well-intentioned listeners would cry or recoil. No one wants to have to take care of the person who is supposed to be listening and helping them.

TERMINATION

The patterns of termination seem to be no different than others. Some people leave early, others come and go over an extend period, while some stay for a long time. Brief therapies treat people in fewer sessions and those with open-ended time frames have highly variable lengths. Perhaps this is as it should be.

SUMMARY

It is likely that individual psychotherapy will remain an indispensable option for helping first responders. Certainly, the efforts of many mental health workers for 9/11 first responders demonstrated the flexibility and potential effectiveness of that modality. It is useful to consider modifying aspects of traditional techniques, such as how one introduces the option for individual treatment, how boundaries are managed, listening and speaking with extra sensitivity to context and language, or setting the criteria for the goals of treatment. The same effective messages provided to the general population overall—normalizing, depathologizing, and validating experience—are also useful at the level of individual psychotherapy.

CHAPTER 7

Finding Comfort in Groups

T HERE ARE many reasons why group interventions are efficacious in the aftermath of trauma. Groups provide an opportunity to join with others who have survived similar circumstances and support one another in healing. Group involvement interrupts the isolation that so often is an accompaniment to trauma. In addition, groups provide an efficient use of resources; many, or at least several, people can be seen at one time.

Group interventions are not new in the treatment of trauma but rather date back to interventions designed to aid in the recovery of returning World War II veterans. Subsequent to this, the literature describes groups addressing personal trauma such as rape, sudden traumatic loss, sexual and physical abuse, and other horrific life events. Similarly, there are multiple examples of groups in the aftermath of natural and man-made disasters. These range from on-scene intervention groups, such as debriefings conducted in the acute stage of response, to cognitive behavioral, exposure, and psychodynamic interventions that can range in time from months to years following an incident.

The range of possible group interventions following trauma will not be reviewed in detail in this text. Rather this discussion will focus on the specific issues that emerged when offering group interventions to different subgroups within the FDNY community. It will address issues of timing, composition, and structure as well as the context in which groups were offered.

It is common within the world of employee assistance practice to dismiss the use of group intervention based on a belief that people who work together are unlikely to be comfortable disclosing the level of personal information called for in an ongoing group. Possible exceptions to this include psycho-educational support groups and single-session interventions, including debriefings. Employee assistance programs (EAP) frequently have staff trained to offer debriefings on scene when a particular workplace suffers a traumatic incident or loss, such as a robbery or accidental death. These interventions help coworkers to talk about the event and its impact on the workgroup and also serve to convey the concerns and support of the organization's leadership.

Group intervention within the context of FDNY CSU has always been somewhat different from the more typical workplace setting. Firefighters for the most part are accustomed to and comfortable in groups. It is how they do their work and a part of the culture in which they live. For years prior to 9/11, CSU had offered a program for early recovery from alcohol and drugs that ran primarily on a group intervention model. Here firefighters dealing with similar issues met on a daily basis and freely disclosed much about their personal lives and struggles. These groups worked in part because they brought together firefighters dealing with a specific set of problems. Often membership in the Brotherhood was felt to hasten group cohesion rather than impede it, as the more typical EAP concerns would dictate.

The conditions that support group intervention in the aftermath of disaster mitigate some of these concerns as well. Trauma groups, across most accepted models of intervention, are primarily focused on an event and the individual reactions to that specific event. They are more about the shared trauma, and thus the present and recent past, than the disclosure of earlier, historic material. They generally do not focus on the interactions between members or on the patterns of behavior displayed in the group which may be problematic in an individual's life. Such groups come together for the purpose of mutual aid and support and in this way are consistent with, rather than antithetical to, the culture in which firefighters live with one another throughout their careers.

WHY GROUP INTERVENTION?

In his seminal text on group psychotherapy, Yalom (1970) talked about *curative factors,* those aspects of a group that helped patients get better. While all are potentially present in any specific trauma group, some of these curative factors are particularly relevant to the effectiveness of trauma groups across the intervention spectrum:

- Installation of hope
- Interpersonal learning: learning about oneself from others in group
- Catharsis: the opportunity to speak about the event and express reactions to it without judgment
- Universality: learning that you are not alone and that your reactions were shared by others

- Normalization: learning that your reactions are normal to the event and not pathological
- Group cohesion: experiencing an increased sense of belonging
- Imparting of information
- Existential factors

THERAPY GROUPS VERSUS SUPPORT GROUPS

Most trauma groups are not therapy groups but rather fall under the general heading of support groups. The members come together based on a difficult, shared life experience rather than an individual psychological problem. Support groups operate on the basis of mutual aid and the belief that in helping others one helps oneself. It is the members of the group who are the experts on the shared feelings and experience, the role of the leader is as facilitator. The group provides safety by allowing members to choose the level of participation they feel comfortable with. There is no pressure or expectation for individual change, but rather support and acceptance are offered along with a place where one can talk about those things that are not possible to talk about elsewhere. In the case of 9/11 this ranged from the discussion of body parts and body handling to the expression of ongoing, unrelenting grief in the face of outsiders asking, "Aren't you over it yet?" An additional important aspect of support groups in contrast to therapy groups is the allowance of contact between group members outside of the group meeting. These features are especially important in assisting with recovery from the typical trauma symptoms of isolation and alienation. The importance of social support in the recovery process cannot be overstated.

TRAUMA GROUPS

Temporal Considerations

Trauma groups vary considerably depending upon the timing of the intervention in relation to the event. As you move from the acute (emergency) phase through the early (postimpact) phase and finally the middle and later phases (restoration and recovery) the locus of intervention, purpose of the group, and methodology change considerably. For example, initially groups will be held on site mainly for the purpose of conveying information. The main tasks for the leaders of the group are to listen empathically, contain the process, assess members in need of crisis intervention, and educate regarding anticipatory reactions. As groups move off site and into a more private venue, the purpose shifts with it. Groups at this stage and in this setting afford opportunities to share the traumatic experience and/or the traumatic response.

The purpose of the group may be to improve coping mechanisms, manage intense feelings and symptoms, or increase understanding about the impact of the event on one's life. Leaders at this stage facilitate this process by encouraging emotional expression and educating members about the relationship between feelings of anger, guilt, loss, grief, and the trauma they have experienced. Similarly they can help to link emotion to thought process and address distortions and changes in belief systems and world view stemming from trauma. Still later, groups may form or continue for the purpose of creating meaning from the traumatic experience, integrating the experience into the narrative of one's life, and establishing a *new normal*. Leaders at this point in the process assist members not only with disclosure but with introspection as well (Buchele & Spitz, 2004).

In the aftermath of 9/11 the protracted period of time that FDNY remained working at the site extended the time line of each of these periods. For the purposes of this discussion, *acute/emergency* refers to the immediate aftermath on the day of the event and the days following, during which time rescue workers continued to believe they might find survivors in the rubble. The *early/postimpact phase* began when the work at the WTC site was changed from rescue to recovery. This too is a difficult date to establish. While it was gradually accepted that no survivors would be found, firefighters were committed to working 24-hour shifts until all remains were recovered. In late October, the mayor attempted to change this pattern, creating furor within the FDNY community who met with him to protest turning the site into a *construction zone*. Eventually a compromise was struck that left FDNY in charge of the operation. This phase lasted an unprecedented amount of time, until June 2002, when the last firefighters left a broom-swept site and walked away knowing they had not succeeded in bringing home the remains of all their brothers. It was after this that the *recovery and restoration* work of the middle and later phases could truly occur.

Along with the protracted time frame of the overall event, there was also a personal time line of recovery which varied based on each individual's involvement in the direct recovery work. To accommodate this there was overlap in the offering of phase-specific interventions to provide what was needed to those beginning and completing different phases of the work at different times.

ISSUES OF MEMBERSHIP SELECTION

Group selection varies across this temporal continuum with more consideration given to controlling membership as you get further away from the event in time. Basic triage techniques make it possible to screen out anyone exhibiting extreme signs of traumatic stress from the on-site acute phase group. However, the fact that at this point members are largely unscreened and unknown is one of a number of factors that speak to caution in the amount of processing encouraged at this stage. In groups where trauma exposure remains the single most important inclusion criteria, it is increasingly possible after the acute phase has subsided to screen potential group members not only for inclusion but exclusion as well. Generally inclusion criteria are quite broad and focus on the individual's capacity to relate to others, commit to the structure of the group, and tolerate the feelings that may be expressed. A desire to participate is important. Selection criteria may vary depending upon the purpose of the group and the type of intervention utilized. For example, prolonged exposure groups require a higher degree of screening as the capacity to tolerate intensely affective material, both one's own and that of others, is required. Compliance with attendance, homework, and so forth, may also become aspects of inclusion criteria for these groups.

STRUCTURAL CONSIDERATIONS

It has been our experience that time-limited groups were most useful. This was especially true when groups were developed relatively soon after the event while the situation continued to be in flux and members remained relatively unscreened. This made for an easier transition into new group formations, where purpose, membership, and other group dimensions could change based on circumstances. This is not to suggest that ongoing groups cannot recontract around these issues, just that it is more difficult.

All of the groups we ran, with the exception of the following bereavement and activity groups discussed, had certain structural similarities. They were time-limited, generally 6 to 12 sessions, and offered psycho-educational material along with group interaction. Emphasis was placed on discussion and the expression of feelings and ideas related to the event that might lead to some modification of attitudes and behavior. All of these groups were co-led in order to minimize the impact of vicarious trauma by encouraging coleaders to process the groups together after each session. Cofacilitation also allowed for ongoing scanning within the group to assess the impact of traumatic material on others. It permitted one of the leaders to be available to any individual member in need of attention outside of the group without entirely disrupting the group process.

At times a newly defined population would be invited to meet once in a rather informal setting, often firehouse style over lunch, to explore their interest in participating in a multi-session group. This was consistent with the importance of building safety and control into the process of trauma treatment. Especially when we were not drawing primarily from those who had participated in individual treatment and felt a certain degree of safety at CSU, this introductory session was often of help. At times a multi-session group formed, at times not. In this case individual treatment was always an alternative for those who had not yet utilized this service. The possibility of a group forming at a later time always remained as an option.

ON-SITE INTERVENTIONS

ACUTE/EMERGENCY PHASE ON-SITE INTERVENTIONS

As discussed earlier, acute phase interventions for the most part will occur on site. In our experience, during the earliest, emergency phase, group intervention is not the best choice for firefighters. Rather what can be described as *the walk around* is beneficial. This on-site, informal method of intervention is a form of psychological triage that can be used to identify a first responder who is experiencing significant psychological symptoms in need of intervention: dissociation, suicidal ideation, confusion, significant numbing, and the like. It begins the process of education about the signs and symptoms of trauma and allows for the disbursement of information about available services (Phillips & Thomas, in press). This verbal information can effectively be supplemented by handing out pocket-sized cards listing the main symptoms of acute stress reaction that may be a cause of concern and a phone number to call for more information or assistance. This can easily be slipped into a pocket, may be forgotten about, and may serve as a reminder when rediscovered at a later time.

Caution: This is an on-scene intervention, and thus only those with formal access and auspice should be handing out such information.

This preference for individual as compared to group intervention at this earliest, on-scene phase is specific to our assessment of the FDNY population and should not be automatically generalized to other populations. In considering this it is important to recognize that firefighters, unlike many others who are seen on site following a disaster, will at some point return together to the firehouse. Here they will sit as a group and talk among themselves. This behavior is as old as any of the traditions of firefighting. An appreciation of this natural group opportunity may help to mitigate the helper's need to put people together in groups on location. In addition, all of the factors discussed earlier in this volume that relate to the importance of staying focused on mission come into play in staging a response in the earliest acute postdisaster phase. Any mental health presence at this stage must not intrude on the work; this is an emergency, and first responders are appropriately preoccupied with doing their job. Information, along with providing a protective individual outlet for those becoming overwhelmed, is useful. So too is knowing that firefighters will naturally gather together for support when their work for the day is done.

For those who do not naturally have the opportunity to come together off site as a group, an on-site acute stage group before disbursement can be advantageous. This may apply to first responders, such as EMTs and paramedics, who unlike firefighters are not returning as a unit to a single location, as well as others exposed to the traumatic event. There is a great deal of controversy regarding such groups especially related to the potential for trauma exposure and contagion. It is therefore important when conducting such groups to be clear about their purpose, which, consistent with the concept of psychological first aid, is to offer support and compassionate listening in order to reduce acute psychological distress and facilitate additional support when needed. It is primarily intended to offer information rather than to elicit it. That is not to say that it is not appropriate for group members to talk about what they are experiencing but more to support the idea that no member of the group need speak and that a skilled group facilitator needs to monitor the impact of individual catharsis on the members of the group. It is generally recommended that groups either be small and homogeneous as to trauma exposure or larger and more heterogeneous, with greater limitation on the amount of personal disclosure. Follow-up opportunities for those who need and/or desire them are always a part of this early group intervention (Everly et al. 2005).

Early/Postimpact Phase On-site Groups

Over the course of the 9 months during which firefighters continued digging at the site, the walk around continued as CSU peers and, whenever possible, clinicians visited the site, spoke to the men, and disbursed information. During this phase, firefighters were able to volunteer for a 30-day work assignment digging at the site. This was not an opportunity for overtime but rather substituted for their usual firehouse tours. It meant they worked different hours, at a different location, and most importantly with different firefighters and officers. In sync with these 30-day World Trade Center work rotations a CSU clinician and peer offered a formal group meeting along the lines of group psychological first aid to those beginning their tour and separately to those completing it.

Some groups were more talkative than others. For those beginning their rotation there was often little to say. The hope of being successful in their task of recovering remains that might bring some small amount of comfort to a grieving family was complicated by the feeling of apprehension as to what one might encounter to make that possible. Meeting with those ending their rotation was different. Many talked about the frustration of digging all those hours and finding nothing. Others talked about the strange mixture of reactions in finding a foot, a finger, a wallet—anything identifiable that might have meaning to a family member. It mattered less if anyone spoke and more that they sat together, in some way marking the experience they were about to have or had just completed. Unquestionably, finding human remains increased trauma exposure, however, not finding anything increased the feelings associated with failing to accomplish the mission. While no data are available to support this, we would hypothesize that it was the latter group who experienced greater difficulties following their World Trade Center rotation. It was important that they knew how to access help when they were ready.

If the line between acute and early stage groups as discussed above seems blurred, it is. Disasters and the time lines that follow do not easily lend themselves to neat demarcations of phases or time that allow prescriptions for intervention. For firefighters in the aftermath of 9/11, the ongoing work at the site created multiple time lines in which the *acute* phase for some might be thought about as the time immediately following the collapse while for many not present at that time it was the postimpact phase of rescue activity marked by searching for survivors at first and digging for bodies later on. The ongoing recovery work was so protracted that it can be difficult to think of as a single phase of the event. Gradually the recovery work at the site became more organized, although it was never routine. For those working a 30-day rotation digging for remains, it indeed seemed *early* in relation to the event, and it is for this reason that we think of the early phase as extending until the closing of the site in June 2002. However, the time from the event was a continuum that stretched out over numerous activities and varied considerably from one member or unit to another. To avoid confusion about the timing of intervention in relation to this, it may be helpful to think about the location of interventions along with the time frame in which they occurred. Acute phase interventions occurred on scene either at the WTC site or in the firehouse. On-scene interventions continued throughout the early/postimpact phase and into what some might have begun to think of as a middle phase, lasting until the site was officially closed in June 2002. Office-based groups also began during this time.

All future events will have their unique features that require thoughtful consideration and assessment as to what type of group interventions make sense, for whom and when. Our experience was that, for as long as the mission continued, some type of on-scene educational and informational group was beneficial in addition to individual opportunities.

KITCHEN TABLE GROUPS

While difficult to categorize, it is important to recognize the significant role of the informal kitchen table groups that occur on a daily basis in the firehouse. As part of the fabric of the culture, these groups existed during all phases of the 9/11 experience as they did before and continued to after. They are unstructured, naturally occurring peer groups based on being present in the firehouse. One can join the table or depart from it at any time. Participation is voluntary, although peer pressure at times can exert a powerful influence. These groups can be educational, self-revealing, confrontational, retraumatizing, supportive, and healing as well as many other things for individual firefighter participants.

They perhaps more resemble a large family group or college dorm than the professional groups we are more familiar with. Generally the members of these groups know one another's strengths and vulnerabilities. They know when it is okay to tease and about what and when to pull back, be silent, or offer support. They most often know when outside help is needed.

These groups operate outside of our professional radar. They are helpful to some and not to others. At times a professional may be invited to join the group, but, as is true with any leaderless peer group, the moment this occurs the group as it was no longer exists. It is participation in the informal group process that makes most firefighters such good group members. It is important to recognize the existence of these groups and employ them as an ally. It is at the kitchen table that those who know one another best take note of how each other is doing and, using the buddy system of referral, let it be known when a brother needs help.

OFFICE-BASED GROUPS: MIDDLE AND LATER PHASE

In our experience, when firefighters did decide to come into CSU for help they really wanted individual time. Often they were saturated with the informal, and at times endless and potentially retraumatizing, kitchen-table talk. When they came it was not for mutual aid or any of the curative factors of group. They had experienced the catharsis of the kitchen, generally felt themselves to be part of a cohesive group and at that moment did not feel that they emotionally had much to give or get from other firefighters. Most often what brought them to counseling was a need to own and process their individual, unique, personal experiences, which many did not share at the kitchen table. It was often something held back during these discussions: some experience, question, regret, or other disturbing, private memory that haunted them and led to the sleeplessness, isolation, bursts of temper, and other trauma symptoms from which they sought relief. It helped to talk about this with someone outside, in the private, confidential space that is the hallmark of individual therapy. (For more on individual therapy of firefighters see Chapter 6.)

It was later, after a period of individual work, that the possibilities for shared experience and empathy reemerged. When this occurred, it was the homogeneity of the group that mattered most: collapse survivors, morgue workers, chauffeurs, dispatchers, EMS workers, family liaisons, and others who shared a common experience related to the event although they may not have shared that experience together. This was a different aspect of shared trauma. Unlike those who were actually, physically in the collapse together or shared the losses of a particular firehouse together, these individuals felt isolated from others who shared their experience.

Groups seemed to work best for those who had experienced something different from the firefighters or coworkers they saw every day. Those struggling with feelings of regret, self-criticism, or survivor guilt often felt unable to find the specialized camaraderie they craved at the kitchen table because, in their view, their experience had been different, unique, or apart from the others. They often found relief in the commonality provided by a group where they could give voice to the particular unspeakable aspects of their experience and feel they were not alone. It was important to share common experiences while recognizing and exploring the individual meaning the particular experience had to each member. Even when a group followed a period of individual treatment, verbalizing these thoughts and memories in the presence of other firefighters was a powerful aspect of recovery for many.

We experienced less success when offering more general trauma groups targeted to those who worked at the site during the long recovery period but had not been present at the time of the collapse or participated in a particular distinguishable role either the day of the event or subsequently. All who worked at the site had witnessed and endured horrific sights, smells, and conditions. They felt and in fact knew that most all of their fellow firefighters had endured the same work. Everyone shared the experience of digging and of loss. It is difficult to know if they felt undeserving of this additional service or simply felt they did not need it. Perhaps they felt that they had sufficient opportunity to share these experiences with other firefighters both on scene, in the firehouse, and often, unfortunately, at the bar.

We can speculate about this but may never know. It is likely that there are many reasons why some join groups and others do not. We know that often firefighters entered CSU minimizing their need for help and expressing concern that they might be taking a time slot away from a brother more in need— always the helpers. We also know that many felt a tremendous sense of survivor guilt and that the inability to successfully bring their brothers home made this sense of unworthiness even greater. Was this part of the reluctance to participate in discussion about their work there? Was there an element of protection, a feeling that holding their own visual images was enough without exposing and being exposed to others? Whatever the reason, our experience was that for those who participated in the recovery effort by digging at the site along with so many others and whose trauma was connected to the sights and smells and images from that work combined with the loss of so many they knew and worked with, individual rather than group seemed to be the modality of choice.

Perhaps what is most important is the idea that if we listen well, our clients tell us what they need, what makes sense, and what is not helpful. We found that often it made sense to offer something several times, typically at different times, and that if we felt there was sufficient outreach and still no response, the message was clear and we could move on. There was much to do and many different ways to do it.

IMPORTANCE OF HOMOGENEITY IN GROUP FORMATION

Unlike individual treatment that FDNY members accessed at the six CSU locations as well as through a large number of individual therapists, the groups, with few exceptions, were offered directly by CSU at our offices and at times at other convenient locations. The primary reason for this was the desire for homogeneity in terms of trauma exposure and group membership. CSU had access to the entire FDNY membership and community. We were seeing hundreds, eventually thousands, of firefighters in our six locations and were able to help people find the homogeneity and therefore safety they were seeking. It is, of course, only the extraordinary and thankfully atypical scope of the event that lent itself to the ever more specific homogeneous groupings we were able to offer.

We found the desire for homogeneity to be true for others in our population as well. As described elsewhere in this text, the family members of surviving firefighters had an experience so unique that they felt isolated and alienated from friends and families not part of the FDNY community. Most firefighter families lived outside of New York City in communities that fairly quickly returned to a sense of life as it had previously been lived. For them 9/11 entered their home only on the news and in the papers. They were of course relieved to learn that their firefighter neighbor or coach had survived but rarely stopped to think of the ongoing impact on the life of his family. That he spent weeks and months digging for dead friends, often not coming home at all or not speaking when he did, was not visible to others. Firefighter wives, grateful to have a husband still alive, did not share these concerns with many. They would not find groups outside of the FDNY community that met their needs.

While there were many groups in place for those who lost relatives in the collapse, we found that most relatives of the deceased firefighters wanted not just to be with others who had experienced loss, or even 9/11 loss, but specifically FDNY 9/11 loss. Occasionally such groups were offered by others, such as when a private practitioner found that several clients they were seeing individually might benefit from meeting together in a group and there was no CSU group that met the particular need by virtue of relationship or location. In those cases, the group was encouraged, endorsed, and supported by CSU.

The process of listening to emerging themes and developing time-limited, homogeneous groups in response has continued in subsequent years. Typically a specific problem area or life situation would emerge that was unlikely to offer the individual a naturally occurring group in the firehouse. The resulting isolation was likely to trigger unresolved feelings of loss and/or trauma related to all that had occurred since 9/11. Coping skills during this time had been stretched to the max so that any new life stress, especially those connected to trauma and loss, were more difficult to endure alone. Groups dealing with divorce, anger management, military deployment, and retirement are a few that have been offered to date.

TRAUMATIC BEREAVEMENT GROUPS

Many communities offer bereavement groups to those seeking additional support during painful life transitions related to loss. Often such groups are offered under the auspice of hospital, hospice, or faith-based organizations. Some are peer driven by those who have previously experienced the loss of a child, sibling, or spouse reaching out to help others facing a similar situation. The loss suffered by members of these groups may share certain characteristics. Loved ones may have died from cancer or another particular illness or all may be parents who have lost a child. Still each has experienced a separate course of illness or sudden trauma. It is only in the aftermath of a catastrophic event that impacts a particular community that bereavement groups comprised only of members from that community, who have suffered the same unique loss, can come together in an attempt to help one another cope with the enormity of the event and the ensuing loss.

When the bereaved community is large enough, it is possible and often preferable to offer groups that are specific to the event and the surviving population. These traumatic grief groups are prepared to address the specific and unique aspects of the event that has created them. Loss that follows a specific traumatic event, be it an accident or act of terrorism, can lead to grief and bereavement that is complicated by symptoms of posttraumatic stress. Traumatic memories of the event filled with anxiety, fear, and avoidance may at times interrupt, derail, or prolong the mourning process. These memories need to be processed in order to fully mourn the loss of the individual and the relationship separate from the horror of the event surrounding their death. In our experience this takes a very long time and is rarely complete. It has been extremely difficult for family members to privately mourn the husband, father, son, or brother who died when the public eye remains so focused on the firefighter hero they have lost.

Groups can assist members in processing both the trauma and the grief. These are not separate and neat treatment components; one does not first process trauma and then grief. In our experience the two are inextricably interwoven with themes related to each moving in and out of focus as the groups continue. At first trauma triggers were omnipresent, often fueled by the fascination of the media with both the event and the role of FDNY in relationship to it. While this has somewhat subsided, traumatic reminders of 9/11 continue to confront family members on a regular basis even now, 4 years later. Throughout this long ordeal, private ordinary citizens have had to cope with public celebrity and scrutiny during what certainly will be their most horrific life experience. It is understandable how a group composed of others coping with the same set of circumstances can at times be experienced as the only safe haven.

PROCESS OF GRIEF AND BEREAVEMENT

One often hears the expression *grief work* without a clear understanding of its meaning. There are a number of different ways that researchers and theoreticians have articulated the concept. Worden (1982) describes the tasks of grief and healing in a four-stage model. It is important not to think of these stages as linear but rather descriptive of the work involved in moving forward in one's life.

Accepting the reality of the loss.   Unquestionably the more sudden, unexpected, and traumatic the death the more difficult this task becomes. The absence of remains to bury adds to this difficulty and has elsewhere been referred to as *ambiguous loss* (Boss, 1999). When the circumstances surrounding a traumatic loss are as incomprehensible as those of 9/11, it is yet more difficult to fully acknowledge the reality of the loss. To fully grasp the impact of this it may help to think for a moment about how difficult it was for most people not directly or personally affected by 9/11 to accept the reality of the event. For example, even months later people in New York City would often look up to where the towers used to stand and exclaim, "I still can't believe it." How then does one come to believe that a loved one is gone along with the buildings?

Experiencing the feelings related to the loss.   Many feelings are associated with loss, and it is important to acknowledge and talk about them. They can include angry feelings of rage and protest, feelings of sadness, joylessness, and despair, and feeling helpless and hopeless in relation to the loss of meaning and function in one's life. At times, these feelings can seem overwhelming and unbearable. At such times, focusing once again on the unfathomable event that led to the death can shift focus away from these extraordinarily painful feelings. Being part of a group of individuals who are struggling to give voice to these feelings can be beneficial.

Adjusting to the environment without the deceased.   Life changes in many ways without the deceased. Often roles, responsibilities, and tasks need to be re-arranged and reallocated. This is a slow and gradual process. Often subtle and unexpected reminders, such as a trip to Home Depot or a Little League game, can create waves of grief as one goes about the routine tasks of daily life and is suddenly confronted with some seemingly small thing that the deceased always took care of. The number of such items can seem endless; thus this process has no clear beginning or end.

Emotionally relocating the deceased in memory in order to go on with life.   This may be thought about as a shift from the loved one being always in our heads to always in our hearts. It is not that the loss or memory leaves us; in contrast, it is that the person lost is always with us. However, on a daily basis we gradually become less preoccupied with the loss and thus have more psychic energy to invest in our current life. Sadness and reminders will continue to be part of the landscape of our lives, but the disruptive quality of this does shift with time.

These tasks outlined by Worden provide a useful framework in which to think about the complicated process of grief. However, the more dynamic dual process model presented by Stroebe and Schut (1999) adds additional dimension and complexity to our understanding of this process. For example, along with accepting the absence of the deceased, there is emphasis placed by them on the acceptance of a changed world. This perhaps has additional relevance in the wake of a trauma that indeed created a changed world even for those less directly affected. In the wake of 9/11, families of the deceased needed to adjust to a personal world changed by the loss of their loved one in the context of a public world forever changed by the trauma that created the loss in the first place.

Another contribution of the dual process model is an emphasis on the importance of taking time away from grieving along with confronting it. This is an important addition that helps both client and clinician to not see *grief work* as something to be engaged in 24/7. Furthermore, it adds to the understanding of the length of the bereavement process. By breaking down the often unwelcome phrase *moving on* into the more descriptive *development of new roles, identities, and relationships,* they help those involved in the experience to know better what they are trying to accomplish and why it is so difficult. The dynamic process of oscillation between loss and restoration-oriented coping and between avoidance and confrontation of stresses is described as necessary for optimal adjustment. This is supported by our observations in working with the FDNY's bereaved community and is further developed in Chapter 8 when Christ describes her work with young FDNY widows and their school-aged children. She further illuminates the oscillation process for this population as occurring between trauma/grief reactions and tasks of restoration, the active process of finding ways to confront and tackle new roles and new tasks (both practical and emotional). Identity restructuring (developing a new view of self within these roles, goals, and relationships) is a newly identified challenge for young widows with dependent children that is stressful and becomes evident over time.

MEETING THE FAMILIES OF THE MISSING

Several days after the tragedy, FDNY invited all of the family members of the missing to a meeting at a hotel in Manhattan. The idea of such a meeting was a bit daunting as emotions were raw and little real information was available. CSU was invited to be present at this meeting to provide crisis intervention if needed, but it also provided an opportunity to begin to make contact with the families. Different from our expectation, the meeting was remarkably calm, and the comfort and support that family members derived simply by being together was immediately evident. This was the first of two such meetings hosted by the fire department during the early weeks.

Seeing the family members together made it clear that organizing support groups in areas where families lived was a logical next step. In October we hosted a series of such meetings in seven different locations. Outreach was to any member of the family of the missing, as the deceased were referred to at that time. Meetings were organized initially to feature a speaker, external to the department, who specialized in traumatic grief. When possible, a member of the FDNY clergy attended as well. We anticipated that family members might attend with several support persons and wanted to offer information and support without any pressure for active participation. We planned to then follow this with a second meeting at the same location one week later that would follow a more traditional support group model.

Our experience was somewhat different from the expectation. For the most part family members came alone or in groups of two or three: perhaps a widow and her mother-in-law, a mother and her adult children, or a widow escorted by her firehouse family liaison. Initial gatherings were quite small; most people wanted to talk although beginning to do so was quite difficult and emotional. Outside *experts* were not needed. Caring mental health practitioners who knew the culture and would be available for the long haul were, in hindsight, much more helpful as were members of the community who previously had lost firefighters in the line of duty.

> A young woman in her late 20s arrives with an older woman—obviously her mother. The mother stares over her shoulder at the door . . . saying quietly— I shouldn't be here—I shouldn't have come. Her daughter encourages her— practically carries her to the table—where she sits and says little for about an

hour. When she talks she verbalizes for the group the enormity of the pain of the loss of her son.

In those locations where attendees indicated a desire to return, we continued to meet. At times we consolidated locations. It was in this way and without the usual pregroup planning regarding group composition, contract, structure, time frame, and so forth that our bereavement groups, some of which are still meeting 4 years later, began. We do not recommend beginning in this way to others. Even in the midst of crisis and pressure, it would have been beneficial to offer homogeneous groups limited by number of members and sessions in order to better assess the needs going forward.

Initially we met with whoever attended, most often sitting around a table supplied with coffee and tissues and offering members an opportunity to put words to what they were feeling and gain comfort in knowing that others shared their experience. Parents sat with widows and siblings, fiancées, and occasionally friends from the firehouse. In some locations widows from earlier FDNY line-of-duty deaths attended to lend their support and bear witness to the possibility of surviving. Their presence was a great comfort to the wives, although it would be years before they would use the term *widow* and apply it to themselves. Gradually the groups grew and gained some stability. Some people came regularly, others only sporadically. Few knew each other before even if their husbands or sons worked together in the firehouse. It was membership in the FDNY community and the sharing of such incomprehensible loss that created an almost instant group cohesion that was so different from the typical beginning stage of a group.

The early groups were notable in their sense of disorganization, which seemed reflective of the inner chaos that most participants were experiencing. This was a time of extreme disorientation where nothing made sense and one day simply ran into the next. Time was at once endless and fleeting. Within the group some members spoke a lot, others barely at all. They talked about their loved one, who he was, where he worked how he came to be a firefighter. This was the common bond that brought these individuals together as a community of grievers. It was difficult for most to listen, concentrate, relate to, or empathize with anything different from their own experience. There were some situations that everyone reacted empathically to: a widow with four or five very young children; those pregnant with a first child; a mother who had previously lost another child; the family who lost not one, but two sons in the towers. What could they do for or with one another? How could the group help? What about the leaders?

Sitting with such a group is not easy. There is a strong pull to want to make it better, to soften the pain, to offer reassurance. This must be resisted. It is difficult to be in the midst of such overwhelming grief; it is also a privilege to be allowed in. There is little that one can say or needs to say. Rather the task is to assist members in giving voice to the pain and the many unanswerable questions that fill their minds. Being in the group helps each to recognize that they are not alone, not going crazy. Their reactions are normal, the event is incomprehensible, and answers are not available. There is no road map, no right way to grieve, no time line they can follow. When possible, it helps to point out the minute differences that are observable week to week: the ability to verbalize the pain, get dressed in the morning, comfort a child, or say no to an unwelcome demand. These are signs of survival and strengths to be noted and appreciated. Somehow, even when they are not sure they prefer to, they will survive.

Different Voices of Grief

Gradually differences began to emerge. Those with children, especially young children, were understandably overwhelmed with questions and concerns about them. Talking about children was at times painful to parents who had just lost their child and to those newly married or not yet married who had now lost the possibility of sharing this experience with their firefighter. Siblings sat listening to their parents' grief wondering at times if anyone recognized their loss or if perhaps their parents felt that the wrong sibling had died. For most, the need to separate and meet in more homogeneous groups became evident.

> "A parent's grief is the worst," states one mother who lost her son. "I wanted to scream when she said that," says a widow later, adding, "if we didn't split the group I never would have continued."

The need for homogeneity expressed by most extended not only to the relationship between the deceased and bereaved (spouse, parent, sibling, etc.) but also to a separation between FDNY bereaved and other 9/11 families. Those who attended our groups often expressed the discomfort they felt when attending other community events where all 9/11 families, as they came to be known, gathered for support. These feelings were often based on the perception that FDNY families were given more attention, more material goods, and more support than others. While much of this perception was fueled by the amount of media attention focused on FDNY, in terms of support it was true that FDNY was able to design services specifically and exclusively for its community via CSU. Evaluated in the context of community, this was perhaps no different from services offered within a particular geographic community that had significant losses. Still this perception was one additional thing that the FDNY family members had to deal with as they began to venture out of the house and into the communities in which they lived. While later opportunities fostering connection and reintegration might be important, initially this experience further supported the need to offer specialized services.

THE WORK OF THE GROUP

Group cohesion happened quickly. Perhaps this was a function of the enormity of the experience of loss that members shared; perhaps in addition it was a function of belonging to the FDNY family. In any event the groups moved beyond their awkward, often silent, beginnings to a time, perhaps a month or two later, where *group*, as most referred to it, became an established part of the week. Members looked forward to coming to group at a time when they looked forward to little else. In a way it helped begin to organize the week. Membership became more stable, yet given the nature of the FDNY community, the groups remained open. At this stage, when occasional members dropped in it was somewhat disruptive to the work of the group. At such times, sessions often became more about catching up and the traumatic themes were prominent and often repetitive. Frequently it was some media event or anniversary that was the impetus for the person to return to group in the first place.

The traumatic elements of the event are what differentiated the work of these groups from other bereavement groups. It was both the enormity of the event and the unfamiliarity of the issues that family members were called upon to deal with in the aftermath of the disaster that made groups so important. This loss was like no other. The lengthy process, ambiguity of the recovery, and relentless media attention especially separated 9/11 family members from others who lost a son, a husband, or a father under different traumatic circumstances. It was within this specialized, homogeneous group that these issues could be raised, confronted, railed against, and hopefully put in some perspective. Topics unimaginable in any other context became common place in group: body parts, dismemberment, media hounds, mediums, instant wealth, family feuds, bias and hate, mounting anger, tattoos, loneliness, and despair, to name a few. Members were often haunted by images of the end. Where was he? Was he conscious? Did he suffer? These were unanswerable questions, but most had an unquenchable thirst for information. Some attempted to get answers from the surviving firefighters, the medical examiner, or the funeral parlor director who handled the remains. Then there was the anger, but anger at whom? The perpetrators of the event? The officials who did not predict it? The department that did not protect its members? The deceased who did not choose them over the job they loved? At times the thought that he died doing what he loved brought some comfort or at least made it easier to fit the trauma into the narrative that was his life.

There were no rules, no guidelines, no one way to see it or to react to it; just understanding that much was a relief and was of help. In fact much of the work was about helping individuals to listen to themselves, to trust in their reactions, and to begin to make independent decisions. Group members helped one another set limits and establish guidelines that were important in beginning to handle the external world, which now was often overly involved in their day-to-day existence. Group meetings became a marker of time as the group developed a history that allowed members to reflect back on anniversaries and remind one another how they were doing this year as compared to last.

Differences

Groups initially formed on the basis of commonalities. What they shared was initially of far greater importance than any observable differences. These were support groups, not therapy groups. Members were polite and careful with one another. They recognized the assault each had experienced and were aware that many were being further assaulted by others telling them what they *should* do. It was a long time before they felt able to openly disagree with one another or directly suggest what another might do to ease a difficult situation unless directly asked. Still, differences were allowed, respected, and unchallenged. They existed on many levels. As discussed earlier, differences in relationship to the deceased surfaced early and most groups realigned accordingly. Where the need existed, we ran separate groups for spouses, fiancées/significant others, parents, and siblings.

Other differences emerged more slowly and were visible within the group. Some were based on values, attitudes, lifestyle, and life stage. These differences emerged in discussions on parenting, finances, relationships with parents and in-laws, responding to advice, visiting mediums, dating, attending ceremonies, and ritualizing anniversaries, to name but a few. It was impressive how members came to accept these differences in one another. They showed enormous respect for one another's values and decisions and in the midst of such intense grief showed great tenacity in holding to their own family values. If at times they seemed a bit reluctant to question or confront one another, this was offset by the degree to which they supported one another in the truest sense of the word and understood that assisting one another in feeling confident in continuing to confront life was most important of all. Certainly this was true for the widows suddenly having to make all decisions related to themselves, their children, and their future without the partner they had so much relied upon.

Some issues related to the event divided the group, such as a separation between those who had a recovery of remains and those who did not. Members at times expressed their difficulty in discussing how *lucky* they felt that they had something to bury, knowing that others in the group had nothing. With encouragement these issues led to important explorations of the multiple issues related to the recovery of remains. Group members were able to see the various ways in which these complicated, emotionally charged issues were handled and that not everyone felt any particular way about them. How could one family ask to no longer be notified while another waited anxiously for anything? Should one go to the medical examiner's office and look at the file? If I do, will I forever be haunted by what I see? Will it be better or worse than what I imagine? Can we go together? Why are the firefighters trying to protect us, don't they know we have already withstood the worst? Why do you hear from your firehouse while I barely hear from mine? I don't really want to go to their Christmas party, but dare I say no? Why are parents excluded from the notifications, don't they know he was our son first? How do I approach my daughter-in-law about seeing my grandchildren more? How do I explain I just can't go to her house yet?

Every question had no answer and many answers. Themes would recur. At times the meetings began to resemble those of other bereavement groups. The talk was of loss, emptiness, and worry for the future. Stories were told, and members began to know the deceased through the memories of their loved ones. Pictures were brought and stories told. When looking at a vacation picture taken just prior to 9/11, a group member spontaneously and poignantly said, "You look so happy, I've never seen that smile." They shared in one another's grief and attended one another's memorials, funerals, street namings, and fundraisers. Each type of event marked another year in the seemingly never-ending cycle of grief that had become their lives. Then suddenly, most often triggered by some outside event, the trauma would reemerge. Discussion would again center on the unfathomable circumstances surrounding the death and the equally unsolicited, unwelcome, and unbelievable celebrity that had become their lives. In a flash it was once again September 11. They railed against the department that had not *properly* notified them about the death because it had been unable to find a way to dispatch a senior officer to 343 homes in a timely fashion. Would that have made a difference or eased the pain? Raising such questions was not important, helpful, or appropriate. The rage and anger related to the unreasonableness of the event and the catastrophic loss needed to find an outlet. There was perhaps no way to *properly* notify a family about such a loss, but opportunities to express this rage were necessary and important albeit difficult to tolerate. At first the return to *trauma* talk seemed a disruption to the grief work or bereavement process. Later the importance of revisiting and reworking the traumatic memories as a means of reducing traumatic symptoms became clearer. Each revisitation allowed for the expression of a wider range of feelings, a host of previously unasked questions, and a sharing of the internal images that haunted the members. It gradually allowed for greater acknowledgement of what could and would never be known.

The groups proceeded in this way not for months but for years. There seemed to be two parallel tracks: trauma and loss. This was a different type of oscillation from that written about in the dual process model between loss and restoration-oriented coping or Christ's oscillation between trauma/grief reactions and the arduous tasks of restoration/identity reformation. Before these additional themes emerged, there seemed in the groups to be an oscillation between the trauma and the grief. An oscillation between the horrific events of the day and the traumatic circumstances of the death and the feelings related to the loss of the person they loved and the role he played in their lives. Over time the trauma responses about the event decreased and the grief about the loss increased, but there was much interaction between the two responses.

Because the loss was so public it required a lot of time and took a lot of energy to respond to the various demands that were made. These came in the form of memorials, street namings, scholarships, awards, fund raisers, trips, and other forms of public recognition. People were sometimes retraumatized by so many public memorials that often interfered with individual needs for distance and private mourning. At first, most felt a sense of obligation to participate in all that were requested. Moving back and forth between public and private mourning added complexity and stress and often re-evoked traumatic feelings and symptoms. At times it was easier to tolerate feelings connected to the events of 9/11 and the public loss of the fighter hero, in contrast to the more personal pain of losing a loved one, which was more difficult to access, more painful to talk about, and seemingly more impossible to endure. The calendar was filled with anniversaries of all types. Not just September 11, but the day of his memorial, the day they found his remains, the day of the funeral. Then there was his birthday, their wedding anniversary, Father's Day, the day he became a firefighter, and on and on and on. Some marked the private and personal life that was lost, some the more public figure. All were painful, all were noted, and all were shared by the group in support of one another.

RECONSTITUTION

While the old themes never disappear completely, at some point the group discussion began to shift more toward how one will continue with life. Gradually the focus must move from back then to now and, eventually, to tomorrow. The oscillation now is between loss and reconstitution. It is not only young widows with children who must find a way to move forward with life and forge a new identity. Older widows with grown children struggle to replace the retirement plan they must set aside, while young widows without children—along with fiancées and girlfriends—try to reenter the single world they have no desire to rejoin. Siblings struggle with a loss they feel is invisible to others yet profoundly has affected their definition of self: how to express their loss, the absence of a shared childhood, and the sense of oneself as an only child or a member of a smaller family. Perhaps most confusing of all is the identify reformation of the parent who lost an adult child who at the time of his death no longer had been a part of daily life yet without whom one seems to have become a different and unknown person.

No one is spared the need to dig deep to find meaning in life and the motivation to forge ahead.

Almost without their noticing, life has continued. The passage of time is noted as children get older, graduate from one school to another, leave for college, get married, and have babies. Each transition is bittersweet for each member of the family. How can I enjoy this grandchild, who is named for my dead son? How can I bear his joining the fire department, of which his father would have been so proud? Time continues, and members of the group experience the deaths of a parent, a friend, a spouse. These events precipitate discussion of the differences between anticipated loss and sudden loss, the gift of getting to say goodbye, and the comfort of a casket that holds a complete corpse and allows for a proper burial. Ultimately each transition and life event leads to questions about oneself: What about me? How do I want to live my life? What do I do now? Each person's journey is explored and experienced by the group. Often this extends outside of group to friendships that have formed and support systems that have grown to include children, family members, and a few close friends who have found a way to understand the experience.

Eventually, as is appropriate, the importance of group begins to change. Attendance may become more sporadic as individual members choose a fun event over coming to group, cancelled groups no longer need to be rescheduled, and some members decide to leave for good. This is not resistance, as might be the case in a treatment group, but most often indicates that the purpose of the group has been fulfilled, at least for some.

Those who choose to continue at this stage are often faced with having to defend this decision as outsiders question if perhaps coming to group keeps them from *moving on*. Often missed is the complexity of the tasks involved in moving on, as described by Christ. Also, as time moves forward many of those affected feel as if it is the rest of the world that has *moved on* and left them behind. They often feel that group is the only place where they can talk about their ongoing grief and the struggle to accept and succeed in their new life. In our experience this is an important function of group in the later stage. The feeling that most people in your life *don't want to hear it* can be an isolating and painful experience. By offering a specific time and place to deal with their grief and the traumatic reminders of 9/11, group can help members to contain the experience and as a result begin to connect with others outside of group in a different and more satisfying way.

This can be a difficult phase in the life of the group as decisions about the future are faced. In our experience there is no *right* way to handle these decisions. It is important that the changes be noted and discussed with the members. Some believe that a formal termination process is extremely important as a way to help group members focus on the loss of the group and in this way experience a planned ending in contrast to the sudden and traumatic loss that created the group initially. While there is a great deal of merit in this idea and it seems to have worked well for those groups that moved in this direction, others feel that a support group should remain in place as long as the members find it helpful. Allowing members to have control over how long the group continues, how frequently it meets, and when it should end recognizes that members are at different places in their journey toward a new life and have different needs for support along the way. Here too the group opts to support the development of control and mastery over one's life and environment that was so damaged by the traumatic loss each person suffered. Counselors need to be mindful of the many counter-transference elements evoked not only throughout the group but particularly in regard to termination (Phillips 2004). Most group leaders have formed powerful relationships with group members over a sustained period of time, and they too find the idea of ending difficult.

Whichever choice a particular group makes, we believe that all of our post-9/11 bereavement groups have been a source of support, confidence building, and friendship for the members while at the same time supporting the importance of members reconnecting with support systems outside of the 9/11 community, not only those that existed before but new relationships as well.

SINGLE-SESSION GROUPS

THE USE OF ACTIVITIES AND EDUCATION IN COMMUNITY BUILDING

Activities can be used to develop relationships between individuals and build cohesion in a group. They can help to improve communication and to create a link between strangers (Northern and Kurland 2001). Used during times of extraordinary loss, activities can assist in validating the importance of play and laughter even during difficult times.

> It is early in the aftermath of 9/11. We have invited the children who lost firefighter fathers to one of our suburban offices. Acupuncture and massage are available to the adult women while children are engaged in a variety of crafts

and sports activities. Neither group is urged or expected to talk about how they came to be here. The office is set up is like a house; the main room here is furnished like a living room. Still new to this, we hadn't even thought about the pictures scattered about the room, especially the 9/11 photo of the 343 deceased. Late in the day we see kids of all ages who had spent time playing together taking one another to the photo and pointing to their dad:

Even in a single-session group there is comfort in knowing you are part of a larger community that shares your situation and has endured the same loss. This awareness, especially in the case of children, need not be verbally acknowledged. Some might suggest that these single-day events are not really groups. In contrast, we believe there is value in thinking about these programs as groups and not just outings. While membership is not fixed, there are criteria for inclusion. These are open groups whose membership is drawn from a defined, larger community. The purpose of each event is consistent with Yalom's curative factors. Each meeting is designed as a separate, individual event that allows for movement in and out of the group and encourages members from the larger community to participate in what has meaning for them. Participation in activities encourages taking risks by trying new things and supports the development of competency and mastery. Even in the course of a single meeting, the stages of group process are present, albeit condensed. When attraction between members exists, as is often the case with participants who define themselves as part of a community with which they identify, group cohesion occurs. In this way there is carry over between discrete events that builds trust and a sense of community for the future. CSU provides connection to the FDNY culture and transmits that connection within and between each single session. Mothers will say, "I want my children to know this culture, to be part of it; I want them to have that from their father."

The *Kids Connection* program has used this format to build a community for the 389 minor FDNY children left fatherless when the towers collapsed. Based on past experience, it is anticipated that as children revisit the issues related to their father's death at different developmental stages the family may turn to CSU for help. The historic and traumatic nature of this event is likely to make these reworkings even more complicated for all family members. Developing a community that can offer support into the future without an expectation of consistent or ongoing participation is the goal. Events are organized based on age or geography.

A newsletter and web site are available at home. Kids are encouraged to contribute their ideas. Older kids are asked to help out with those younger. Some events are open to extended family members, the cousins missing their uncle or to friends you want to share this part of your life with. Other events are just for those who lost a dad. Kids can come alone, with the FDNY Big

Brother or Big Sister they have added to their life as a result of the mentorship component of the program, or with a grandparent in specially targeted events. Adults attending are offered wellness services, such as auricular acupuncture, massage, and reflexology, and given an opportunity to spend time together while children are engaged in activities with firefighter helpers.

Relationships also build with CSU staff who are able to assess ongoing needs and target programs accordingly. They are available for individual consultation when needs arise and can make appropriate suggestions or referrals. Over time individuals see progress and movement in others and eventually come to see it in themselves as well. Overall the program seeks to develop and support hope for the future.

A series of workshop for widows, named by one participant as *Managing Me,* offers single-session workshops in support of the arduous identity restructuring process that most are engaged in 4 years after the event. Focused around specific topics, they offer opportunities to remain connected to other widows, discuss topics of mutual concern, and also explore new areas of interest: home repair, gardening, interior design, dating, single parenting, and others. As support groups come to an end, these single-session events provide opportunities for CSU to continue to assess the ongoing needs of this population and offer new, time-limited interventions as needed.

The use of single-session activity groups in the service of community building has been applied to other subsets of our population as well. *Stay Connected,* FDNY's program for retirees described in Chapter 10, has a similar structure and rationale. More recently *Community Connections* has been developed to offer single- and multiple-session wellness and educational activities to the active-duty workforce and their families. Even single-session informational groups are known to reduce anxiety and lessen isolation via interaction with others who share a similar stressful situation. Recognizing the additional stress that FDNY members and their families have experienced since 9/11 has suggested a need for CSU to focus on developing and strengthening the coping skills that are necessary for families facing the *new normal* that is today's FDNY.

A FINAL WORD ABOUT GROUPS

The healing power of groups cannot be overemphasized, nor can their complexity. In our opinion, groups should occupy a significant place in the continuum of posttrauma intervention. It is important to consider the wide range and variability of trauma intervention groups and be thoughtful in their development and implementation. Not every client is a good group candidate, and not every clinician is skilled in group intervention. Care should be taken on both sides of the selection equation. We believe it is important to offer groups to trauma survivors and to train and support staff in their use. When identifying community practitioners to partner with in the event of a disaster, we strongly recommend the selection of those with expertise in group intervention. Groups promote the development of natural healing communities and, in the case of postdisaster intervention, underscore the belief that trauma response is not pathological but rather the understandable, normal reaction to abnormal, horrific life events.

CHAPTER 8

Providing a Home-Based Therapeutic Program for Widows and Children

O N MARCH 1, 2002, 5 months and 20 days after September 11, 2001, we interviewed the first family, and the FDNY/Columbia University Family Assessment and Guidance Program officially began. This home-based service was offered to families with dependent children in which a firefighter father was killed. Most families were past the initial acute stages of confronting the reality of the loss, but they were still involved with the search for remains, attending multiple memorials, reacting to terrorist threats and the war, and other continuous reminders, as well as making preparations for the first memorial. By then CSU had accomplished the Herculean tasks of providing immediate support for active-duty firefighters who were both working and searching for remains; initiating bereavement groups for parents, wives, and children of the 343 firefighters who died; and implementing a broad range of individual mental health counseling services.

Mothers of bereaved children were becoming increasingly concerned about finding ways to help their children cope with the loss and the ongoing stresses and requested help. Their apprehension was not surprising when one considers even a short list of stress-related behaviors and grief reactions children were exhibiting, which had enormous variations depending on their developmental level and resilience or vulnerability. These included sleep problems, difficulty concentrating at school and in sports, a drop in grades for most, withdrawal from peers, loss of behavioral and emotional control, behavioral regression, unusual increase or decrease in weight, increases in separation anxiety, phobias of all kinds, and anger management problems. For some children these symptoms were severe and prolonged, causing major disruptions in school and at home. For most they were intermittent, but ongoing and persistent. Many older children shut off all discussion of the death with adults, and some younger children did as well.

CSU recommended the FDNY/Columbia University Family Assessment and Guidance Program as one response to these requests. This family intervention program provides in-home parent guidance services as well as ongoing monitoring of bereaved children's functioning. Parents are given feedback about how their children are doing in comparison to bereaved and nonbereaved children their age and guidance around identified problem areas. Initially bereaved families chose this intervention because they wanted support for their children and information about their children's progress over time.

UNDERSTANDING THE EXPERIENCE FOR MOTHERS AND CHILDREN

As visits to the family began, it became apparent that the first step in providing effective help was to try to comprehend the widows' and bereaved children's unique and profoundly distressing experiences since the disaster occurred. This bereavement situation was like no other. Acknowledging that reality was important for families and counselors. This meant that while we were experts in the grief and trauma processes involved, we needed to be constantly open to new information and engaging families as teachers and reporters of the experience as well as recipients of help and support. We quickly learned that some of the difficult features of this disaster included traumatic elements: the long period for recovery of bodies, deaths of family members and multiple friends, the special role of the firefighter father as "Mr. Mom," the continuing intrusive reminders, and the public scrutiny.

TRAUMATIC ELEMENTS

The first days following the World Trade Center (WTC) disaster were unbelievably chaotic and nightmarish for firefighter families. Many did not know whether their husbands had gone to the site of the tragedy. Some finished their tours at 9 a.m. and should have returned home soon after that. Some were assigned to firehouses that were far from downtown Manhattan. The unease and terror grew as there were no calls from the husbands that evening, in the middle of the night, or even the next morning. The firehouses where some were assigned were still sorting out the rosters. This was complicated because some of the firemen who were going off duty joined a fire truck that was headed downtown. Gradually, more and more firehouses or close friends of the firefighters called saying the husband was seen entering one of the towers and was still missing. Mothers and teenage children sort of accepted his probable death after several days.

> One boy said, "I knew something bad had happened. I saw Mom was smoking. She stopped years ago."
> Many said, "When I got home, I had heard about the WTC. When I saw Mom crying, I knew something bad happened to Dad."
> A 13-year-old boy had been told his father died, but when a fireman in uniform arrived in his father's car, returning it from the train station where it had been parked, the son ran toward it, shouting, "He's home," then dissolved in despair when he saw that the driver was not his father. "It was awful!" his mom reflected 2 years later.
> Some younger children clung to fantasies that he was still alive, often for months. One thought superhero Spider-Man had rescued Dad, that he had been hit on the head and had amnesia, and that some day soon he would snap out of it and come home.
> Another felt certain that he was buried in a small hole, surviving by eating bugs. He would be rescued and come home.
> A number of the very young ones, those 1½ to 2½ years old, continued to ask for Daddy months later. Some would wake suddenly out of a deep sleep in the middle of the night alarming the household with their screams "Where Daddy!"

Schoolchildren described hearing an announcement during second period, usually by the principal over the school intercom, explaining that there had been an attack on the World Trade Center and the Pentagon and that there would be a school lockdown so no one was allowed to go out or come into the school. Children could not leave until a parent came to pick them up.

> A 15-year-old girl remembered that her mother was also working near the World Trade Center that day. The teachers allowed her to be taken home by her father's best friend, a neighbor, who came to the school and asked to take her to be with friends and neighbors while they awaited news on both parents. Two years later her younger brother and sister demanded to know why they had not been allowed to go home with her, as they had also been very worried about their parents. Their mother was one of thousands who walked out of Manhattan over the Brooklyn Bridge and finally arrived home early that evening.

Because of the totally unanticipated shocking nature of this disaster, the fear mothers experienced of more loss and more harm to their children was intense. Some even worried that if their young children had an accident the mother would be viewed as an incompetent parent and their children would be taken from them. "They are all I have now," mothers would say. "It's all on my shoulders. If something goes wrong, it's my fault." Such a profound and shocking loss robs one of the certainty that one is able to help and guide children in a way that will prevent later adverse consequences. This fear was especially acute when they had a number of young children and surveillance by a single parent was not easy. Sometimes their fears were exacerbated by experiences in their own childhood of parental illnesses and threatened separation from them. These heightened fears of further loss also contributed to their reluctance to leave children in the care of anyone except family, hence increasing their need and desire for home visits.

THE LONG SEARCH

Many surviving firemen seldom came home in the months after 9/11. After work or on their days off they went to the World Trade Center site to help search for survivors in the first few days, and then for bodies or body parts. As the days stretched into weeks and then into months, for many families nothing was found. The spouses of the deceased found themselves engaged in gruesome discussions they never imagined having with their children, especially about body parts, dismemberment, and the process of dying. "What is in the dust?" asked a 10-year-old girl when she heard about the closing of the site. "What will happen to Dad now?" One widow, an amazingly articulate raconteur and mother of two girls, described the horror of these months:

> We kept hearing that they had found several bodies. At first I called the firehouse. Later they called me. I learned to say immediately, "Is this business or social?" My heart pounded too much before I knew. If it's business it means they want to ask about my husband's body, to see if there is a match with a body part they have found. If it's social, it means they are calling to ask how I'm doing. Those are two very different conditions and I need time to get myself ready for each discussion. Once they called to say they'd found an arm with a tattoo and knew that Dave had one. It wasn't his. Then they found his shield—this helped because then I knew where he had been at. It was the first tower that crumbled—I knew then he had not known that his tower might crumble when it actually happened.

A 12- and 14-year-old brother and sister had been worried for months that their father might have been frightened at the end when the building crumbled around him, but they had been unable to ask [their] mom that question because they didn't want to upset her even more. When they visited the World Trade Center site with their younger sister (age 10) before it officially closed, they asked a fireman who was taking them around, "Do you think Dad was scared when it fell down?" The fireman said, "No, it took seven seconds from the time it started until it was down. No one had time to realize what was happening or to feel pain." He then took out a stop watch, put his hand up, then lowered it after seven seconds. The younger sister repeated this several times, nodding. Not only these children but many others who heard about this felt some relief that their fathers had not likely suffered.

Over time it became clear that while all family members wanted something to be found, finding remains did not remove the pain of loss, and not finding remains did not necessarily compromise grief. Families were inventive about rituals, and rituals were helpful to all families. Lisa, whose four children were ages 1 to 11 years on September 11, 2001, described an innovative ritual she used and published in the FDNY newsletter, *The LINK*. Her husband's body was not recovered.

The Locker, by Lisa Jordan
Visiting the firehouse was always a special treat for my children. Because we lived in Remsenburg in Suffolk County and my husband, Andrew Jordan, worked at L132 in Brooklyn, the trips were usually limited to a few a year. Even though the children loved the sliding pole, backyard, and TV room, going to my husband's locker and opening it up to see the treasures he kept inside was what they waited for the most. They loved to see how many coins he had saved in the cigar box on the shelf, which tools he kept on the side, and what recent picture of them was taped on the door.

After September 11, the vast loss of my husband and his presence was too much to bear. We would look for him everywhere. The objects in the garage he used, we used; the clothes he wore, we held on to; and the car he drove, we would sit in, and start up, taking in the scent of the memories the Dodge contained.

Our first visit to the firehouse was at the end of November 2001. At that time, the children had collected some of their best artwork and asked me what to do with it. It occurred to me that they could share this with their father by decorating his locker with it. "Save it for Daddy's locker," was and still is the phrase we use when a special award comes from school, a picture is drawn with love, or a snapshot taken.

The children love to visit my husband's locker still. They continue to look through his treasures, which we haven't removed. I plan to leave this personal "memorial" for as long as we can. My hope is that our youngest son Sean, who was born fifteen days after the attacks, will be able to get a good sense of who his father was by visiting the firehouse and sharing in Daddy's locker.

I am sure, over the years, there will be more awards, pictures, and drawings to add to the locker. I hope my children Andrew, Matthew, Kelsey, and Sean will always feel a connection with their father when they visit the firehouse and when they become adults with children of their own.

DEATHS OF MULTIPLE FRIENDS AND ACQUAINTANCES

An academic sitting next to me at a conference on the psychosocial impact of terrorism asked, "What's the difference between 1 death and 10 deaths?"—

implying that it is the same grief process, therefore no difference in the impact on survivors. A colleague sitting next to me responded, "The difference between 1 death and 10 deaths is nine." Mothers attended multiple memorials and burials of firefighter friends during the first year. These were always wrenching, as the mourners grieved each time not only for the family friend, but for their own husbands. The "Mother of all Memorials" on September 11, 2002, was conducted in a highly evocative way that was effective in engaging a distant public but difficult for grieving families who were trying to contain overwhelming emotions in order to achieve some sense of control in their lives. Although the families wanted the firefighters' heroism memorialized and remembered, some felt that public grief delayed private mourning. Few felt they could choose not to participate in memorials during the first year. One mother described her experience:

> My husband made many friends, not only in his current ladder where six of our friends were also killed. At first I would go to a funeral and it would take me right back to where I first was. It would take me three weeks to come back up again, but after a while, with a funeral every two to three weeks, I'm just not coming back. This week I've hit rock bottom.

MEDIA SCRUTINY

The 9/11 attacks were such a public event that families were flooded with unending references to their loss for a prolonged period of time. Many families turned off the radio and television, avoided newspapers, and stopped opening mail and answering phone calls as an attempt to assert some control over reminders of this public, but privately very painful, event.

They continued to receive massive amounts of mail over the course of 4 years, especially around the time of the anniversary.

> One mother tried to open holiday presents that arrived from strangers before her children could see them. However, around the time of the second post-9/11 Christmas, she was outside when 13-year-old Kenneth arrived home and excitedly opened a large package that had arrived from a stranger addressed to him. His excitement turned to profound distress when he pulled out a sculpture of a crushed firefighter's helmet. He remained depressed for several weeks.

The public nature of the event and the firefighters' heroic rescue of thousands of people before they themselves died gave the widows a celebrity status after the event that also made demands on their time and had a profound impact on their grief. Some felt they would dishonor their husbands if they stopped grieving—it was their public duty. Over time the media went through periods of being critical of the widows, and also the active-duty firefighters, by magnifying any behaviors they deemed disrespectful or exploitive. This was enraging, but there was really no way to counter the critique—the mothers learned to believe in and define themselves. As one mother said, "I won't let them change who I am." Widows were also called on to speak to media outlets. This was welcomed by some but could become overwhelming.

> Nine months after the World Trade Center attack, several widows were invited with other family members to listen to their husbands' voices on a tape that recorded the messages from a special communication device that one husband, a firefighter chief, was able to use to communicate with the command center. On the tape he described the situation he found on the 72nd floor in the second tower, just below where it was hit by the airplane. He had climbed the stairs with over 100 pounds of equipment. As it turned out, the firefighter was with another widow's husband, a businessman whose legs had been broken by falling beams, a helpless victim with no way to follow his colleagues down the stairs. The firefighter reported the businessman's name as well as the situation of other casualties on the floor, and requested more assistance. The firefighter's widow expressed relief along with sadness as she listened to the tape. She now knew where her husband was when he died, and he seemed to be going about his business trying to rescue people without fear or anxiety, doing what he was trained to do. The businessman's wife, wept with relief that her husband was not alone in his injured condition. The fire chief was there with him, reassuring and organizing help. I met the widow of the businessman at a professional conference at which she was speaking years later. She poignantly told the audience that although no remains of her husband's body were found, she and her daughter would be forever grateful to that firefighter because her husband did not have to die injured and alone but was with someone who had come to rescue him and was trying to help.

Later, on the day of the audio tape review, the firefighter's widow gave a statement to the press about the relief she felt that her husband was unafraid. She also described her desire, while listening, to tell him to "Hurry, hurry." Clearly he was unaware of what was about to happen. She wished there had been a different outcome, but she said, "What's done is done." That evening reporters called her nonstop on the phone and wandered around outside her house. One even attempted to crawl through a window. With great forbearance she explained, "Don't you understand? I know this is a very public issue for you, but for me right now, it's a very private moment."

The Special Role of the Firefighter Father

Firefighter fathers were often very active parents by choice, affectionately called "Mr. Mom." Their schedule of two 24-hour tours of duty per week made this possible. They could get a second job to supplement the household income or the spouse could work while the firefighter took care of the children. Both arrangements occurred. True co-parenting was not uncommon, and at times the firefighter functioned as the primary caregiver while making home improvements on his days off. Children generally react more strongly when they lose a primary caregiver (Raveis et al. 1999; Kwok et al., 2005; Harris et al., 1986; Tremblay & Israel, 1998). Almost no families had any experience with hiring outside help for child care or household chores. This strong ethic of managing children and housekeeping on your own made it difficult for widows to engage additional help they often desperately needed in order to maintain the family as single parents caught up in a major public phenomenon, even though the outpouring of donations from a grateful public made it financially possible to do so.

> Several mothers who had children under seven years of age when their husbands died described how they reluctantly hired a cleaning company to help with the house that was in disarray months after the death. They became upset if the cleaning company parked their truck in front of their homes, fearing that neighbors would be critical of them for paying for someone to do their household chores.

Most mothers of young children discontinued jobs or careers in which they were involved in order to make sure their children were stabilized. Many in the program expressed a powerful determination to help their children survive and thrive through this experience. As one mother stated:

> I told myself that I cannot let things get any worse for my children. This has to be the worst thing that has happened to them. I could not change what had happened, but I was determined to make things better.

DEVELOPING CSU SERVICES FOR BEREAVED FAMILIES

As described in Chapter 3, 9/11 was a transformative experience not only for the FDNY and all its members, but for New York City, New York state, the entire country, and indeed the world. The deaths of two to six firefighters in 1 year is a calamity, but the loss of 343 in one site, in 1 hour, along with the survivors who were devastated beyond belief, presented an overwhelming challenge. For CSU, it required a profound identity change while retaining those goals and commitments to the firemen and their families that had successfully evolved over the years.

The Oklahoma City bombing experience alerted CSU to two important challenges: (1) the traumatic effects of the Oklahoma City disaster were still being observed 7 years after the event, suggesting that longer-term services should be planned, and (2) some of the most exposed and high-risk individuals rejected traditional mental health services. New models of service needed to be considered for different groups.

Initial support groups for all of the bereaved including mothers, fathers, wives, siblings, and other family members were offerred. Many family members quickly asserted a preference to meet with individuals who had similar life circumstances to their own or a similar relationship to the deceased. It was very hard to fully honor other relationships to the firefighter who died when consumed with one's own particular loss. Widows would say: "If I hear her say one more time 'there is nothing worse than the loss of a child,' I think I'll scream. Here I am having to raise four small children without their father, what could be worse?" It was from observations such as these that widows' groups were formed along with the broad range of Kids Connection activities and services. This also led to the acceptance of the FDNY/Columbia University Family Assessment and Guidance Program as a service CSU would recommend to widows with children.

CSU confronted two overarching and equally daunting tasks in providing help to the bereaved: (1) fund raising and (2) defining subgroups of individuals with special needs in order to create services they could use. While ongoing collaboration between these two domains was essential, each task also required full-time direction in order to optimize senior staff functioning in such a crisis environment. The fund-raising effort is often underestimated, yet it proved critical to being able to put programs in place in a timely fashion and to extend them over a long enough time interval.

Developing a Program for Individual Families

While programs had been developed for individual family members, there were none focused specifically on individual families. There were groups for widows, which began about 2 weeks after 9/11, referrals to community child bereavement programs, and individual parent and child mental health counseling. Many families also used school-based services if they were available. Accessibility and quality of services in the school depended on the school's resources and the prior training of staff assigned to help bereaved children. CSU directly provided a broad range of financial and practical solutions to urgent family needs. A bimonthly newsletter, titled *The LINK*, was begun in January 2002. It was filled with information and resources for emerging issues confronting widows, parents, siblings, and other relatives of the deceased firefighters. The FDNY/Columbia University Family Assessment and Guidance Program, which offered home-based services, provided a new service with a focus on individual families.

The reluctance of families who experienced such shocking, multiple losses to engage traditional mental health services was not surprising. Previous disaster literature documented that higher-risk families did not utilize services at a level of frequency and intensity commensurate with their risk and symptomatology (Allen et al., 1999; Pfefferbaum et al., 1999). The reason frequently cited for underutilization of mental health services was the symptom of *traumatic avoidance* of the sad, painful, and frightening feelings evoked when discussing the event. Others suggested that the location, timing, structure, expectations, presentation, and focus of services offered also played a role in their being underutilized (Allen et al., 1999). Such traditional office-based, individually focused services may not be appropriate for the immediate and longer-term needs of disaster-affected families. CSU also wanted to expand options for engaging families for longer-term follow-up because of their previous experience with young children who showed few behavioral problems at the time of a firefighter's death but returned for help in an emotional crisis as adolescents.

CHALLENGES TO DEVELOPING APPROPRIATE SERVICES

While some families were underutilizing services, CSU received a virtual flood of requests in the first few months for individual therapy for each child in the family, each widow, and each active-duty firefighter. These came from diverse sources, including therapists, families, and other firefighters. How individual services could address identified needs was unclear. CSU staff worried that only the most vocal members of families were receiving help and that the more silent sufferers might be neglected. They received offers by professional services to visit families with young children in their homes. However, without a specific intervention plan families could accept or reject, CSU staff were reluctant to sanction and recommend unorganized or unsupervised home visits. They feared negative effects in vulnerable family systems if the goal of the intervention and follow-up was unclear.

CREATING A PRELIMINARY MODEL FOR THE FDNY/COLUMBIA UNIVERSITY FAMILY PROGRAM

MODIFYING A PREVIOUSLY EVALUATED MODEL

The FDNY/Columbia University Family Assessment and Guidance Program is a family-oriented and strengths-based model built on an intervention previously evaluated at Memorial Sloan Kettering Cancer Center (MSK) for children who confronted the terminal illness and subsequent death of a parent from cancer. The MSK intervention was used by more than 120 families, the majority of whom found it helpful during the stresses of a parent's terminal illness and at 14 months postdeath (Christ et al., 2005). It gave families the option of home interviews, which were generally used by participating families when the ill parent was no longer in the hospital and after the parent's death. In addition to documenting the efficacy of this intervention, the study found that bereaved children experienced their highest levels of anxiety and depression before the parent died and had rapid decreases in distress levels after the parent's death occurred. This finding, subsequently replicated with adults, supports the value of preparation and suggests the possibility of helpful anticipatory grieving when death is expected (Bonanno et al., 2005). Unfortunately preparation for the loss was not available to FDNY families.

The quality of child care after parent loss and the child's relationship with the surviving parent/caregiver have consistently been found to affect the course and outcome of children's bereavement (Bifulco et al., 1987; Breier et al., 1988; Harris et al., 1987, 1996; Saler & Skolnick, 1992; Sandler et al., 1992; Tennant, 1988; Kwok et al., 2005; Worden, 1996). Therefore, an emphasis on parent guidance was chosen as the theoretical approach in the MSK intervention. In this model the goal was to affect children's adjustment to the loss by enhancing the surviving parents' abilities in several areas: (1) sustain competence in providing support and care for their bereaved children; (2) provide an environment in which the children felt able to express and contain painful or conflicting feelings, thoughts, and fantasies about the loss; and (3) maintain consistency and stability in the children's environment. Parents were given support, knowledge, and insight that would enable them to promote conditions that would foster their children's necessary grief work and help them to effectively reconstitute their lives. Interventionists also supported the parents through their own grief work in order to expand their capacity to function effectively during this family crisis (Christ et al., 2005; Siegel et al., 1990). Follow-up evaluation was relatively short term, taking place 14 months after the parent's death.

Although parents were satisfied with the MSK program, their suggestions and the specifics of the World Trade Center disaster were incorporated in the new FDNY/Columbia University Family Assessment and Guidance Program after the 9/11 tragedy (Christ, 2005). These modifications included three key points: (1) a greater focus on direct, individual work with each child; (2) more flexible intensity and frequency of contact depending on need; and (3) a longer term of engagement with the family to assist with troubling later symptoms in children. Finally parents were provided feedback information about the results of their children's assessments with standardized measures rather than using measures only for research purposes as occurred in the MSK intervention.

PRELIMINARY TRAUMA, GRIEF, RECONSTITUTION MODEL

In recent years bereavement specialists and theorists have tried to move away from a focus on rigid models that identify phases and stages of recovery from a loved one's death. Too often these are portrayed or viewed as linear or occurring in a sequence through which one must progress. A corollary is that such models have led to linear sequential prescribed treatments. There is a growing awareness that there is much more variation in coping with loss than these models suggest. Also emerging is a new appreciation of the importance of specific stresses surrounding the loss, the meaning of a particular loss, the influence of the social context, and the characteristics of affected individuals, which in this instance are young widows and children. Currently, the two most frequently cited theories of the grief process include the task approach of Worden (2001), and the more dynamic dual process model by Stroebe and Schut (1991, 2001). This study of young widows and their children exemplifies the importance of this emerging perspective.

Worden's grief process includes four tasks: (1) accepting the reality and permanence of the death, (2) experiencing the pain of the loss, (3) adjusting to an environment in which the deceased is missing, and (4) memorializing or locating the individual in memory and moving on in life. Stroebe and Shut expand these tasks in their "Dual Process Model" (1999). They add to Worden's tasks the following: (1) acceptance of a changed world as well as accepting the absence of the deceased; (2) the importance of taking time away from the pain of grieving as well as confronting it; (3) the need to reconstruct the subjective environment; and (4) the need to see *moving on* as more complex, including the development of new roles, identities, and relationships. Specifically they propose that bereavement includes a dynamic process of oscillation between loss and restoration-oriented coping and between confrontation and avoidance of stresses. They describe it as a dynamic back and forth process that is postulated as necessary for optimal adjustment over time.

Our experiences over 4 years of working with these young widows and their children support the basic elements of both the dual process model and the task approach. However, our experiences also suggest modifications for this specific population. It has been recognized that young widows are at significantly greater risk than older widows for adverse psychological outcomes (Stroebe and Stroebe, 1993). These modifications of the model clarify the arduous tasks and bereavement processes we found more characteristic of young widows 20–40 years old with dependent children confronting this traumatic situation. The following tasks may account in part for their greater risk.

Both mothers and children need to integrate the traumatic aspects of the loss and the many ways in which this public catastrophe changes not only their lives, but also much of the world. This brings continuous reminders of the trauma and loss and adds unique psychological challenges that have to be addressed.

Disynchrony in coping with trauma and grief was prominent as parents and their children at different developmental levels had different needs for expression, confrontation, and avoidance of stressful aspects.

They also experienced a different pace and timing from each other that was often painful and contributed to family conflict in some (Christ, 2000; Crook & Eliot, 1980). Both mothers and children need to confront the loss and at other times need help to learn to avoid its reality in their lives. The oscillation between confrontation and avoidance is continuous. For example, young children asking questions impeded the mother's ability to avoid troubling affects and grief topics. At other times it was difficult for mothers to express their grief because it distressed the children. Not only do children have less tolerance for prolonged exposure to intense emotions, but children at different levels of cognitive and emotional development have differing tolerance. In general, children needed smaller doses and different modes for expression of grief. Mothers were challenged to titrate their own pace of confrontation with that of their children.

We use the term reconstitution to encompass 3 steps in adaptation that describe the activities of these young mothers: (1) restoration, (2) reorganization, and (3) identity restructuring. They are described more fully in the following discussion.

The need to reconstruct family life, to fulfill tasks, and functions for and establish a new norm for each family member is a major challenge for these young families. The process of developing new roles, identities, and relationships is also arduous for young widows as they confront the ways in which the experience changed them and forces them to consider how to direct their lives going forward.

Although we observed the oscillation between a focus on loss and reconstitution orientation and between approach and avoidance coping, we also observed a change in emphasis over time with an increase in discussions that attended to life changes, new pursuits, and identity restructuring and a diminution of emphasis on grief related affects. Grief often recurred, and the process of mourning during these first 4 years was not finished for either mothers or their children. It is important to recognize that both loss and reconstitution are stressful and painful processes.

These processes are incorporated in the preliminary loss and reconstitution model (see Figure 8.1) for these families post 9/11. It also suggests varying

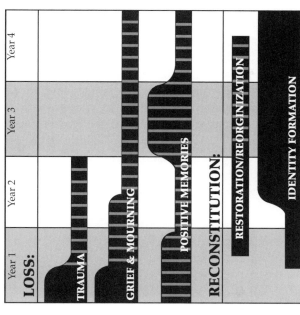

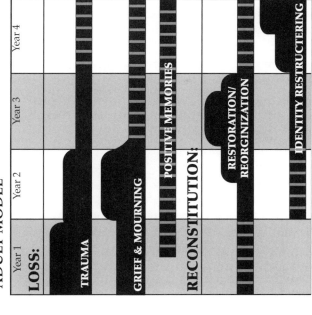

Figure 8.1 Preliminary model of loss and reconstitution.

levels of intensity of responses of children and adults as they cope with bereavement over the course of 4 years. The model is based on the experiences
of the families. The individual experience varies depending on pre-existing
conditions and additional stresses.

This model emerged from the work with the families and reflects their experience. It broadens the concept of the bereavement process to incorporate
trauma more fully, and it gives legitimacy and value to the struggle in each
phase or aspect of recovery. Individuals often ask, "Why is this taking so long?
Just how long is this going to last?" We have found that those asking these
questions view the whole process as composed of grief and mourning. This
perspective lacks the realistic understanding of the complexity of the later
reconstitution process. We used different words to describe that complexity.
As mentioned previously, it is important to keep in mind that our population
is limited to young widows who are consistently found to be at greater risk for
adverse psychological consequences following traumatic loss than are older
widows.

Definitions of the Process Depicted in the Preliminary Loss and Reconstitution Model

Trauma and grief.   The first reactions to the death of the fireman father/hus-
band in the WTC event were trauma, grief, and mourning. They included a
devastating inseparable amalgam of traumatic responses and grief responses.
We identified this in the young widows and their children; our coauthors also
reported this in the older parents of the firemen. Separating intervention to
deal first with the traumatic responses and then with grief responses, as has
been recommended, was impossible in most situations (Cohen, 2004). Uncon-
trollable grief reactions provoked traumatic responses and event reminders
elicited traumatic responses which were comingled with painful grief. We
found the concept of traumatic/grief responses closer to the picture the widows and the adolescent children conveyed to us. A temporary shift in intensity
of traumatic or grief responses could be related to the frequency and intensity of reminders, memorials, negative or positive mediators, and associations
that elicit reminders of pre-9/11 traumata.

One definition of trauma refers to the external event: the sudden, unexpected nature of a loss; violent or gruesome conditions surrounding it; the
presence of threat to oneself and one's family and friends; and continuing
losses or threats (American Psychiatric Association, 1994). A second definition
refers to emotional responses to any perceived severe threat: these include
troubling intrusive reminders of the stress, hyperarousal or loss of emotional
and behavioral control, avoidance of activities and/or discussions that might

evoke the fear, or constriction of functioning and emotional withdrawal. Typical reactions include loss of a sense of safety/security or one's *assumptive world*. It may be identified as a loss of innocence. Both grief and trauma are responses that can recur when predictable or unpredictable reminders or triggers occur in one's daily experience. We refer here to the first as a traumatic event and to the second as traumatic responses.

Positive memories.   Quite soon after the event children began to welcome intermittent positive stories and memories of the father; at first in small doses, larger doses in 3–8 year old boys and girls as well as 12–14 year old girls. Mothers, on the other hand, even in the third year found that positive memories could easily elicit more painful grief responses. In general we found that the younger the children, the more intermittent the nature of not only positive memories, but also traumatic and grief responses. If more persistent responses of the adults were observed in children it could indicate a more worrisome exception.

Restoration.   The first step in the process of reconstitution was one of slowly identifying and fulfilling functions that had been done by the father. Not uncommonly part of the distress this triggered in the widow was grief, but also anger. Mothers must now make all parenting and household maintenance decisions. But the challenge is not only to fill practical tasks, but emotional ones as well. This means deciding, for example, how the children will be nurtured, disciplined, and taught. How will the father be remembered and memorialized? How will grief be expressed and managed?

Reorganization.   As these changes became more routine, the second step of reorganization began to emerge. The psychological process of reorganization could be identified by moments of satisfaction and effectance, "I planned the whole trip, I got us to the airport on time, to the boat, the whole nine yards!" or "I think the kids are really surprised at how well I am managing things." Within the family the need for each member to find a new acceptance and comfort with the family unit without the day-to-day presence of the father leads to the change from restoration to reorganization.

Restructuring Identity.   This third step for the widows is the process of evolving a new view of oneself, one's roles, life goals, relationships, and activities that incorporates the reality of a new life without a husband. For some the change may be dramatic, the person may develop a new career, new intimate relationships and social networks, new hobbies, new religious interests, a change almost as profound as a changed identity. It also may be more subtle and internal.

They may view themselves as a more independent person, a stronger person, a more vulnerable person, a more artistic or musical person, a stronger parent or a more altruistic individual seeking to help others. Individuals may return to previous careers or jobs, but generally with altered goals. They may develop new commitments to help others in ways they were helped or wish they had been helped or to assist others to make up for what they perceive as past mistakes. Identity restructuring sometimes came as a surprise when the question of giving up parts of the new identity occurred, for example when thinking about the possibility of remarriage. Widows recognized they had a degree of independence and self assurance they had not previously experienced.

In children and adolescents a major difference is the very significant role played by the processes of development. With mothers we speak of identity restructuring, however in children the positive relentless push of development is better captured by speaking of identity formation. We were impressed by the clarity with which a few of the more articulate early and mid-adolescent girls described this process. They clearly identified the positive contribution their father's life and memory as well as the experience of his death had on their maturation and identity formation. This normal process is affected by the fact of the parent's death and by the absence of the parent's day-to-day influences on what they do and how they view themselves. Yet there is evidence that the emerging identity of older school-age children and adolescents is continuously influenced by their views of who the deceased parent was and what the parent would have expected of them as well as by the fact of the absence through death. Are they stronger, more vulnerable, more different, a victim, an orphan, a survivor? Are they wiser and more mature, more thoughtful, more compassionate, more empathic, more caring? Are they more determined to achieve in areas that would please the parent, or do they now value relationships more than performance? Do they react more strongly to separation, loss, rejection?

Described in the following is the program that emerged and some of the unique features developed as a response to the realities of the post-9/11 world of the firefighters' wives and their children. This section describes how the family's experience and needs, the previously developed model, and the CSU service structure influenced the development of the family intervention.

IMPLEMENTING THE FAMILY PROGRAM

The Family Program was implemented by an interdisciplinary team of CUSSW faculty and doctoral students. In order to address the broad range of stresses and behaviors of bereaved children and parents, the team consisted of social workers with individual, group, and child experience; psychologists including an educational psychologist; a psychiatric nurse; and a child psychiatrist. The program is structured to consist of the following elements.

The Family Assessment and Guidance Program

- Four bimonthly, then monthly interviews in home during the first 2 years. More frequent contacts provided as needed or requested.
- Two or more interventionists meet with family members in the home.
- From the third year on use flexible interview and measures schedules with frequency based on family needs.
- Conduct a complete battery of measures twice during the first year and then annually, on mother and children over age seven.
- Provide feedback to families on measures and evaluation.

This program is a family-focused therapeutic intervention that aims to help families master the challenges of adaptation to the sudden highly stressful, traumatic loss of a parent. It is predominantly a supportive, preventive intervention. Unique features of this program include the evaluation of children with feedback to parents, individual sessions with varying frequency, a normalizing approach, and encouragement of families to use other available services they found helpful.

- Four initial interviews are used to clinically evaluate each family member and obtain responses to standardized measures. Extending the evaluation over several weeks provides opportunities to spend time getting to know the family, to begin working on identified issues, and to titrate the use of measures that may be evocative. Standardized measures are completed twice during the first year by the mother, children, and their teacher and then once a year for subsequent years to provide an ongoing check of the clinician's assessment of the status of each individual's adaptation. The results of measures are analyzed and family members are given feedback on the results of the evaluation. Possible approaches to parenting challenges and child coping are discussed with the mother and with the children.
- The evaluation sessions are followed by individual therapeutic sessions with each widow and each child. Although we tend to schedule monthly sessions, the frequency is determined by the needs and/or requests of the families. If more intensive individual help is needed, the program assists to find and access appropriate referrals.
- A normalizing or nonpathologizing approach is integral to the family program. Experience and research suggests that, however devastated and depressed the young widow is in the first years, it is realistic to assume that her behaviors and responses are probably adaptive. This nonpathology approach means our first goal is to learn about and interpret

affects and behaviors in the context of the current situation. The clinician asks why is a particular behavior necessary to a mother or to a child in their adaptation and recovery? Given the peculiar nature of this traumatic event, we had to remind ourselves that all behaviors, reactions, and responses are best viewed as being normal under the circumstances unless proven otherwise. Important is helping family members understand and value their own needs and accept their pace of recovery. While learning what other widows are doing from the bereavement groups or *The LINK* was extraordinarily helpful to mothers, they needed to appreciate that their needs and timing would be different around such issues as when to do the memorial, how to relate to relatives, how to provide child care, if and when to date, and many, many more.

- Multiple services became available to families over time: individual and group counseling for mothers, school-based counseling for children, bereavement programs for children in schools and community, activity groups, and camps. We encouraged the use of available services that were helpful and accepted by families. Families were referred for additional services only when they requested or when the normalizing approach was unsuccessful in reducing symptoms for an extended period of time. Because the Family Intervention Program team is interdisciplinary, additional evaluations of children and adults could often be completed without having to send them to yet another agency.

INTERVENTION GOALS FOR CHILDREN AND ADOLESCENTS

Outcome assessment is an integral part of the therapeutic aspect of this program. Outcomes of the intervention are evaluated by repeated standardized measures of psychological adjustment (see appendix), and by the therapeutic clinical interviews that assesses each individual's gradual return to pre-9/11 levels of functioning in multiple domains. The following are goals that defined outcomes for children, adolescents, and parents that guided the intervention process throughout.

- To reduce general distress symptoms and symptoms of complicated grief
- To improve children's communication and relationship to the surviving parent
- To facilitate children's return to levels of functioning comparable to pre-9/11 functioning in multiple domains:
  - Psychological, including grief management (i.e., an increasing ability to talk about pleasant experiences of the parent)
  - Development of skills in dealing with planned and unplanned re-

minders, reduction of the impact of reminders on functioning, and a decrease in the amount of time the child is distracted by the reminders
- Functioning in the home with parent and siblings
- Functioning in school work and with teachers, in relation to peers, and in structured and unstructured after-school activities

The results of the measures served as a support, a check and modification of the clinical assessments. On occasion, they suggested a possible unexpected finding. They were also helpful in concretizing improvements or declines in areas such as depression and anxiety; change in complicated grief scores; and change in the intensity of the impact of external reminders.

INTERVENTION GOALS FOR ADULTS

- Gradual improvement in widows' depression, anxiety, and symptoms of complicated grief
- Increase in confidence in their parenting skills as single parents with children experiencing bereavement

Gradual improvement in the widows' satisfaction with their reconstituted lives in multiple domains including the following:

- Grief adaptation and memorializing of spouse
- Regaining control of their own emotions
- Financial management of the family
- Competence in functioning as a single parent with bereaved children
- Sustain empathic connection to children
- Relationship to parents and in-laws
- Relationship to peers and friends
- Current and future plans in relation to their own education and career
- Ability to enjoy recreation
- Dating and future plans in relation to establishing intimate relationships
- Ability to begin to make long-term plans

As with the children, the results of the measures filled out by the parents quantified the extent and breadth of their distress and supported or questioned the clinical assessments of both improvements and declines.

THERAPEUTIC APPROACHES

While overall goals of enhancing parenting competence, communication, and consistency in families were retained, a broad range of established parenting

200 PROVIDING A HOME-BASED THERAPEUTIC PROGRAM

skills training approaches were used to accomplish them. For example we encouraged identification of differences in individual responses and understanding the impact of developmental changes and external stresses as a way to increase empathy and warmth between parents and children. We explored options for ways to reduce the impact of stressful events and situations on children. For example, we supported parents gradually becoming comfortable with children declining to attend some memorials. We encouraged reduction of negative stressors, such as family conflict and parental depression, as well as reduction of children's psychological symptoms often related to cumulative stress, developmental change, and traumatic and grief reminders. We supported active listening skills, individual time with each child, and development of positive family activities. Positive parent-child relationships were encouraged through the establishment of stable routines and effective discipline. We worked with parents to understand their own and their children's grief reactions and to find ways to bridge the differences in timing and intensity. For both parents and children, we challenged negative thinking by using positive reframing of views toward the self and others.

Children are helped to recognize and express their emotions: sadness, disappointment, anger, fear, guilt, and shame. But they are also helped to reframe, contain, and control overwhelming preoccupations with the trauma and the loss. Skills for coping with the impact of so many changes in their lives and finding ways to create more satisfying experiences are major foci. The first year after the disaster was so distracting that most children and adolescents thought they had lost a year. "What happened to 14?" asked one adolescent who was a high school sophomore in the second year after 9/11. For most 9 to 14-year-old children and adolescents, the second year was therefore one of intense focus on catching up with peers, school work, sports, and hobbies. Skills in understanding emotions, grief, and trauma (their own and their parents') and especially learning to deal with multiple reminders of the loss were integrated in the work with children. Of central importance was improving the communication and the relationship between the child and the mother, reducing conflicts, improving mutual understanding, increasing empathy, warmth, and open discussion, and identifying and accepting that Dad's way of doing things was changing.

FINDING FOCUS

Although we developed a broad outline of topics for use by clinicians in work with families, our program's clinicians found it was critical to follow the direction of mothers and children in order to reduce perceived areas of distress. During the first years there was a greater focus on family members' grief and the external events that magnified their internal experience of loss and fear.

Such events included, for example, the continuing search for remains and the participation in multiple memorials. Mothers were concerned about how to deal with children's stress-related behaviors such as repetitive questioning ("When is Daddy coming home?"), sleep difficulties, aggressive behaviors, avoidance behaviors, and school difficulties. Some mothers wanted help with their own emotional highs and lows. Help was also provided through locating resources to assist with household chores or child care, clarifying and reframing behaviors and events, suggesting ways to reduce family conflict, facilitating communication around bereavement, improving the relationship with a child, or assisting in communication with the school about a child's behavior. Familiar cognitive behavioral approaches were used with both parents and children to help prepare for reminders, reframe events in ways that relieve guilt and feelings of victimization, normalize reactions, and encourage stress reduction techniques such as relaxation, desensitization, and downward comparisons. Negative appraisals of the situation were also challenged: "He must have suffered," or "I could have kept him from going to work if I didn't get out of the car," or "The pain will never end," or "My friends don't like me any more," or "I'm stupid because my grades aren't as good as last year's grades."

ENGAGING THE POPULATION

In the first year after the 9/11 attacks, mothers struggled to find a way to survive amid the memorials, the terrorist threats, the war, the publicity. Those who requested the family intervention program wanted support for their children, but their own ability to survive the daily traumatic events and the demands of single parenthood often needed to take precedence. Only by being helpful to each individual in ways they needed in the moment could a trusting relationship develop in such a crisis environment. Clinicians asked themselves: What is it this mother or child needs or wants to talk about right now? What might be helpful given the most troubling issues? Are they reacting to the three memorials that just occurred, some media revelation about another firefighter, distress over having to prepare their family's story for the compensation board, dealing with a child's school problems, sleep difficulties, a son's meltdown at baseball practice, an anniversary, a birthday that evokes anger and sadness rather than joyous celebrations, or the usual amalgam of several or all of these stresses?

Mothers were encouraged to trust their own ability to identify areas of concern and need, to value their judgments and their own thoughts and experiences in this totally new situation. In time the family gradually came to trust the clinician's ability to assist in working toward solutions for some of the challenges they were facing. During the first years, anger and mistrust were ubiquitous in families' reactions and responses and a challenge to the process of engaging them in free dialogue. Just knowing that anger is part of the adaptive process helps to deal with specific critiques or complaints. Engaging and reengaging families with this level of anger and fear is a continuing process that takes place through carefully identifying, validating, and resolving some of the most urgent problems that families experience. Consistency in initiating communication and responsiveness to their needs is also vital.

Beginning in the second year, clinicians found they were becoming an unwelcome reminder of the intense emotional pain of the loss. Older children and especially adolescents said, "We don't want to be 9/11 kids anymore." What was once special was now different, and that was not good. Shifting the focus to reconstitution issues, improving children's daily lives, and developing more positive experiences within the family and within the meetings sometimes helped to change children's identification of clinicians as reminders and as bringers of pain.

INTERVIEWING IN THE HOME

The family intervention program is conducted with mothers and their children primarily in their homes. Families requesting the program are given the option of being seen at a local counseling office, but thus far 100 percent have requested to be seen in the family home. Some reasons are obvious, others less so. With 1 to 10 children in a bereaved family, scheduling therapeutic sessions outside the home in addition to helping children keep up with school work, activities, and friends was a virtual impossibility for bereaved widows. In addition, in a situation of continued threatening events that occurred throughout the first 2 years after the World Trade Center attacks, mothers' anxiety about being able to protect their children was extremely high. In response, many left the home only for necessities.

Professionals used to working in an office often forget how much more relaxed and comfortable children can be in their own homes. This comfort makes discussion of threatening topics more possible, especially with younger children. The children can use their own toys, bring pictures of Daddy, make drawings to put on their refrigerator. In the Family Intervention Program the home visit generally involves two or more clinicians so that each family member can be seen in a relatively short period of time. Typically, individual children chose a place in the home for interviewing, either their own room or a family room that permits private conversation. Most children want a private interview rather than meeting together with brothers or sisters or with mother. Joint interviews are often less productive because children are guarded in expressing their thoughts to siblings or parents, fearing they might upset them, be criticized for their reactions, or be put on the spot to discuss embarrassing topics before they are ready to do so. Concern about upsetting or alienating other members of the family by expression of thoughts or emotions is ubiquitous after such a sudden and shocking loss. Still there are a few families who value joint interviews on agreed upon topics.

Special challenges of meeting in the home concern the travel time of clinicians; fitting the interview into the family's schedule and rhythms; managing distractions of the setting; and balancing an open, honest, and more social contact within a clear set of appropriate boundaries. In many ways the professional has to deal with more discomfort in the client's setting than in an office. However, there are also opportunities for greater effectiveness.

Travel time and fitting their schedule. Firefighters often lived in outlying areas in order to obtain sufficient space for their families to live adequately on their relatively low salaries. Travel requires 2 to 4 hours of driving to and from the home. The use of travel time is maximized by having a team of two or more clinicians audiotape their discussion with each other in the car on the way home. This includes bringing each other up to date on their analysis of what they have observed and learned and discussing plans for subsequent interviews. Clinicians have found that these postinterview sessions provide peer supervision and support, facilitate collaboration, and provide an unusual learning situation for each clinician.

In the home, clinicians almost automatically become involved in events that had occurred that day. They try to respond helpfully and view this not as resistance but as an opportunity to further their understanding of the family and as a way to continue to build a trusting relationship. In fact, such events give a much more real dimension to the intervention.

One mother was delayed in returning home from an event in the city on the day of the Family Assessment and Guidance Program appointment. The children (ages 10 and 13) were home waiting for the clinician and for the babysitter to return from an errand. As the clinician arrived, a caravan of cars pulled up behind the babysitter, whose car had clearly been in a fender-bender accident. The car she was driving was an old car that had belonged to the firefighter and was used by her for errands. The caravan was the large extended family whom the mother had quickly notified by cell phone to go to the scene of the accident. "The last time I saw my Dad was in that car, he dropped me off at school on September 11th," said the 13-year-old. The children were clearly distraught by the damage done to their father's car and at the same time frightened that their babysitter could have been seriously hurt in the accident. Both drivers were unharmed by the accident. The grandfather was very reassuring that the car could be easily repaired. The clinician focused on helping each family member, including the babysitter, regain a sense of calm, validating their anger and fear but emphasizing a realistic appraisal of this situation, their safety, and their competence in being able to handle such events.

Honest communication and setting boundaries.   Being in the home facilitates a more social communication appropriate to the setting and to the events of the day. As with adults, an open, honest, and direct approach is particularly important in building and maintaining trust in the context of sudden and multiple loss of life and continuing threats.

> During the first year of the intervention one of the clinicians experienced the sudden death of her own mother, causing her to cancel two appointments. One widow was informed that the clinician's mother had died when the program's coordinator explained the cancellation. The widow expressed sympathy to the clinician at their next appointment, was curious about what had happened, and developed a closer, more trusting relationship, saying she felt that they had more in common now. One family had experienced multiple losses, and the clinician, wanting to spare them more news of loss, simply told them she had a family emergency. This led to a more distant, less trusting tone in the next interview.

It is important that clinicians not pursue a personal, social relationship with the widows and children even though, as clinicians working with anyone in the FDNY community found, one might value the personal friendship. Being in the comfort and warmth of the family home of stressed and needful individuals can elicit a desire to blur boundaries and become, in fact, a helping friend. While one is friendly and personal, one is not a personal friend. Families may want to know about the clinician's illness that caused a cancellation of an appointment. They may ask where you live, where you work, if you have children. Adolescents might ask if you like sports, music, art, or teaching as a way to explore different lifestyles. Ongoing discussion with children about their own life gives them the opportunity to explore and reflect on their life rather than talking about the death of the father exclusively. Over time more focus is placed on exploring the children's own life course. Boundaries are maintained by providing only personal information that is directly requested or that is specifically germane to the situation. Another important way to establish helpful boundaries when interviewing in the home is to set limits on the amount of time spent there, generally we found this to be no more than 2½ hours. This assures that family activities are minimally disrupted.

Benefits of the home interview.   The most obvious benefit of meeting in the home is the opportunity to see how the family is actually functioning and interacting with each other. Behaviors such as memorializing the lost loved one, their movement and gradual change in the type and placement of memorabilia, their resource needs, their social networks, and their emerging identity and role definition also can be observed and assessed.

Initially inundated with welcomed memorabilia, most families began to reorganize and reduce the presence of objects placed throughout the home after each anniversary. Gradually they asked children to select pictures of special meaning to them for their rooms and reserved one particular section of the home for large photographs. Mothers explained that especially adolescent children were finding the presence of too many reminders upsetting and an unwelcome distraction from their daily chores and preoccupations. But there was variation, with a few mothers maintaining multiple memorials and others removing almost all. These observations aided discussion of each mother's understanding of her own and her children's grief process, assessing the impact of their approach, and identifying possible alternative ways to process it with the family.

Home interviews were especially helpful for families with multiple children and those with younger children. For once, scheduling did not become an overwhelming challenge to the mother. Every child in the family is seen, although younger children for shorter periods of time and often for observation and play. It was touching, however, when a child who was 2 years old on 9/11 became 4 or 5 years of age and announced to the clinician, "Someone should be talking to me now."

ASSESSMENT

There are three aspects to the assessment process: the clinical interview, the use of clinical measures, and additional specialized evaluations. With most mothers and children the clinical interview assessment and the measures are sufficient. At times additional, more specialized evaluations are requested related to special symptoms or areas of functioning.

The domains for assessment of children in the clinical interview were developed from findings in the practice and research literature with bereaved and traumatized children and the child development field. All domains are assessed within a developmental context and over time.

Assessment Domains for Children

- Psychological state and behavior (mourning, separation reactions, self-esteem, internalizing and externalizing symptoms).
- Functioning in the home with parent and siblings.
- School competence (grades and academic functioning) and overall cognitive functioning.
- Behavior (in relation to teacher and classmates).
- After-school activities and hobbies.
- Peer and classmate relationships.

Clinical intervention: The assessment of the child is not separate from intervention. As children discuss their situation the clinician listens for and observes what is most troubling and begins to label and clarify issues. So, for example, efforts are made from the beginning to increase children's sense of control and self-esteem and reduce their negative views of themselves. Taking time in the assessment and building a sense of control and an ability to move away from intense emotion are essential. Sometimes the grief for the father is in the foreground of the child's thinking, but often over time it recedes into the background. Their concerns about day-to-day activities and exploring their own life course are increasingly front and center. While these two preoccupations interact, it is often helpful for children to feel permission to focus exclusively on one or the other, on grief or on current events.

Use of measures in the assessment process: All children and adolescents from 7 to 17 years old are asked to complete the measures twice in the first year and once per year afterward. Most are able to complete them the first time, and some are willing to repeat them. However, over time many children, especially boys and adolescents, indicate it is too upsetting to complete them and either refuse or are reluctant enough that the interventionist does not pursue the issue. This was sometimes consistent with their feeling of not wanting to be "9/11 kids" any more. What was initially felt as special becomes over time a sense of unwanted difference with a connotation of victim. While encouraging children to complete measures, it is important for clinicians to be respectful of their reluctance and of the fact that children have the right to give assent to completing these kinds of assessments.

The assessment process was a critical part of the family program because the primary motivation for mothers choosing it was to have their children evaluated over time. Therefore the assessment needed to include measures that could provide comparisons with national norms of nonbereaved children, with other children in the program, with their own children's scores at different time periods, and on specific areas of child/parent interaction. While measures encourage children to more fully describe what they are experiencing, they still want the opportunity to discuss it and to tell their story in an open-ended interview. Often measures provide specificity and corroboration to the child's story and clarify what is most troubling to him.

The use of measures also provides an additional check on clinicians' judgments with both children and adults. Too little is known about the interaction between grief and trauma and its relationship to psychopathology to rely on clinical judgment alone. Almost nothing is known about these phenomena in such a catastrophic situation as the World Trade Center disaster or the longer-term trajectory of the recovery process. Observations in the home, from parents, schools, and from comparisons with national and group norms provide important triangulation of information that gives greater support for one's judgments and decisions.

Specialized evaluation: Each clinician in the team had an area of expertise that could be tapped, including social workers with a PhD in psychology or educational psychology, a board-certified child psychiatrist, both master's- and doctoral-level social workers, and social work doctoral students. The judicious referral to outside expertise, or for neuropsychological or neurological evaluations, was carefully discussed with the mothers and the children, as were results, recommended treatments, and extended follow-up.

LESSONS LEARNED

The goals of the program were based on findings from studies in child bereavement, child traumatic stress, spousal bereavement, and parenting skills training approaches. However the World Trade Center disaster raised unique questions and challenges related to the particular circumstances of this disaster that informed the program: the interaction of trauma and grief, coping with reminders of the loss, and the importance of the longer term perspective.

1. *Trauma and grief following a public catastrophic loss.* Knowledge about responses to trauma and to grief have developed quite separately. Concepts and knowledge about trauma evolved from war veterans and victims of domestic violence and child sexual and physical abuse. Knowledge about grief evolved primarily from studies of spousal, child, and parent death from illness. Only recently has the connection between the two responses been recognized and examined (Malkinson et al., 2005; Cohen, 2004; Brown & Goodman, 2005). Work with survivors of the World Trade Center disaster suggested that focusing on one set of responses (i.e., trauma) to the exclusion of the other (i.e., grief) was often impossible as there was continuous interaction between grief and trauma in both adults and children. Trauma and grief often needed to be addressed simultaneously, and approaches to accomplishing this are emerging.

One mother of two young children had worked in the city before 9/11 but remained at home with the children afterward. About 7 months after her husband's death, she revealed on questioning that she was having difficulty sleeping at night for the past 2 months and was becoming sleep deprived. After exploration she described that she was kept awake by the image of her husband when he died. On a video just moments before the collapse, he was

shown in a stairwell huddled with two other firefighters from the same ladder. She believed that meant he was frightened and sad, and she felt tortured
by how he must have felt just before he died. The clinician suggested she substitute thoughts of him praying with his friends, since he was a religious man,
and also of him having a sense of peace, a state that can occur with brave
people when they recognize the end is inevitable. She readily accepted the reframing of the experience, which she believed fit his personality and way of
responding. Her sleeping improved.

Children also can be traumatized by their grief or their grief can lead to an increase in fear and sense of vulnerability.

Seven months after September 11, 2001, a 9-year-old boy who was having
marked traumatic stress symptoms and an increase in difficulty controlling his
aggression at school asked sadly with tears, "I want you to tell me this, how
long is this going to last . . . no more laughing, no more fun, no more jokes?"

A 12-year-old girl deeply mourned her father's death; he was her buddy and
a major help with her school performance, even leading her Brownie troop for
awhile. She experienced an increase in her fears of someone breaking into the
house when she thought of being without his reassuring presence.

A mother described her 12-year-old son crying for 2 hours as they sat on the
beach with his sisters around the time of the first anniversary. He was unable
to be consoled.

While facilitating children's expression of grief was an intervention goal, the
perspective of trauma clarified the critical importance of building children's
confidence in their ability to contain and control overwhelming emotions.
This was done by helping children know when to stop describing their grief
and teaching them how they could put it aside by thinking about something
pleasant and then returning to it at a later time. While accepting children's
emotions, clinicians learned that it was also necessary to help them interrupt
the flow, to experience their ability to put it away for awhile so that they could
break it down to small doses that are easier to digest. Some children needed
permission to *not* think about dad during the day. Mothers assured them this
was not disloyal but was the mind's way of giving them a rest.

Deciding when to facilitate emotional expression or to employ a broad
range of containment and control techniques was especially challenging in
the first year. Teaching mechanisms for control while exploring affect and
helping to contain it was useful. In the third and fourth years, children and
adolescents were affected by developmental changes, cumulative stresses,
and often unanticipated trigger events that became traumatic reminders of
their losses. Children were helped to identify external causes of their renewed

experience of grief, to develop positive appraisals of themselves and the situation, and to learn ways to cope more effectively in the face of changes in themselves and the family and continuing reminders of their fathers' death.

2. *Reminders after this catastrophic event.* One of the most stressful aspects of this event for survivors was the public involvement with it over time and the media scrutiny of survivors' lives. While the attention was clearly helpful in mobilizing support, both children and adults had to find inventive ways to cope with the continuous reminders of the threat and the loss. Using avoidance, distraction, and other coping strategies that have been found helpful was not so easy to do.

Some of the first-year memorials were exceedingly evocative and designed to engage the public rather than grieving family members.

A 16-year-old daughter walked up to receive her father's flag at one of the many memorials that first year after 9/11. However, her mother reported that when she got to the podium she turned her back and refused to touch the flag. Fortunately her mom was right behind her and put out her arms to receive the flag. All realized that the emotion of the moment was way beyond what most adolescents could tolerate and she had a right to her protest.

By the second year, mothers had gained more confidence in their perspectives and judgments, and all survivors demanded that the memorials be low-key and personal. They had learned the importance of making space for their own private expressions as well as meeting obligations to a grieving and supportive public.

A few possessions of the husband of one mother with two young children were found several years after the event. The CSU representative brought them to her house. Later she described her thinking: "I didn't want to open the box while the FDNY person was there. She was very nice, but I know I would shape my reaction because of her presence and this time I wanted a pure response that was my own." She had learned over time the validity and importance of her own personal grief response.

Early after the event, reminders were caused by outside events: memorials, street namings, terrorist threats, declarations of war, deaths of soldiers, media coverage of firefighters' lives, and finding remains. Reminders of the loss were birthdays, holidays, anniversaries, and events that Dad would have attended. Over time, however, the reminders became in some ways less predictable and expected, mixed with many other emotions and experiences, and often more powerful in their effects.

Later reminders included children reaching a new stage of cognitive and emotional development, moves from dad's house, changes in dad's house, separations, other stressful events, other deaths, rejections and disappointments, changes in the family, mom's dating, or classroom discussions of the World Trade Center disaster for which the student had not been prepared.

Adolescents were particularly reactive to cumulative stresses and unexpected trigger events.

> One previously resilient adolescent was overcome by having to attend multiple sweet 16 parties and watching daughters dancing with fathers. This overlapped with street namings, family gatherings for memorials, subsequently her having to plan her own 16th birthday party, and finally, watching her dad's favorite baseball team lose the World Series. These cumulative stresses created a feeling of hopelessness, and she thought she was becoming mentally ill since these feelings were emerging 2 years after the event. Understanding the influence of the accumulation of stresses, the relevance of trigger events, and the need to discover new coping approaches gave her a sense of control and direction. Her mood was lifted quickly.

Reminders could also be such ordinary events for children that they are completely unexpected.

> A 9-year-old boy said he becomes sad now when he sees cars lined up in the street in front of neighborhood houses. He remembered several days after 9/11 coming home from school and seeing many cars parked in front of his house. He was excited because his father was a "party man," and he thought his father had come home and they were having a party. It turned out they were there to tell his mother they had found his father's body. Seeing the cars now reminds him of that time and makes him sad.

3. *Benefits of a longitudinal project.* Following families over a longer period of time was invaluable. Not only did we learn about later appearing behaviors and responses, but we could understand the relationship of later responses to earlier reactions. In the context of the use of a broad range of services and supports, severe stress responses observed in mothers in the first 2 years that might indicate enduring problematic conditions improved remarkably in most widows in the 3rd and 4th years. In general their relationships with their children also improved as evidenced by children's behaviors and their rating of their parent's competence on a measure developed for that purpose. Later stress responses in previously asymptomatic children were instructive about the enduring impact of reminders in such situations and the vulnerability of adolescents to cumulative stress. We were alerted to the changing responses of chil-

dren as they matured and to their sensitivity to separation, loss, rejection, and disappointment. But we also began to observe their greater comfort with being "9/11 kids," their growing empathy and compassion for others in need, their advanced maturity in social and emotional functioning. Adolescents now say "9/11 is a part of my life, but it's not all of it." Rather than feeling "different" and stigmatized by their greater awareness of what's important in life many have become proud of their maturity, perspective, and insight. Most continue to achieve: taking jobs, receiving awards, achieving in sports, spending time with friends, and trying out new activities.

It was impressive to observe how mothers were able to set aside their own grief for extended periods of time in order to focus on their children's needs. Although the demands of being a single parent in these situations is daunting, they made good use of the distractions and demands, building skills and mapping out new directions for themselves and their family. For many their confidence in managing both has vastly increased.

The execution of a long-term intervention is indeed challenging. The generous participation of the families made this possible. Only through continuing study of such experiences can we build a solid knowledge base to inform planning for major disasters.

CHAPTER 9

Strengthening Connections within the Family at Home

Looking around the room it is difficult to recognize the couples arriving for breakfast as the same people who had entered this room looking tentative, scared, and awkward with each other and with those they encountered a mere 24 hours before. Yet there they were . . . the young woman laughing as she helped herself to coffee was the same woman who yesterday helped herself to tissues as she talked about the change in her marriage since 9/11. She and her husband seemed relaxed as they chatted with the older couple next to them, perhaps comforted by the presence of this officer whose 20-year marriage had undergone a similar, yet unique struggle of its own. Another couple sat alone, talking with the type of intensity that suggested others not intrude. As the program facilitator, I remembered them as having four young children and not having been away alone together since the oldest, now 7, was born. I was pleased to notice yet another couple, who clearly were in a lot of distress, some of which predated 9/11, talking to one of the staff and later learned of their request for additional help. Gradually, the room began to fill. They came in pairs, carrying their overnight bags, nodding to one another in recognition, helping themselves and each other to food, and then choosing a table and waiting expectantly for the day and a half program to resume.

I breathed a sigh of relief—each couple who arrived helping me to let go of my fear that no one would return now that the free hotel, dinner, and theater were behind them. It had been a long journey getting to this room. A journey based on the knowledge that 9/11 itself, combined with the recovery effort, had placed significant stress on firefighter marriages and that our effort to address this was having limited success. Like many offers of help, our earlier attempts required that people with no time make time to attend to what they were trying to avoid. This program was different in that it offered time—time away from routine and from distraction—and promised to combine looking at difficulties with time out for relaxation and fun. We were just beginning to learn what a powerful and important lesson this could be.

B Y TRADITION, firefighters have two families: the family at home and the family at the firehouse. To marry a firefighter has always meant that holidays may be split between time at home and time in the firehouse, last-minute requests to change schedules to help a brother firefighter might be granted without consultation, and help for any home repair could be sched- uled within 48 hours but might go unfinished for months. Most couples man- aged over time to strike a balance between the two, understanding the events that were nonnegotiable within each family system and living by a calendar that carefully tracked the commitments of each.

In the days, weeks, and months following 9/11, the firehouse family domi- nated the lives of most firefighters. First there was the physical necessity of digging at the site, attending funerals, and continuing tours in the firehouse— for many the only *normal* activity that remained in their lives. Beyond that there was the emotional necessity of being with one's family at the time of loss, in this case the firefighter family, which lost 343 *brothers.* It was months before the impact of this on the family at home began to emerge with tears, anger, worry, and concern from the family members who until then felt unable to ex- press their feelings since, after all, their firefighter had survived.

Complicating this was another strong tradition within firehouse culture em- bodied by the slogan posted in most firehouse kitchens, which simply states "What's said here stays here." For many this slogan extends beyond the pro- tection of personal confidences shared at the kitchen table and includes a more global policy of never discussing work at home. For some, this stems largely from a desire to shelter one's family from the daily trauma that inhabits a fire- fighter's work life. Somehow by not talking about what goes on, firefighter families build a myth of safety.

If one doesn't talk about the daily danger faced on the job, all can pretend that unquestionably one goes to work and returns safely at the end of each tour. Women from firefighter families who grow up to marry firefighters are well schooled in coping with the unspoken danger that exists each time her husband leaves for work. Those who marry into the culture generally describe a period of adjustment during which they come to realize that to think about their husbands at work, listen to the news, or imagine the unimaginable is an unbearable way to live. Gradually they settle into a routine that often includes enjoyable rituals that mark the time they have all to themselves or later with the children: girls' night out, pancakes for dinner, movies rather than TV. These coping strategies sometimes included behaviors that reflected the fear lurking just beneath consciousness, as with one wife who noted that it was not until her husband retired that she realized she had never gone to bed when he was at work without first cleaning the kitchen "just in case."

Prior to 9/11, when something happened to break through this denial, a serious injury or line-of-duty death, firefighters simply reassured their families that their firehouse was safe and that they were cautious, looked out for each other, and were extremely experienced and well trained. The fact that this type of false reassurance was generally successful seems surprising until considered in light of the psychological necessity and healthy denial required to go off each day to face unknown dangers and potentially life-threatening situations. On 9/11, all of these defense mechanisms crumbled along with the towers. No longer could wives, children, or families believe that their firefighter would of course return from work. Neither experience, nor judgment, nor teamwork had spared the most senior FDNY members that day. The list of fatalities included top-ranking chiefs from headquarters, 102 officers, and many members of special operations units. It included not only those on duty but many off duty who fled to the towers from wherever they were at the time they heard the news.

Each funeral, each photo, each encounter with 9/11 widows and children reverberated with the message that no one was immune to the dangers of the job. As firefighters attended memorial after memorial, many wives went along to offer support. They watched silently as women and children grieved for the firefighter, whose remains were often missing from the coffin at the front of the church. As they watched, they barely understood the impact that facing their worst fears over and over again in the faces of these other women was having on them. In the fire department it is not six degrees of separation but one. Each memorial service could be you, your children, your husband. Wives were mostly in touch with their feeling of extreme gratitude that their firefighter had survived. They stood by understanding that the men had a job to do and that this was a time when the needs of the firefighter family took precedence. They struggled to deny the feelings of concern, fear, and resentment as time passed and their husbands continued to be absent from home. This was not a time that wives dared to think of themselves. If any family time was available, it was the children who needed their father's attention. Most wives put their needs and feelings on hold as they kept the house running by filling in the gaps left by a husband who had previously shared many of the household and child care tasks. Any acknowledgement of feeling overwhelmed, lonely, or upset was rapidly replaced by feeling guilty for daring to feel anything but grateful for her spouse surviving.

By the Thanksgiving and Christmas holidays, scenes like the following (written for a CSU video) began to be reported with increasing frequency by the men coming to the counseling unit for help and also by the peers and firehouse clinicians talking to the men at the kitchen table.

The scene depicts a firefighter and his wife at home while he is getting ready to leave for work. He's searching around the house for his keys, complaining that the kids leave their things all over. His wife tosses him the keys, letting him know that they were exactly where he left them when he came home, and then comments that he is the one who can't remember anything.

SHE: You were supposed to meet your folks for dinner. It was your mom's birthday, remember? I told them you were working.

HE: I forgot. I have a lot on my mind. I had to take Mara and the kids to a ceremony at the Parish. They were giving her an award for Mike.

SHE: You know you spend more time with those kids than you do with us. Your kids haven't seen you for days, and they see you almost every day.

HE: Let's not start on this again. Mara and kids will never see Mike again. I'm just trying to help out and you're giving me a hard time . . . that's really nice! You know if something happened to me—those guys would be there for you. Don't you forget that!

SHE: I know that. And that's why all fall I said nothing. Every day you were gone, digging at the site, going to a funeral, helping out Mara and the kids, and I said nothing because I knew you needed to get this done.

HE: That's right.

SHE: Christmas came and went and I thought, you know, it will get better. The holidays are over and you're still gone; the funerals are over and you're still out there somewhere. Even when you're home, you're not here. I talk to you and your mind's not here. Your kids miss you; last week you missed their awards ceremony; your mother's birthday you missed. Something's not right.

HE: I'm going to be late for work. I got to go; we'll talk later.

SHE: I love you. I want the old you back. I want our life the way it was. I want our old life back.

HE: I don't know if that's ever going to happen. I'm not the same. I don't know if I ever will be the same again. I just don't know anymore. I used to think I had all the answers; now I just don't know anymore. . . . I got to go.

THE IMPACT OF TRAUMA ON RELATIONSHIPS

No one goes through trauma alone. When an individual is dramatically affected by an event, that event will impact those closest to him or her as well. Each of the classic symptoms of trauma creates an understandable disturbance in intimate connections.

Avoidance The *necessary numbing*, where one can't cry, can't feel, can't talk about it, precludes intimacy and involvement through constriction of feelings.

Reexperiencing   the presence of intrusive recollections of the traumatic event in thoughts, images, nightmares, and flashbacks—takes one away from participation in the here and now.

Hyperarousal   reacting physically, neurologically, and psychologically as if still in danger—makes the normal routines of family life nearly impossible to tolerate. The sound of children's chatter, infant crying, sibling squabbles, and the like often lead to angry outbursts, overreactions, and ultimately isolation.

Coincident to these difficulties in emotional regulation is a disruption of beliefs about the meaning of life. Trauma changes and often damages the sense of self. Consequently relationships with everyone, especially with those most intimately connected, are also often disturbed. It is not always possible to predict who will be most affected in the aftermath of trauma, and some traumatic events are so catastrophic as to leave their mark on most everyone exposed. However, researchers tell us it is the ability to derive comfort from another human being that ultimately determines the aftermath of trauma, not the history of the trauma itself (van der Kolk et al., 1991). For this reason an individual's support network is of critical importance in the recovery from trauma. When the self has been assaulted, healing is facilitated by a safe, secure, and predictable environment. In the final analysis, those who deal well with trauma are those who can turn to others for support (Johnson, 2002; Herman, 1997). Ultimately this support does not come from the professional resources that rally to provide assistance but rather from our closest family and friends.

This understanding of trauma underscores the importance of addressing the family members of those directly exposed to trauma and including them as central figures in any recovery plan. The magnitude of the World Trade Center disaster had shattered the necessary illusions by which firefighter families previously coped with the dangers of the job. The physical and emotional distance from the family at home during the long and difficult recovery process precluded the development of new coping mechanisms for the couple. Not surprisingly, this disconnection paved the way for the increased use of destructive coping strategies—alcohol, food, affairs, and so forth—most typically (though not exclusively) on the part of the firefighter.

While it is true that firefighters have the advantage of a brotherhood steeped in the tradition of turning to one another, it is equally true that turning toward the firehouse family often meant turning away from the family at home. This behavior can also be understood as consistent with the concept of the *trauma membrane,* where those experiencing a trauma feel it is possible to relate only to those who have shared their experience (Lindy, 1985). Ultimately recovery from trauma necessitates crossing this membrane and reconnecting with those who did not share the traumatic experience in precisely the same way. In the case of the firefighters, the most critical reconnection was with the family at home, whose experience, though different, had most often been traumatic as well. For most firefighters, it took a long time to develop any awareness or understanding of the trauma experienced by their spouse and children. Not acknowledging it meant that it did not exist and they could imagine that everyone at home remained untouched by these horrific events. This belief reinforced the distance between home and work and created walls of silence within many families.

If the *best defense of all is to have a loved one stand in the dark beside you*, the importance of the recovery effort including not only firefighter brothers but spouses and other close kin is underscored (Johnson, 2002). It is helpful to educate both the sufferer and the loved one about the connection between withdrawal and anger at home and the fear and vulnerability felt in anticipation of letting one's emotional guard down. It is especially powerful to explain that one is likely to feel most vulnerable when relaxing in the presence of a spouse. This information replaces a paradigm of distance with one of closeness and connection simply by reminding the couple of the closeness they were accustomed to sharing in the past. We believe that the implications of this clearly point to the importance of finding a way to include the family at home, who comprise the immediate support network, as a critical component of a comprehensive psychological recovery effort.

We have found that through culturally sensitive and specific psychoeducation family members can be helped to understand the typical range of reactions to trauma. By normalizing these, family members can be helped to assist more directly in the healing and recovery process. Videos depicting scenes such as the one described previously, which speak directly to the viewers' experience, help to depathologize family problems and encourage more open dialogue. This type of education serves to defuse the anger that results from personalizing traumatic reactivity. Understanding the behavioral implications of trauma can assist the nontraumatized spouse in multiple ways. For example, reframing distance within the relationship as traumatic avoidance minimizes self blame and can help partners join together in the recovery process. Often arguments can be avoided by understanding angry outbursts in the context of the trauma within the self rather than issues within the family. This information is also useful to a spouse needing to help children understand why Dad is angry or unavailable in contrast to past behavior.

REACHING OUT TO FAMILIES

In the post-9/11 FDNY environment, bringing this information to families was more complicated than one might think. First, unlike many disaster operations, where first responders are deployed to assist in the recovery effort while family members, with no direct exposure to the event, wait at home for their return, some aspect of this event was directly experienced by all family members. Exposure ranged from direct witnessing to the protracted uncertainty of the fate of one's spouse to the direct loss of close family members or friends. Yet few recognized their own trauma as they attended to the business of daily living and their concern for their surviving firefighter spouse. Second, while CSU services had always been available to family members, relatively few were aware of this. In addition, the long-standing stigma attached to seeking help prevented many family members from reaching out on behalf of themselves or their husbands. Initially, the entire community focused its emotional attention on the families of the perished, while a kind of collective survivor guilt prevented many from focusing their attention on their own family unit. Third, access to family members was difficult. While peer counselors rotated through work locations providing information to FDNY members, including information for their families, by and large little of this made its way home.

Supported by a long tradition of separation between the two firefighter families, the traumatic avoidance and desire to protect one's family made it unlikely that material describing psychological phenomenon or services would be transported from one kitchen table to the other. This left many family members completely in the dark about what, if anything, was being offered to the workforce, thereby increasing both the concern for their spouse and also their anger at the job for doing nothing. Fueled by media attention about PTSD and heightened concerns about the dangers of the job, families found themselves torn between constant ineffective confrontation and equally ineffective avoidance.

The dilemma for those on the psychological front lines was how to effectively build a bridge connecting two families that were often perceived as competing for the same scarce resource, namely the time and attention of the surviving firefighter. Efforts to reach out independently to spouses were often met by direct resistance on the part of firefighters who were suspicious of their wives coming together to talk about them or the job. Thus information communicated through the firehouse rarely made it home, and mail sent directly to the home was not only a huge and costly undertaking but also remained in the name of the employee. Outreach to the couple or family unit was designed to cut through some of these difficulties. In addition, a psycho-educational approach about the impact of trauma on relationships was important information for all, not just for spouses.

Early efforts took the form of a series of psycho-educational meetings offered in the community to anyone wishing to attend. Programs were offered during the day while children were in school and also in the evening after dinner. A panel of experts was prepared to talk about trauma and traumatic grief and help attendees understand its impact on individuals, relationships, and children. The attendance at these meetings was disappointing, however, those present did seem hungry for the information provided. This was not the first poorly attended program, nor would it be the last. It was often difficult to predict what kind of a response a program would get. Each time it left the same question: was it the wrong program or the right program delivered at the wrong time or in the wrong way?

DEVELOPING AN EFFECTIVE INTERVENTION

Contemplating this question was often worthwhile. Time and again listening attentively during program failures began to lead us toward a more effective program. Letting go of a program that seemed to not get a response and going back to further explore the need it originally attempted to meet was critical to the process of building successful programs.

In this case, the poorly attended programs in the community led us to reexamine what our clients had been saying that initially prompted the psychoeducational programs:

He's a different person than he used to be.
She doesn't understand what it's like.
He doesn't even try and talk to me.
This didn't just happen to him; it happened to all of us—the kids, too.

Surely these individuals were not unique, but rather were expressing aspects of the collective community experience. However, this was not the only voice that needed to be attended to. We also heard from the families:

He is never home; I have to do it all.
When I finally get home she has a list of things she wants me to do.
The kids miss their father; it's almost as if he died, too.

While the first set of voices led us to offer a program, perhaps the second set offered clues about why people found it difficult to get there. The dilemma was how to offer a program that people needed but were too busy or overwhelmed to attend. If we responded to the latter, people might not only attend but be more receptive to what they heard. If the message was that families were feeling disconnected, a program that helped them to reconnect could be healing on many levels.

The choice of the couple rather than the family unit was difficult. Firefighters have a long tradition of family focus; clearly the comments above spoke to the issues of parental absence. However, on the other side was a strong belief in the importance of the marital bond in promoting the security of children and setting the tone for the family. A family retreat, which we had offered to the family liaisons who were working closely with the families of the deceased, generally created a child-centered program focused around activities involving both parents and children. While time at these events was set aside for some group discussion with the adults, the focus was not the marital relationship. We opted instead to take the limited time and resources available and create a couple-centered program that would not only talk about the impact of trauma on relationships but offer a context in which couples could take this information and begin to repair the disconnection they had experienced. Supported by a grant from the *New York Times* Foundation, this was an example of a program developed through close collaboration between a CSU staff member and a specific outside consultant, Suzanne B. Phillips, PsyD, CGP. (For more on collaboration models see Chapter 4.) The first couples weekend workshop was held in July 2002. Over the next 3+ years more than 15 such weekends were held, reaching more than 400 FDNY couples.

THE COUPLES CONNECTION WEEKEND

The Couples Connection program invited 30 FDNY couples to spend 1½ days away from their home focusing on their relationship and what had happened to it in the wake of 9/11. In addition to the workshop, it offered them overnight accommodation in a Manhattan hotel along with dinner and theater. The workshop was designed to utilize all the available time to impart information and allow each couple the opportunity to process it. By building on a carefully crafted progression of dialogues, couples who arrived with little understanding or empathy for their partners' post-9/11 experience were helped to reframe the experience allowing them to enter into a different dialogue with one another. By the time the first day ended, most were able to utilize the recreational part of the program for genuine reconnection, which for many represented their first post-9/11 recreational outing as a couple.

Breakfast Program

The weekend begins at 10 a.m. with a breakfast talk about trauma and its impact on relationships. The talk is very specifically about the FDNY 9/11 experience and begins to clarify the trauma of each spouse and the possible impact on significant relationships. These commonalities help to connect those in attendance, most of whom do not know one another. This is especially helpful to the wives who unlike their husbands are unaccustomed to being with others similarly affected. It clearly states that 9/11 was traumatic not only to firefighters to but to firefighter spouses as well. It lets everyone in the room know that they are not alone and that the presenters understand their unique experience. It is this commonality that differentiates the program from more typical marriage encounter weekends. It is also what necessitates that any replication of the program be tailored to the specific experience and needs of the population being served. Consumer feedback consistently indicated this cultural specificity as an important aspect of satisfaction.

The morning program is designed to help each couple take the psycho-educational material and digest it in a way that helps them to apply it to their situation and begin to make whatever adjustments they feel are necessary in their relationship. It is not intended to address long-standing marital discord or complaints of the past. Rather, it is focused on recognizing the shifts that have occurred post-9/11 and deciding together how to address them. Couples enter this process in very different places along the connection ←→ disconnection continuum. However all report that to some degree they have not sufficiently talked about the impact of this event on themselves, their marriage, and their family life. The goal of the morning program is to help each individual process this new information in a way that allows them to enter into a different dialogue with one another.

GENDER-SPECIFIC GROUPS

Because men and women most often entered the process in a different place (the men having benefited from time and talk in the firehouse, the women most often isolated from others in their situation), the psycho-educational lecture is followed by separate men's and women's groups. The video clip described earlier is used as a trigger to begin the discussion within these groups. Comments such as *it could have been filmed in my house* are often heard. These gender-specific groups offer comfort in hearing one's experience reflected in the experience of others. They remind all participants of the comfort derived from a same-sex peer group.

Initially the men most often talked about themselves as they might at the firehouse kitchen table. They had a need to identify where they were on 9/11, the direct losses they suffered, and their role in the recovery effort. Workplace issues related to changes in the firehouse, union and departmental politics, and the good old days often emerged before a focus on home and spouse was possible. Often the male group leader had to work hard to help the men focus on how the experiences they described had impacted them in relationship to their family at home and how in turn their families might have also been affected by these powerful events. It is interesting how many of the men never realized the impact that the tragedy itself had on their spouse. They recognized the impact of their absence, but the idea that the women had been directly affected by witnessing the event on TV, losing friends, or fearing for the future was slow to come. When asked what had changed at home, some were able to recognize the impact of their anger, impatience, and withdrawal from the life they knew before. Others could not see beyond their wives' demands, complaints, and fears and held fast to an insistence that only fellow fighters could understand. These men continued to feel distant at home, often finding comfort only at work. Allowing all of these reactions to emerge within the group at times enabled the men to begin to see a different perspective. It was not simply the way a professional would view things but in fact the way another firefighter viewed them. For many this marked the beginning of a lessening of defenses that would continue throughout the program and often beyond.

In contrast to the men, the women, although strangers to one another, most often felt such relief at being with other firefighter wives that they instantly shared personal information and intense emotions. Tears were a frequent accompaniment to the extreme isolation, fear, and anger that they had held to themselves for so long. This was as true in October 2004 as in July 2002. Frequently it was the first time a wife had *told her story* recounting the long wait to learn of her husband's safety and the still longer wait for him to return home. Many felt that the man who left home that morning had yet to return and indeed might never. For others it was not the story of that day but of the many months of absence while digging at the site. They talked of men who changed clothes in the garage for fear of contaminating their families and of those who cried out in their sleep or did not sleep at all. They shared stories of memorials attended, the feelings of awkwardness when approaching the newly widowed women they had known for years, and attempts to explain the unexplainable to children afraid each time Daddy put on his uniform and went out the door. Most always the story was about the loneliness of not being able to share these feelings with their spouse due to fear, guilt, or anger that he just was unable to hear her. They felt isolated from family and friends whose lives had long ago returned to normal after the initial intensity of 9/11 wore off. Many were weary after months or years of putting the needs of others above their own and continuing to handle responsibilities that in prior years had been shared. Some had left part-time jobs that had afforded them not only additional income but often meaningful time away from the house in the company of colleagues. Uncertainty and fear for the future were typical themes that echoed in these groups, and yet it was not unusual at some point in the discussion for one of the 12 to 15 members to say, "I feel so lucky—if anything I think my marriage is stronger." This idea—that trauma also has the potential to transform, to create growth—is an important message to all. The 1 hour and 15 minutes devoted to this group is never sufficient. Still, it is important to not devote too much time to reinforcing gender differences, as the goal of the program is reconnection.

These gender-specific groups—while necessary—have the potential to po-larize the male/female experience. More often, however, they helped partici-pants to recognize that the range of human reaction to trauma and grief is not always gender specific. Not all firefighters shut down; some talked to their wives, some cried. Not all spouses wanted to hear about what it was like in the building or digging at the site, a conversation others seemed to long for. Some women appreciated their husbands' effort to protect them, while others felt angry and shut out by this behavior.

The feelings expressed in these groups were most often intense and con-veyed the difficulty that most couples faced in finding a way to communicate effectively about all that had happened. The difficulties described and the ques-tions asked are characteristic of trauma and its impact on intimate relation-ships. These were the stories that illustrated the psycho-educational material presented at breakfast, and in hearing them people began to feel less isolated and less guilty for being unable to resolve their problems alone as they were accustomed to doing previously. Now, in the safe space created by the group, they could turn to one another and ask questions such as the following:

> If he is shut down, how do you find a way in?
> If she keeps asking what it was like, how do you convey your inability to talk about it?
> How do you express what you are feeling when you don't know?
> How do you express your anger when you are feeling guilty that you should only feel joy at being alive?
> How can he/she possibly understand what it is like?

The potential value if each could hear the conversion occurring in the oppo-site gender group was immense. The question was how to make this happen in a way that maximized the opportunity to learn from others.

> I recalled sitting in the room with a handful of people at one of the commu-nity education program "failures." The presentation and discussion was in-formal given the size and mix of the group. And then it happened, at first so subtle as to almost be missed, then more clearly. Ann, the wife of a firefighter who had come to the meeting alone, listened attentively as a firefighter she had never seen before talked about his situation, and then she said, "Wow, you know my husband has been saying that to me for months and I just ig-nored him, but listening to you maybe I understand."

The idea of encouraging men and women to enter into a dialogue without the additional emotional load created by the presence of their own spouse illustrated in that room went on to become a major component of the Couples Connection program.

Mixed-Gender (Nonspouse) Groups

Following the men's and women's groups, participants are reshuffled and assigned to a male/female group but not with their spouse. These mixed-gender nonspouse groups have provided a crucial step in working toward developing understanding and empathy for the other's experience and position.

The group begins with a recap of themes reported in each of the prior gender groups. Since within the group there are members of each of the separate gender groups, it is possible to get the full range of ideas expressed earlier without focusing on any one individual's situation. Men and women are asked to listen without interruption while the opposite gender report about their group experience. During the presentations they are asked to make notes in their workbook about anything they want to ask about or return to later. This instruction is intentionally designed to demonstrate an important communication skill to be built upon later in the program when couples are asked to explore both the benefit and difficulty of listening without interruption. After both the men and women report back, the group is open for discussion and men and women are encouraged to ask questions of one another in an attempt to clarify behaviors and ideas they have found difficult to understand.

In this group when men report about not wanting to talk about their work at the site of the collapse they are likely to have their assumptions gently challenged by a woman they have never met before.

> Joe: "I don't want to tell her about what it was like down there, and I don't
> think she wants to hear."
> Karen: "Have you asked?"
> Sue: "Why don't you think we can take it? Shouldn't that be up to her?"
> Kevin: "My wife did want to hear . . . it shocked me but she did."

Even compliments don't go unchallenged. When Sean says, "I couldn't have made it through those months without her," Lois says, "Have you told her?"

As members feel safer with one another they share more of their personal experience using the members of the group to help shed light on their partners' puzzling behavior:

> Why does he talk on the phone or to the neighbor but never to me?
> I get the funerals . . . but every collation? [the food and drink offered after
> the service]
> What does she expect of me? Why can't she understand that I just need time?

Time and again, participants comment on the power of this particular part of the program in helping to shift perceptions, offer new insights, or simply help understand some basic gender differences and thus be less angry about them. For some it may offer an opportunity to practice asking a question long avoided while others find a new appreciation of their spouse who, in contrast to others, may seem less extreme in his/her reactions. At times it is the reverse.

RECONNECTING AT TABLES FOR TWO

Whatever the experience in the more than two hours they have spent apart, when asked to rejoin their spouse for lunch most have much to talk about. They are usually surprised to find the tables for two, which ensure that couples lunch together rather than break off into the greater comfort of same-sex conversations that returning to their earlier group table would encourage. The room is usually buzzing with spontaneous conversation.

For those with more strain in their relationship, there are also structured prompts to help ease or guide the conversation. Earlier in the day, by means of introduction to the weekend, each had been asked to think of a particularly positive memory related to their relationship and to guess how their spouse might respond. They are prompted at lunch to share their response; this offers those not ready to discuss the content of morning groups with a different, lighter, and more positive context for table talk.

Following lunch the couples stay at these tables and are guided through a series of communication exercises, which offer them a more structured opportunity to talk about some of the post-9/11 issues they have been thinking about throughout the day. Male and female facilitators role-play a couple using all-too-familiar poor communication skills to lighten the tone and engage the participants in giving constructive suggestions to the mock couple. The facilitators will describe and demonstrate active listening skills and then allow couples to practice the skill by applying it to something each found important to discuss with the other. Each partner is given an opportunity to begin the dialogue. The time-limited structure, while at times frustrating, provides safety along with a glimpse of a different type of dialogue. The focus of group discussion is on skill and not content. Couples are able to comment aloud about the difficulty of listening without interruption as well as the comfort in trusting that they will be listened to. This ability to process feelings and reactions without revealing content parallels an important point that is frequently made in both single-gender and mixed-gender groups. As men come to understand that it is possible to talk about their experience of 9/11 in a meaningful way without graphic detail, the dialogue between the couples opens in a new way. This idea helps support healthy boundaries, allowing couples to define for themselves what is private between them and what each is comfortable sharing with others.

Purpose of the Evening Activities

When they leave for the day at about 4 p.m. there is a feeling of having worked hard, and thus the group is sent off for the evening entertainment with an instruction to leave the heavy discussion behind and try to reconnect on a more playful level. This is one of many places where the program structure attempts to model lessons that we ask participants to take away and apply to their everyday lives. They are reminded of the importance of time alone as a couple but cautioned not to use that time to bring along a serious agenda. They are given a suggestion to tell one another something about themselves from childhood that has not been talked about before, something relatively insignificant, light, or humorous, as a way to highlight the ongoing process of discovery in marriage. No matter how well you think you know one another there is always something new to discover.

Problem Solving and Group Empowerment

The group reconvenes at 9 a.m. The task for the day is to apply the lessons of day one to a series of hypothetical situations first as a couple and then as a couples group. This problem-solving process takes situations familiar to all but by putting it outside of oneself begins to demonstrate how many different ways there are to come at a problem and begin to solve it. Spouses not only hear this from one another, but in talking with four or five other couples they begin to understand how different couples approach situations. They witness the way in which other couples talk to one another, agree, and disagree. Most often the discussion allows for a lot of self-disclosure as couples reveal their struggles to one another and take charge of the process of problem solving and recovery. The professional at the table mainly serves as a facilitator while participants talk about the lessons learned, apply new skills to the situation presented, and eventually stand before the larger group and report on their work. Ending the program in this way makes it clear that the answers lie not with the professional but rather within them and that there is much they have to give to one another.

Participant Feedback

At the conclusion of the program couples are asked for feedback about their experience and also offered additional services closer to home. Most often couples whose marriage is in serious difficulty will linger to discuss a referral.

Anyone requesting additional services is contacted within 1 week. Often times couples exchange contact information with others who live nearby. About 40 percent request some type of referral information for self, spouse, children, or couple. Almost all indicate a desire for additional workshops for couples.

Comments from Male and Female Participants

- Many of the same things were happening in other homes; I felt normal for the first time in a long while.
- My husband and I have erected walls around us and this was a giant step toward knocking them down. It won't be easy, but thank you for giving us tools we can use.
- The firehouse has always been about family, so this was a natural way to help heal from the events of 9/11.
- I loved this group [mixed-gender/nonspouse]! When the men heard my point of view as a woman, I felt I was helping his wife or girlfriend.
- The weekend put a light at the end of the tunnel for me. It has given me hope that we will get through this and be stronger because of it.

As is often the case with retreats, conferences, and so forth, the high that one feels at the end of the program is difficult to sustain. Attempts to offer briefer follow-up programs have had limited success, not for lack of interest but because they re-create the initial programming dilemma of limited time, wavering commitment, and so forth. The need to continue the Couples Connection dialogue in the current climate of uncertainty is clear, and efforts to find a packaging that meets the need are currently underway. The basic program has also been adapted to meet the specialized needs of particular groups within our population—for example, retirees and military families.

Most recently, via a mental health and wellness grant from the American Red Cross September 11th Recovery Program, we have begun to offer a range of programs to active-duty members and their families. A focus on couples is one important component of this *Community Connections* program. Couples from throughout the FDNY community are offered opportunities to come together to support one another in recognition of those aspects of their family life that are unique to first responders. Programs are teaching and supporting the importance of stress reduction, relaxation, leisure activities, and other wellness services. They will allow those interested to come together in the spirit of the Couples Connection program to continue to learn communication skills and focused dialogue techniques that support healthy marriage and, we believe, will go a long way toward helping in the aftermath of additional tragedies, be they large or small.

LESSONS LEARNED

The overall impact of 9/11 on FDNY marriages has been impossible to determine. If one looks at the general population statistics, there is no reason to think they are any different within the fire department. Since we have no preincident divorce rates there is no way to determine if they have or have not increased in the aftermath of 9/11. Regardless of the rates, it is reasonable to assume that, to the degree that trauma affects one's fundamental belief systems and world view, for some the event triggers a recommitment to appreciating what one has and for others a feeling that life is too short to continue in a less than satisfying relationship. Both of these positions have been articulated frequently in individual, marital, and group sessions. It is important to recognize that these are, and need to be, personal decisions, which should not be externally judged. However, offering access to information and services that help people understand and sort out their response to trauma in a way that allows them to make difficult decisions with a clearer understanding of what underlies the choices they make is not only possible, but necessary.

To that end, even as a solo intervention, the benefits of the Couples Connection program are clear. Important messages from the weekend are embodied in a workbook distributed to each participant that can serve as a transitional object to be looked at and utilized by the individual or couple as a reminder of the experience. The educational message, sharing of a common experience, and awareness of available services can have a significant impact on a couple's understanding and decision making in the aftermath of trauma.

The FDNY experience has a number of implications for the development of services both pre- and postdisaster. It has underscored the importance of preincident education for families as well as the importance of including the impact of trauma on the family at home in education offered to all members of the department. Including families early on recognizes not only their vulnerability to secondary traumatization but also their primary role in trauma recovery. The ability to understand what is happening to them and their families in the aftermath of disaster is a valuable tool that can help to mitigate the negative spiral that many families experienced by not recognizing problematic behaviors as trauma symptoms and not knowing how to help. A qualitative study conducted with eight surviving firefighters and their families looked at the various stressors and coping strategies of the firefighter, spouse, children, and family system. One of the important and interesting findings was the extremely high incidence of both trauma and stress among spouses. Figure 9.1 offers a conceptual model of spouse coping and underscores the importance of early intervention to support resiliency and offset chronic distress (Linkh, 2005). We believe that preincident education directed toward family members can do just that. An additional important benefit of such education

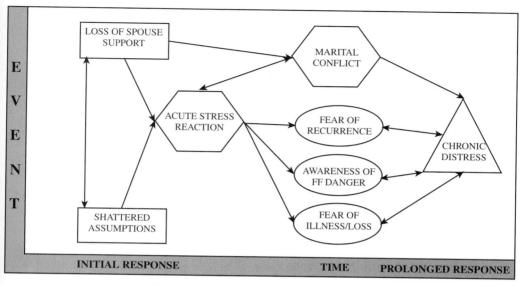

Figure 9.1 Trajectory of spousal coping.

comes from greater awareness of where to turn for psychological help when needed. Also, much of the destigmatization work done in New York post-disaster can be started during this preincident education which opens up the possibility that following an incident more people will seek help earlier, thereby decreasing suffering and increasing positive outcomes.

The experience that resulted from protracted time away from home has implications for how postdisaster work is structured. During the time that firefighters need to continue to be focused on mission, much can be done to support the family at home who in our experience felt overburdened and left behind. In light of all that has been said previously utilization of resources in support of families during this time would be well spent. Rather than seeing the family as a tertiary recipient of services (after the families of the deceased and the active-duty workforce), counselors should view the family as a primary contributor to the health and resiliency of the firefighter and, through education and support, a partner in the recovery process. Responding early on to the needs of family members, including recognition of their own trauma reactions, can maximize their potential availability to assist in the recovery of their first responder.

The Couples Connection program has demonstrated the efficacy of helping couples to reestablish contact with one another in the aftermath of disaster. This type of intervention is best introduced as early as possible following the completion of mission. It should be specifically designed for the target population keeping both organizational culture as well as specific incident experiences in mind. The program has already been used as a model for other post-9/11 populations and, we believe, can readily be adapted to different posttrauma situations. For example, working with couples returning from overseas deployment could help to facilitate family stability on return. Structuring a program around time away from the pressures of everyday life and infused with relaxation and recreation is essential. These program components should not be considered frills but therapeutic agents that add to the recovery process by reintroducing entertainment, intimacy, and escape at a critical time in the healing process. It gives permission for the couple to grieve while supporting the notion that life continues. It helps the couple to reestablish and, if necessary, begin to re-create an identity from which to move forward.

The *new normal* places firefighters and other first responders on the front line of response to terrorist threats and uncertainty on a daily basis. We cannot realistically expect families to return to their pre-9/11 level of selective attention to danger. More than ever those of us who work with this population have a responsibility to offer more extensive support services that address not only the needs of the family at work but also, increasingly, the family at home. Services targeted to couples send a powerful message of inclusion and support that recognizes the centrality of the couple as the foundation of family life and the primary support system of our workforce.

CHAPTER 10

Assisting Retirees in Transition

So here I am at Metro-Tech (HQ) on an early spring morning meeting three FDNY doctors who are going to decide my fate. My fire department journey had so many places still to go: more fires, promotion, maybe getting to work up in Harlem. Retirement just wasn't an option.—37-year-old retiree

WHEN THE LOSSES OF 9/11 WERE COMPOUNDED BY THE LOSS OF THE JOB

When you talk to firefighter candidates hoping for the opportunity to join FDNY, most will tell you that what they hear from current firefighters, both family and friends, is that "it's the greatest job in the world." This phrase, heard often from both current and past members, is reflected in the fact that while a firefighter needs only 20 years of active duty to be eligible for his pension, prior to 9/11 the average number of years worked was 27 for firefighters and even longer for officers. At that time the retirement rate averaged 300 per year. Typically retirement was an event filled with both celebration and sadness. Unlike its corporate equivalent, where a 20-year career might be marked by a plaque or watch presented by the executives, retirement rituals at the department are in the hands of individual firehouses. It is the guys you have worked with for years who plan your send-off. It is a time of reminiscing, storytelling, and laughter. For the individual leaving, regardless of number of years served or plans for the future, it is most often filled with ambivalence about leaving the firehouse family behind.

In 2002, 1,250 firefighters and officers retired from the job, more than four

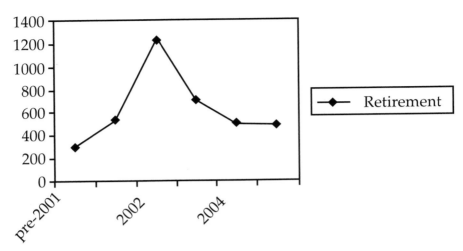

Figure 10.1 FDNY retirement rates.

times the number during the preceding year (see Figure 10.1). While this represents the highest number of retirements within one calendar year, the rates have continued to be inflated and have yet to return to their pre-9/11 level. There are multiple reasons for this dramatic increase, each of which presents different challenges to the individual, his family, and the counseling unit seeking to offer support. Economic realities played one part. During the recovery process firefighters worked a record number of hours and, given the rules of the pension system, where pension is based on income earned during the last year of service, there was an enormous financial incentive for those who had served 20 or more years at that time to retire and receive a higher pension for life. For some this economic incentive was fueled by grief, trauma, and family who feared for the future. For others not yet pension eligible, physical injury and medical conditions prevented a return to full duty in the firehouse. To not work full duty is ultimately to not work for the fire department at all. Lung disabilities of varying intensity, which were connected to the World Trade Center cleanup, often affected young men with young families who never anticipated the premature retirement that was now dumped on them. While their circumstances are different, neither of these groups had planned retirement at this time or in this way. All left the job at a time of great turmoil for both themselves and the department they loved. Some felt guilty for leaving the job and the brothers who could benefit from their expertise. Some felt relief at not having to face a department coping with such enormous loss. All were vulnerable to the combined impact of loss of social support, identity, and meaning.

Already dealing with the loss of the 343 members who died on 9/11, many of whom were the most experienced and best trained, the department faced an enormous challenge because of this record increase in retirements. Unlike the corporation that might choose to reformulate production goals during a time of major organizational transition, FDNY had no such option. The retirement rates put additional stress on a system already pressured to hire record numbers of new recruits and promote new officers, who in turn would face the challenge of training and socializing new members. The result was that less experienced officers were leading companies of less experienced men. The issues faced by these new officers were often colored by the way they were promoted. In a job steeped in tradition, a firefighter might study for years to take a promotional exam. His score determines his rank order for promotion. Given the typical slow rate of retirement, in more normal times the promotional list moves slowly. "Getting made" (being promoted to lieutenant or captain) was thus a long-awaited celebration for oneself, one's family, and friends. In contrast, in the months following 9/11, those on promotional lists were often contacted and told to report the next day for promotion. At first the speed of the promotions caused even the family to be excluded from the ceremony. While this policy was later reversed and family members were invited, there was little time for the usual preparation and celebration. A previously joyous occasion had become overnight a source of emotional conflict because the promotion was hastened by a fellow firefighter's death or illness. As one newly promoted captain said just after 9/11, "Your whole career you envision replacing some guy going off to play golf, not someone whose body has still not been recovered."

Within the firehouse the average time on the job for the most seasoned firefighter dropped during this time from 25 years to its current 15. Along with the obvious challenges involved in fire duty presented by this situation, there are a concomitant number of socialization issues as the department struggles to move forward without losing its connection to the past. Relatively junior guys were now prematurely moved into the role of senior man. In the firehouse the senior man is similar to what group workers would call the informal or indigenous leader. Unlike the officer, this is a peer whose experience fighting fires carries with it a responsibility to translate the norms and traditions of the individual firehouse to new recruits. The burden of this responsibility, now on the shoulders of less experienced men, increased as many houses experienced an unprecedented level of turnover due to death, retirement, and promotion. As the composition of the houses changed, especially those that suffered multiple losses, the traditional method of honoring and remembering the deceased members changed as well. Retirees often comment on stopping by the house and not recognizing anyone on duty, giving vivid reality to the idea that you *can't go home again.* For family members of the deceased, this phenomenon can translate to stopping by or calling the firehouse and not being recognized by the member who answers the phone as the son, spouse, or parent of a deceased member of the company. One firefighter with 11 years on the job and currently the second most senior man in the company was stunned when a new member of his house did not know the names of the six who died in the collapse of the World Trade Center. A retired firefighter commented, "In the old days, that would have been fixed on the spot, or that guy would be gone." Stories like this can be another trigger for shame and conflict over retirement for retirees who believe that the time-honored traditions of remembering the fallen have been lost with their leaving.

THE RETIREE EXPERIENCE

Retirement can be seen as a normative adult transition, most often connected with a time of life when children are grown and obligations to others minimized. Some of us dream of travel, relocation, or simply enjoying our hobbies, grandchildren, and leisure time. Others anticipate a next chapter of work, perhaps quite different from the one we are leaving. Researchers tell us that the retirement experience can lead to new goals, interests, and activities—or stress, physical deterioration, and depression (Floyd et al., 1992). Some see a disruption of a life they love, where others see challenge and opportunity. Most studies report that as many as one third of all retirees report significantly diminished satisfaction with life as measured on global adjustment indexes. These scores are influenced by factors such as perceived health, adequate levels of contact with friends, and sufficient income (Bauer & Okun, 1983). Those who did not think about retirement ahead of time and anticipate its impact appear to have higher levels of depression and frustration afterwards (Walker et al., 1980).

To understand these differences it is useful to consider three Cs related to retirement: connection, context, and control (see Figure 10.2). *Connection* refers to the connection between one's work and sense of identity. It can be thought of as the difference between a job and a career or profession. The more the individual identifies himself as a member of his profession, the more difficult the retirement transition. In short, the more *who we are* is connected to *what we do*, the greater the loss at the time of retirement. *Context* refers to the circumstances surrounding the retirement that affect both the meaning and the impact of the event for the individual. How retirement comes about will have a bearing not only on the immediate adjustments required but on the long-range impact as well. *Control* refers to the issue of choice in the timing of retirement. By all accounts those who choose retirement at a particular point in time do better than those for whom retirement is premature and forced regardless of the reason. Within this division, those who retire for health-related

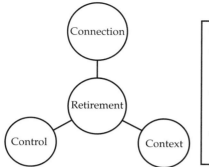

Three Cs Impacting Retirement
- *Connection: How much of your identity was connected to work?*
- *Context: What were the circumstances surrounding the retirement event?*
- *Control: How much choice did the individual have in the decision to retire?*

Figure 10.2 Variables impacting retirement.

reasons consistently report the most stress and adjustment difficulty (Quick & Moen, 1998).

Applying these principles to the situation of the post-9/11 firefighter retirees confirms the idea of them as a high-risk group. For most firefighters, work is not a job but a calling and way of life. It is who they are and how they identify themselves; it is proudly displayed on their clothing and most often how they are known to their neighbors. Leaving such a job can be difficult in the best of times, but doing so in the context of loss, suffering, and rebuilding can be particularly gut-wrenching. Social support is a significant element in trauma recovery, and for most people, work functions as a significant source of social support. When trauma and loss are connected to work and one is separated from that work, a significant healing element is lost. Throughout this volume we have talked about the social support that the kitchen table gives firefighters both historically and specifically in the aftermath of 9/11. The loss of this mediating environment for retirees was significant. Those who left just after the closing of the site and especially those unable to return immediately to full duty after the event were at risk for increased levels of psychological distress as a result of the premature loss of their firefighter family (Cowman et al., 2004; Fullerton et al., 1992).

Many who chose retirement in the face of strong economic incentive were not spared the feelings associated with walking away from a department greatly in need of their expertise. For those who had no choice in leaving, due to illness or injury, the separation was complicated by the additional loss of physical strength that is so much a part of the firefighter persona. Whether retirement was voluntary or forced, planned or premature was not always so clear-cut. Is it voluntary if economics make it impossible to stay or family pressure dictates leaving? Is it premature if you leave 6 months or 1 year prior to your original plan? Are you making a sound decision and clear choice when grief and loss cloud your view so that the job you used to love is at times beyond recognition? What if you leave because you just find it too painful to return to work where you are surrounded by empty lockers, memorials, and young probies you just don't have the energy to get to know?

THE STAY CONNECTED PROGRAM

One indication of the strong connection between the retiree community and FDNY occurred in the aftermath of 9/11 when scores of retirees turned out to help. Indeed, three retirees who showed up to help after the plane crashed into the towers actually died in the event along with their active-duty brothers. Retired officers showed up at headquarters to help man the phones set up to respond to family members. Others reported to their old firehouse to cover nonfirefighting duties and to free their brothers to work at the site. Still others volunteered to work as peers, helping CSU in its outreach efforts not only immediately after the event but even now, 4 years later. Many of these members had been retired for years; many had meaningful work they were involved in. Several lived outside of New York City. They returned to New York as one returns to be with family upon hearing of the death of a relative. They attended funerals, assisted families, and in many other ways helped to fill the gaps created by a depleted workforce.

Working hand in hand with these retirees provided an opportunity to learn more about their experience in retirement. How had leaving the job they loved affected them and their families? Often they described a cycle of initial honeymoon followed by a period of disenchantment and relative isolation. They talked of the need for family adjustment, especially with spouses who had long ago established their routines at home or, in contrast, had more recently begun to focus on their own careers. Those retirees who were young and had left the job following an injury typically described a more difficult transition into a meaningful next chapter.

As the retirement statistics began to climb after 9/11, each of these retired peers began to express concern about the future of those leaving the job during such a traumatic time. They worried about the typical pattern of honeymoon ← → disenchantment and what this would look like for those carrying the additional burden of trauma and loss. They wondered how the guys would receive help while separated from the kitchen table that was the center of outreach and education about signs, symptoms, and available services. CSU listened.

Even the typical firehouse send-off had been altered in the wake of 9/11. In houses where several men might be retiring around the same time, parties were no longer individualized but rather lumped together in a way that unintentionally minimized the significance of the event. The combined abruptness of the decision and departure left many on the other side of the firehouse door without fully absorbing the magnitude of the event and its likely impact on self and family. The belief that the pain of 9/11 could be left behind along with the job added to the difficulty in a number of ways. Often retirees were slow to recognize or connect difficulties to the ongoing trauma and grief, finding it hard to separate reactions to 9/11 from reactions to retirement. Often, the initial relief of being away from the daily reminders in the firehouse was replaced by a feeling of isolation from those whose experience most closely reflected one's own. Without the daily contact there was no one to help make those connections or confront the feelings in a way that only people who have endured the same trauma can. Firefighters are very good at confronting each other with respect; they could and would call one another on denying the pain related to all that had transpired. The loss of a structured place for meaningful conversation among brothers suggested that each retired firefighter ran the risk of isolation, a main contributor to problems in the aftermath of both trauma and retirement.

The *Stay Connected* program was developed by CSU to address the loss of social support that accompanied retirement from the firehouse. It specifically sought to mitigate the potential for isolation as new retirees sought to avoid traumatic reminders of the multiple losses they experienced in the wake of 9/11. Research consistently tells us that it is the individual's ability to mobilize adequate coping skills in the face of life transitions and/or trauma that has the greatest impact on resiliency. Thus, a main goal of the Stay Connected program was to shore up individual coping skills by developing transitional activities targeted to the central elements lost through retirement: peer support, meaningful activity, source of income. Which loss was experienced as central varied for individual firefighters depending upon both the circumstance of their retirement and their current life situation.

- Single retirees faced a different situation than those with a strong intact family.
- Retirees whose social life had always revolved around firehouse activities had a different experience from those with a broader circle of friends and activities.
- Those with a side job they always intended to move into at retirement had a different experience from those who tolerated their side job as a means of making ends meet.
- Those with a formal education who may have considered other careers in the past had a different experience from those who dreamed of becoming a firefighter from their childhood on.
- Those with physical injury or health-related concerns faced uncertainty unknown by those who remained physically fit.

- Those still experiencing trauma symptoms found it more difficult to process this additional loss and needed first to work through their traumatic reminders.
- Those separated from the job years before they ever imagined faced a different scenario than those who had come closer to their original plan.
- Those with financial concerns had a different experience from those with a stable and adequate income.

Attempts to reach out to this varied population necessitated broad programming initiatives that spoke to each of these central concerns. Different from the pre-9/11 retiree organizations, which were organized geographically by peers and primarily social in focus, Stay Connected utilized social and recreational activities to engage retirees into a network that could help to assess and address needs across the broader bio-psycho-social spectrum.

REACHING THE RETIREES

Outreach began by Stay Connected staff attending the retirement seminars organized by the fire department to assist members with their many questions about pension, benefits, and so forth. This preexisting program had increased in frequency to meet the demand post-9/11. It was not uncommon for someone contemplating retirement to attend more than one such meeting, and often they brought their wives to help absorb the complicated financial benefit information. This provided one of the best ways to interface with members before the transition into retirement was complete. It attached a face to the Stay Connected name that would appear on information mailed to all newly retired members. In the earliest days of the program, these meetings provided opportunities for the needs assessment process that helped to shape future content.

Organized around vocational, educational, emotional, recreational, and social interests, the program took a something-for-everyone approach. Attendance goals were modest. Some events were offered in local areas, some were centralized. Unlike other population subgroups of CSU, most retirees had time to fill and were willing to travel. They missed the camaraderie of the firehouse and loved to sit together and talk. Typical of firefighters, they were open to a wide range of programs that brought them together with other firefighters. They enthusiastically encouraged one another to attend events where they could meet new friends and connect with old ones.

Social support in the firehouse is ubiquitous, and its loss constitutes one of the most obvious potential problems for new retirees. While the inflated rate of retirement increased the likelihood that an individual retiree knew of others retiring at about the same time, this did not necessarily create an effective barrier to social isolation. Interaction with retired peers necessitated taking the initiative to organize and plan activities. The energy required to do this was often lacking in those dealing with the multiple losses that were an unfortunate and unwelcome part of the post-9/11 retirement package.

In an effort to reduce the risk of depression, anxiety, and other mental health problems, Stay Connected made it easier to remain involved with other retirees by replacing some of the social opportunities that the firehouse had provided in the past, such as luncheons and barbecues around the kitchen table, tickets to ball games, boat trips, and other outings. Attendance at such events was risk free, not a statement of need anymore than attending a company picnic. It did not publicly label retirees as a group at risk for anxiety, depression, and mental health or adjustment problems. The Stay Connected program recognized retirement as a normal life transition that happened to come at an abnormal time. The events the program offered were fun while also providing multiple opportunities for needs assessment. They played to the buddy system by offering retirees a chance to reach out to one another, especially to those who seemed to be having a difficult time. It is easy to suggest going to a ball game or a picnic, but it is more difficult to broach the subject of attending a support group or a workshop addressing a potential problem.

While all offerings served a social function by bringing retirees together in groups, some were specifically designed to address vocational, educational, or emotional needs. Others were more difficult to categorize and, consistent with a holistic view of the individual, considerable overlap existed. Those most hungry for socialization with peers might attend a vocational program, although perhaps less for the content than the contact. In this way, retirees were often exposed to information and had areas of interest awakened that perhaps would have never been tapped.

Finding meaningful activity to replace employment is important for everyone but perhaps even more so for those who had chosen service to others as their life's work. It is a need that exists apart from the need for income, and for this reason Stay Connected helped retirees explore career opportunities as well as volunteerism and community participation. It offered skill training, such as computer classes, that could be applied either vocationally or for personal interest. Those looking for a second career were offered career change workshops and résumé writing and job search classes along with personal vocational assessment sessions. Additional information on pursuing specific career opportunities attractive to many, such as nursing, was made available in collaboration with local resources.

In addition to information about the vast array of volunteer opportunities available in the city, specific opportunities within FDNY were developed. These included the selection and training of additional CSU peers, who continued to provide outreach to both active and retired FDNY members; Big

Brothers to serve as mentors to children who lost fathers on 9/11; and the Helping Hand Program, which utilized the skills of retirees to assist widows with home repairs.

Through interaction at social and vocational programs, other needs began to emerge. Firefighters are an interesting mix of those who have used their unusual work schedule to pursue other interests and avocations over the years and those who had busied themselves with side jobs and responsibilities without ever taking time to explore genuine interests. Suddenly having time to pursue hobbies and interests is fine for those with clear inclinations. Others felt lost and uncertain as to where to begin. While perhaps normative of the transition to retirement, these feelings are intensified when retirement is sudden. Much like the college freshman asked repeatedly what he plans to do with his life, the retiree often feels pressure to define this next chapter long before having had an opportunity to take stock of himself and his new situation. For this reason Stay Connected began to offer activities that encouraged self-exploration. These took several forms, from the more traditional individual and group counseling available at CSU to writing workshops, cooking classes, and support groups. Reminiscence, especially through writing, was not just about 9/11. More often it became a vehicle to recall many aspects of firehouse life: the kitchen table, cooking a meal, the firehouse dog. This process helped many to replace their last firehouse memories, often filled with the pain of 9/11, with those of earlier, happier times on the job. Never pressured to connect writing to the job, some took the opportunity to recall childhood events or connect with the person they were before *firefighter* became the main label of identity. This was particularly important for those seeking to establish a new identity in retirement.

Reminiscing with other firefighter retirees would sometimes reawaken the trauma and loss of 9/11 as well as other tragedies experienced on the job, which most often remained just out of awareness. It would be a mistake to consider this a negative aspect of the program since these memories frequently created an obstacle to fully embracing a new chapter of life. Talking with others minimized the traumatic avoidance that can ultimately lead to a reliance on problematic coping strategies or PTSD. The informal group has the potential to serve as a holding environment for the memories and affect related to the horrific event that all firefighters shared. As in the firehouse, you can tell as much or as little of your story as you like, you can stay in the room or leave when you choose, you are connected to one another by both the trauma membrane shared by all who experienced the event from a particular perspective and the Brotherhood that creates safety and support for all who are within (Lindy, 1985). Retirement talk was of course inextricably connected to the events that preceded and directly or indirectly caused it. Discussion groups, both formal and informal, often started with one theme and led quickly to the other. Retirees themselves were often surprised at how much was still there, unspoken and at times unfelt. With time, trust, and reconnection to the department via Stay Connected, those who needed to directly process more of this experience were encouraged and able to do so with professional help provided by CSU counselors.

COUPLES

The retirement literature is filled with material about the issues that couples have to deal with during this important life transition. If one spouse retires, both retire from a way of life that they had become accustomed to. It is typical for spouses to experience difficulty working out new rhythms of life. Schedules are different, turf issues within the house are frequent, and the balance between separation and togetherness often needs to be reworked.

Firefighter couples have adjusted over the years to the peculiarities that the firehouse schedule demands. While these demands are often difficult to adjust to early in a marriage, spouses for the most part not only become accustomed to the irregular hours and overnight tours but come to welcome them. They create their own rhythm and activities, which are suddenly thrown into chaos when retirement occurs. Again, this is especially true when retirement is unexpected, potentially filled with emotional conflict, and at times unwelcome and out of sync with the developmental stage of life for the couple and family.

Most firefighter couples entered retirement with all of the post-9/11 baggage described elsewhere in this text. Many had yet to recuperate from the disconnection created during the months of intense firehouse focus just after 9/11. Suddenly they found themselves no longer involved in trying to reestablish equilibrium lost during the post-9/11 period but instead trying to adjust to an entirely new chapter of life. All of the variables discussed earlier affected how the couples navigated the transition. Even wives who were in favor of retirement often held back from expressing this preference, feeling strongly that this was his decision to make and one she did not want to risk being blamed for later. Those who found their young, able-bodied husbands suddenly dealing with limited mobility, most frequently related to pulmonary problems, faced a myriad of daily problems but also, and more important, an enormous fear for an uncertain future.

Within the larger group, there were as many individual adjustment dilemmas as there were marriages. Though often unspoken between spouses, it was typical to find the women carrying the emotional burden for the family and often not recognizing the ways in which this was adding to her stress and/or depression.

- Some wives fled to work, happy to have something of their own to escape to, while others resented leaving sleeping husbands behind while still getting up each morning to face the old routine.
- Some wives happily surrended control of the kitchen, shopping, and laundry, while others felt criticized as if their way of handling things all these years was suddenly not good enough.
- Some told stories of rearranged kitchens, early morning *shopping drills*, and new rules imposed on old routines.
- Those with kids still at home had to renegotiate parenting roles and routines, sometimes feeling that the kids had become the new *probies*, given orders or teased beyond what felt comfortable.
- Some wives felt their alone time was gone forever, including one who described her newly retired spouse following her to the diner where she was having coffee with friends.
- Some wives could not resist the temptation to ask, "What are you going to do today?" while others developed lists of household repairs long enough to keep their husbands busy and unable to think about the future for months or years to come.

For all of these reasons Stay Connected did not limit its programming to the retirees alone but began gradually offering discrete events for both couples and spouses. A *Couples Connection* weekend specifically for retirees was developed following the same format as that described earlier but including education about the potential impact of retirement on marriage. (For more on this program see Chapter 9.) It stressed the idea that while retirement can be traumatic, it need not be. It normalized the reactions that couples have and addressed the complexity of facing retirement with the backdrop of trauma and loss created by 9/11. As with the original program, it offered couples a structure within which to safely discuss some of their transition experiences utilizing new skills.

There were a few notable differences in the retiree weekends. The men particularly were hungry to talk. Their desire for contact with other firefighters was palpable. They shared resources and promoted other Stay Connected programs with those they met on the weekend. The wives told their stories with a mixture of tears and laughter. Their need to talk was clear. This was a different group of wives with different stories to tell. Many still had not given voice to their 9/11 experience, now complicated by the transition into retirement. Sometimes these stories were distinct and separate, other times intertwined; both stories were important and needed to be expressed, heard, and understood.

Requests for additional opportunities for wives to get together were responded to with luncheons, support groups, and wellness days featuring acupuncture, message, reflexology, and so forth. Keeping wives informed of activities available to the men helped to encourage reluctant retirees to participate. It was important for spouses to know what was available, how to distinguish between normal transitional behavior and more problematic responses, and ultimately how to get help when needed. In response to some of what was learned in both the weekend groups and the separate activities, couples were also offered workshops that stressed collaboration and enjoyment of new activities. Cooking classes and wellness events for couples were among the favorites. These programs helped couples shift from feeling confused and overwhelmed by available time and lack of structure and offered opportunities to add to their repertoire of enjoyable couple activities.

LESSONS LEARNED

Underlying the Stay Connected story is a difficult question. In a world of scarce resources, to what degree should the organization take responsibility for its retired members? There is no right answer to this question. Presumably it is via pension, benefits, and often union membership that retirees remain connected to and cared for by the organization they are leaving. When retirement is connected directly to work, this is reflected in the pension allotment via disability.

Why then choose to offer so much more? How does the experience of Stay Connected help to inform this choice? In many ways Stay Connected is a preventive program and as such its real effectiveness will never be known. Are there ways in which Stay Connected benefits the current and future organization? Part of the answer relates to those who chose to remain on the job during this difficult period of rebuilding. For them, watching some of their retired brothers deteriorate and feeling that there was no appropriate FDNY resource in place to help would have been demoralizing. Another part of the answer is embedded in the earlier discussion regarding the family culture of the department. How FDNY, or any organization, treats this generation of retirees, given the difficult circumstance of their separation, lives on in the legacy that remains for those who consider membership or become members in the future. It is part of the story of *the greatest job in the world.*

Looking forward, the experience reminds us that even in normal times retirement for first responders is most often not in sync with the typical developmental cycle. Firefighting is often talked about as a young man's job because of its physicality; most come on the job at a relatively young age, and thus even after 20+ years of service, they are relatively young at retirement. Perhaps even more important for this discussion is the reality that the dangers faced during that career increase the possibility that any individual responder might face a premature, forced retirement. This raises the question of the role and responsibility of the organization via its employee assistance program to help members consider and perhaps prepare for this possibility in lieu of its occurrence even under less extreme conditions than those created in the aftermath of 9/11.

Once the commitment to provide service to retirees is made, the lessons on how to deliver them are more straightforward:

- Enter naturally by replacing the social support that is lost with retirement.
- Recognize that there is tremendous strength in the informal group and thus all types of activities have therapeutic value.
- When possible, help people through the transition by starting before the actual retirement occurs.
- It is never too late to reach out to retirees who have not had a successful transition since to them *the job* is still their best chapter.
- Include family members as part of the transition; their lives change, too.
- Normalize and support the idea of uncertainty, exploration, and floundering as a necessary and important part of the journey. Don't push for a plan prematurely.
- Don't underestimate the need to reprocess trauma and loss before forging a new identity is possible.
- Develop meaningful ways for retirees to contribute to the current organizational situation through either volunteer, paid, or stipend positions.
- Involve retirees in planning for the future—their own and that of the organization.

As we get further from the event it is likely that funding for extensive retiree programming will eventually be limited. In anticipation of this, it is important to remember that CSU had previously extended core services to those retirees who requested them. What has changed in the post-9/11 period is the extensive outreach and the fuller array of services, especially in the social and vocational areas. Hopefully, retiree numbers will gradually return to pre-9/11 levels, and concern for those who left in the wake of 9/11 will diminish because those in need of help receive it. In the past, retirees were not differentiated but rather folded into the existing CSU services. In all likelihood this represents the future direction and is not inconsistent with one goal of all trauma treatment, which is to dissolve the trauma membrane and enable the larger community to reunite. Inclusion of retirees in programs offered to the active-duty community allows for the best possible mix of experience and expertise between retirees and new recruits, including the value of having retiree spouses assist younger women in acculturating to the department and accepting the two-family model. It is akin to the gathering of the extended family network, where all come together yet at times separate by gender and generation for sharing advice, confidences, and camaraderie. For CSU it continues to keep a cadre of knowledgeable, supportive members available to be called upon as peers when needed.

Assisting firefighters and their families with the transition into healthy retirement is an important and valuable function for CSU to maintain and one that should be considered by other employee assistance programs. Targeting services to the larger community whenever possible does not preclude the development and support of a network solely composed of retirees with both a social and vocational purpose. Ideally such a support network can ultimately be largely peer driven and supported, thus requiring only limited funding to sustain its existence within CSU. In this way outreach and support to new retirees can continue and include mechanisms that serve as an ongoing source of needs assessment for future program development at CSU.

CHAPTER 11

Conclusion

T his book is entitled *Crisis Counseling*—a term used to describe many activities performed by caring peer and professional helpers in the aftermath of large-scale disaster. This broad application leaves the space necessary to creatively design a response to meet the unique challenges of each event and each affected population. However, it can also be a misnomer because *crisis* to many connotes immediate and short-term response. In contrast, our experience and belief, consistent with that of our colleagues in Oklahoma City and other response locations, is that postdisaster *crisis counseling* services need to remain available to the most affected populations over a long period of time and be creatively developed, adapted, and applied to each population during that time.

Looked at in this light, crisis counseling encompasses a very broad range of services, which begin with the early interventions that offer support and education in the form of psychological first aid and continue with other on-site services that allow first responders to continue to focus on the ongoing mission. However, over time more is needed, and crisis counseling must then be able to incorporate the more traditional psychotherapeutic, individual, and group interventions known to effectively treat Acute Stress Disorder (ASD), Posttraumatic Stress Disorder (PTSD), and the related anxiety and depressive disorders associated with exposure to catastrophic events. Most people do not readily embrace mental health intervention in the aftermath of disaster. In fact, many believe that somehow nature has automatically provided the most efficient means to recover from them. While natural resilience does exist, it is perhaps unreasonable to expect that many of those closest to such events would not benefit from the conscious efforts of those trained to help. Our experience has been that there is much that can be done in the early stages postdisaster to help those affected begin to recognize, trust, and utilize the help that is available. There are ways of helping that work, other ways that can be useless or even harmful, and others not yet studied enough to be conclusive. Each community has its own natural strengths and support systems. Our work has shown that helpers trained and available to work in concert with these internal systems can make the process of recovery better. We believe that our reflections on providing crisis counseling to a large population of first responders and bereaved family members over a period of 4 years may serve to further illuminate this process and point to directions for further study.

Providing crisis counseling, as described previously, has indicated the value of moving quickly to support and educate but more slowly to label, diagnose, or pathologize. Offering needed mental health services while simultaneously supporting the first responders need to focus on the mission of searching for remains, memorializing the dead, and attending to the needs of their families has resulted in an impressive amount of healing. At the same time, firefighters have demonstrated their capacity to recognize when psychological treatment is needed for themselves, their coworkers, and their families and to accept those services when offered in a culturally sensitive, and geographically convenient, manner. Fortunately, good treatments exist for many of the troubling symptoms that erupt posttrauma. People can often obtain relief from trauma-related sleeplessness, nightmares, hypervigilence, intrusive cognitions, and a host of other discreet problems through well-researched treatments and medications. One indication of the effectiveness of our approach of titrating the level of intervention based on the time postdisaster and the ongoing mission is the increased utilization of the different services available through CSU during different phases of the recovery period. Beginning from a perspective of significant stigma attached to utilization of mental health interventions, 7,684 members of the FDNY workforce have used CSU services between September 11, 2001, and June 2005.

Special concerns emerge when you have multiple deaths that occur under catastrophic circumstances. In our experience this often leads to a protracted bereavement process that is further complicated when the remains of the deceased are not fully recovered and the changed sociopolitical landscape is filled with pervasive reminders, including the seemingly never ending stream of memorials, funerals, and tributes to the fallen heroes. We found it was important and beneficial to help children and adolescents in particular, but adults as well, gain a sense of control over intense emotions, especially in the weeks and months immediately following the event. At that time emotional overwhelm was never very far away and helping to develop containment strategies was more important than initially recognized. An aspect of this in need of additional study is a better understanding of the interaction between trauma and grief and the development of methods to address both simultaneously.

Every disaster, like every person, needs to be appreciated for its uniqueness. No preset formula exists for providing mental health services for large-scale tragedies that would relieve the demands on those in leadership positions from having to make hard choices and find creative solutions. While the conditions faced by CSU in the aftermath of 9/11 were extreme and often unique, as previously stated, we believe that several of these event characteristics are likely to be repeated in other situations and have multiple implications for those responding.

PROTRACTED TIME LINES

Large-scale events are apt to have protracted time lines that vary for different members of the community who are called on to respond. One implication of this is a need to apply a diagnosis of PTSD with caution if the *DSM* continues to utilize a *time from exposure* criterion. In the situation of 9/11, firefighters' exposure began and ended at different times depending upon when they first appeared on scene, how long they remained, and how late into the 9 month recovery period they continued to work at the site. The personal losses each suffered and their involvement with the family of the deceased and the recovery of remains also sometimes altered the calculation of their time from exposure. The impact of multiple and ongoing exposure that results from searching for and handling the remains of known members of one's community needs further study to help inform those faced with making such decisions. This may be especially complicated within those communities where culture dictates the importance of performing this task from within rather than delegating it to others.

For families, the enormity of the event, which resulted in confusion and uncertainty in the earliest time after the event as to who was missing and when notification would occur, set the stage for a protracted period of disbelief and departure from the more normative sequence of events that follow the always devastating news of a line-of-duty death. How to handle the rituals that begin to help one move toward acknowledgement of the loss in the absence of remains opened a virtual Pandora's box of questions, dilemmas, and unprecedented challenges that continue today, 4 years later, as the voices of the deceased return on tapes released worldwide. There were also concurrent stresses, such as the birth of a firefighter's child after 9/11, or the heart attack of the firefighter's best friend post-9/11, as well as previous experiences of trauma and loss that increased the intensity of stress responses and required more time to react. These realities suggest a need for caution in applying preexisting concepts or diagnoses related to the trajectory of the process of grief and bereavement.

COMMUNITY OF GRIEVERS

Large-scale disasters will continue to leave behind a large population of grievers with different relationships to the event and the deceased. Our experience has shown that each of these groups needs separate and specialized attention beginning immediately following the event and continuing long after. Supporting each group, we believe, can help to legitimatize the lengthy struggle to find new meaning in life and hopefully can help minimize the disruption in family relationships that often creates painful secondary losses for all. However, as strong homogeneous support groups develop, care must be taken to assist members in remaining connected to their preexisting support networks. The *community of grievers* is after all a temporary community created to assist but not replace the individual's closest family and friends.

The challenges faced by young widows left to raise children on their own call for the development of interventions that are sensitive to the increased demands of single parenthood and designed to build competence and confidence in this domain. Our experience has been that offering in-home support to both parent and child sends a powerful message that works toward strengthening and restabilizing the new family unit. Rather than respond to the understandable anxiety about their children's well-being, experienced by many mothers at such times, by sending the child out to see a therapist, the person who provides the intervention enters the life space of the family by going into the home and helps to create confidence in the mother as head of household.

The protracted time spent separated from family during the months following 9/11, when firefighters continued digging at the site and attending multiple memorials and funerals, took its toll on family relationships. Based on this experience we would recommend that efforts be made to support connections between first responders and their families while mission is ongoing, including designing work schedules to accommodate the continuation of some normative family involvement whenever possible. The importance of significant relationships in healing from trauma, well documented from many sources, has been supported by our experience. We have also observed that disconnection can result from protracted separation between life partners. While the support from within the work community is significant, as illustrated throughout this text, it can be counterproductive to enhance this support at the expense of the personal family unit where a different and often deeper level of healing can occur.

CRISIS COUNSELING OVER THE LONG HAUL

It is perhaps easier to recognize and respond to some of the early signs, symptoms, and stressors that emerge in the aftermath of disaster than to recognize and understand the nuances of the delayed onset of symptoms and the later-stage issues of recovery and reconstitution that emerge over time. Careful postevent investigation can help us learn more about what types of interventions help whom and when, and may help us also to deploy mental health resources in the most effective and efficient manner. In the absence of such studies we do know from our experience that the need for help does not go away 1, 2, or even 4 years later. Some firefighters are just now reaching out for help for symptoms that may have been present intermittently throughout this time or for others that have just emerged. There is much yet to be learned about the delayed onset of symptoms and their various triggers.

Other responders continue to need help to work through their reactions to this life altering event. Not all trauma recovery is related to disturbing trauma symptoms. The existential sequelae of trauma can continue to surface and disrupt the enjoyment of life years after the event. Healing existential wounds that have shattered fundamental assumptions about life or left one with unanswerable questions about their survival does not come early or easily and does not necessarily end neatly at a discreet point in time. Crisis counseling that is successful in reducing the stigma of accepting help must remain available for those struggling to integrate the traumatic event into the narrative of their life in order to understand not only how one has changed, but how one will go on.

There is to date little understanding or appreciation of the complexity of the later tasks of grief. The experience from the Family Program suggests that for these widows the process was a continuous back-and-forth—or oscillation—of trauma, grief, positive memories, reorganization/restoration, and identity restructuring. The processes of reorganization/restoration and identity restructuring became increasingly prominent over time. Yet the stress, complexity, and pain of these later phases have not been fully recognized for this young adult population. As a consequence, widows sometimes thought they were still grieving 4 years later rather than understanding they were confronting a difficult process of reorganizing their lives and determining how this experience has changed their views of themselves and their future and how they will create a satisfying life for themselves and their family. As is true for most young mothers, the identity as the wife of the husband is a strong one that is not easy to alter. Grief still occurs intermittently, but the major stress may relate to these later difficult personal and interpersonal challenges. It is important to support this as a legitimate part of *crisis counsel-*

ing and not cut it short, inadvertently contributing to the crisis of identity restructuring.

Given the long-term needs that appear to emerge for those populations most affected by large-scale disaster, it would be beneficial to understand more about patterns of utilization of mental health services. Indicating that crisis counseling needs to be available for the long haul is not to say that all who access such services do so for the long haul, although clearly some do. In our experience there are different patterns of service utilization that need to be better understood. Many clients used treatment intermittently as new issues emerged or old ones reappeared in new form. When this occurs, it would be a mistake to question the need for further treatment as related to 9/11, although clearly establishing this link is more difficult and often takes longer as one moves further from the event. Leaving treatment following symptomatic relief should not automatically be interpreted as resistance but rather often seemed multidetermined, especially within a population unaccustomed to, and still not fully comfortable with, utilizing psychotherapy. The process of working through an event of such devastating nature is likely to have a lifelong impact on some. It is not typical, or advisable, for most individuals to enter treatment for life, but it may be beneficial to them to be able to access treatment that is familiar and safe, as needed. This phenomenon changes the traditional concept of the availability of the therapist to concerns of an individual or family moving forward in time. People could reengage with different parts of the service system at different times and leave and reenter as needed. This is not inconsistent with suggestions from current research on bereavement interventions that recommend longer-term engagements with varying intensity of contact (Jordan & Niemeyer, 2003). It is not clear what the optimal level of involvement is, but variability seems useful and patterns of utilization and satisfaction need further study. It is important to recognize that this presents a challenge to providers whose livelihood may be dependent on predictable client contact. Through recognition of these potentially conflicting needs, there is no reason a compromise could not be developed that would address both.

PUBLIC VERSUS PRIVATE MOURNING

Finally there is much still to learn about the impact, both positive and negative, of media coverage of large-scale catastrophic events on those most directly impacted as well as those vicariously affected. Suggestions have been made by others (Malkinson et al., 2005) that the general public, personally bereaved, and other highly affected individuals may be negatively affected by multiple public memorials. For both survivors and families, the media experience can be a rocky and emotional journey. Even as we write, we are facing not only the fourth-anniversary media coverage, but also the more profound impact of the release of the FDNY dispatch tapes and interview transcripts of the responders to the events of 9/11. As we read these media accounts our experience suggests the need for greater sensitivity to this issue along with further study of ways to educate, advocate for affected families, and resolve competing agendas.

One dilemma of a highly public event is responding to the needs of the larger affected community and the needs of individuals who suffer more personal losses. Needs of one group may conflict with the other. Trained to always attend a line-of-duty funeral, many firefighters in the early months went directly from their work at the site to not one, but often two, memorials in a single day. This not only increased their exposure but eliminated opportunities for much needed rest and reconnection with their family. Similarly, shocked by the deaths of so many firefighters, widows felt obligated to stand in for their husbands by attending the memorials of friends. Some of the adolescents were the earliest to say after the first anniversary, "This is too much, we don't want to be 9/11 kids any more." By the second anniversary most bereaved relatives, including the firefighters' widows, were assertive about their need for a more private and low-key anniversary service, and city officials responded. Mothers began to think about how many memorials, street namings, and family gatherings they and their children needed to attend and gave permission for children to attend briefly, if at all. In the fourth year it became more common for families to plan memorials independently based on their previous years' experience and the current requests of children.

Over time, the media seemed to flip-flop in their coverage of firefighters between hero and villain. Initially they lavished praise on them for their heroic service. But in the second year they began to critique them, searching for and highlighting behaviors they deemed unbecoming of a hero. The wives were also initially honored as grieving widows and then critiqued as "merry widows" when they did things the media deemed unbefitting of grief, such as spending money or dating. At times they implied that the somewhat atypical behaviors of a few were descriptive of the entire group, which offended the widows and children, but there was no venue for correcting the emerging stereotype or distortion. Sometimes the media seemed unaware that the message was heard not only by the public, but by the grieving family and children as well. Often the entire community felt upset, adding to its stress load, which was already at its maximum.

We came to believe that it was critical for these differences between perspectives of highly impacted individuals and the larger community to be understood and accepted. Furthermore, increased collaboration with representatives of the families, the responders, and the media may help to inform them of the negative impact of their image manipulation on the most vulnerable victims of the disaster.

THE VALUE OF PRE-PLANNING

We believe that elements of the principles that proved critical to our work can be considered *now,* ahead of time, rather than in response to the next terrible event. You can, we believe, size up your community and in so doing be better positioned if that day should arrive. Whatever community you represent, your constituency is known to you. A given incident may affect all or only some members, but you can begin to think about who might be included. Based on our experience we would encourage you to think broadly about this, not only targeting those who are directly affected but also those who are included in the natural support systems of the affected. Services targeted early on, both pre- and postincident, to these natural helpers can aid in recovery in the aftermath of an event.

We found that making knowledgeable people available to visit a person's home or workplace allowed a large number of people to utilize helping resources. Many reported satisfaction with this system of service delivery. This process allows people to begin to develop trust so that when they are ready for more traditional services they know where, when, and who will be providing them. Bringing education and support directly to firefighters at work enabled them to keep working while monitoring themselves and one another for signs that a break was needed. When time was needed it was given seamlessly by CSU without stigma, bureaucratic procedure, or repercussion. We believe these factors were significant in only 6.3 percent of the FDNY workforce being taken off line for mental health reasons from September 11, 2001, to June 2005, while more than 45 percent had utilized services through CSU during this same period of time.

While the specific site of a future event cannot be known preincident, there will likely be one or more sites that are the epicenter of any large-scale event. Where might yours be located? How will you reach them? This is less a geographic question and more a functional one. It speaks to thinking ahead about possible on-site locations including workplace, home, disaster site, and so forth, and the elements that might be necessary and challenging to effectively provide services within them. The commitment to bringing services to those in need rather than waiting for them to access the more traditional, office-based model of services comes in part from our philosophy of approach. The belief that in the aftermath of disaster most individuals are experiencing *normal reactions to abnormal events* laces a great deal of emphasis on education as a fundamental component of all of our interventions. Psycho-education is highly transportable and can be taken to the disaster scene, the workplace, and the home with little disruption. It can also be infused into a variety of normal community-based activities without risk of retraumatization or intrusion. Education is respectful of the individual's instinct to heal and to know what they believe will help them to do so. While education can be mandated, this is often unnecessary as information is naturally sought by those in need as well as those who care about them and want to help. Knowledge, good information, and guidance can help the healing process. People respond better to a crisis when they can learn more about what they are experiencing. Education after a disaster brings recovery closer.

Perhaps most important for this discussion is the fact that education can be offered preincident to those who are likely to be called on for service and support. Basic knowledge of the signs and symptoms of trauma and grief and how to effectively respond can be helpful to those on the front lines when the time comes. It also can be beneficial for those at home to be better prepared to recognize the imprint of traumatic response before they see it in their responder and to be better informed about responses that can help. In addition, for those charged with organizing community-level responses, we believe that thinking strategically about some of the concepts articulated in this text and how they may apply can be of some help.

Collaboration and partnership as exemplified in this text has been the backbone of our program. Much valuable work can be done before any perceived threat to forge good collaborations between the mental health community, both traditional and nontraditional, and those working directly with first responders who will likely be called into service at such a time. We suggest asking the following questions: Is there communication between first responders and mental health providers in your community? If yes, what more can be done in the area of education and preparation? If not, how can you begin such a dialogue? What unites these two communities is their self-definition as helpers. However each group could benefit from understanding the cultural differences that often divide them. Without a sufficient understanding of New York City firefighter culture, we believe programs and counselors would have been much less effective. Pairing peer counselors with professional counselors benefited both groups and again demonstrated that the teamwork approach favored by firefighters brings more to alleviate a crisis than each group brings individually.

Entering the life space of those we work with, be it at the firehouse or family home, is intensely challenging and personal. It is important that mental health workers have the supports necessary not only to deal with the risk of vicarious traumatization and vicarious bereavement but also to assist in maintaining the important professional boundaries that distinguish professional help from friendship. The more we are able to identify with those we help, the more difficult this can become. Many counselors needed to keep themselves in check not only to ensure they were not seeing people's behavior through the prism of their own culture based on preconceived notions, but also, especially as these stereotypes evaporated, to remember that they were a temporary visitor to the home whose ultimate goal was departure. The psychological needs of mental health workers require attention, which should not be solely relegated to self-care. Mental health systems need to include adequate support for the mental health professionals who respond to disasters.

POSTTRAUMATIC GROWTH

The concepts of recovery and cure are frequently introduced at some point when mental health interventions are discussed. What such concepts mean in the context of postdisaster intervention is not so easily comprehended or resolved. Experience is not an illness. There is no cure for experience. The *fact* of the collapse of the World Trade Center buildings and the resulting trauma and loss cannot be changed. How then to think about the changes that occur as a result of having survived such a life-altering event or having lost someone close who did not?

Opportunities for the development of new growth or other positive changes in the midst of horrific tragedy have been written about in the literature throughout the ages (Tedeschi et al., 1998). Surviving such experiences is frequently reported to impact on values, attitudes about self, and quality of life. Firefighters can be heard to comment on how their friends and coworkers who lost their lives on 9/11 would wish them to live every day to the fullest and not be limited by the grief or guilt or trauma they feel. Family members will note that they know their spouse or son would not wish them a life of pain or paralysis in moving forward. Some report themselves as more compassionate, empathic, self-confident, and able to sidestep the small stuff when reacting to life events. Parents observe with awe demonstrations of their children's empathy and growing compassion for those in need and their ability to find inventive ways to cope with the unending reminders of the loss.

Perhaps the most frequently expressed emotion, more than grief, fear, or trauma, was anger. Firefighters and their related communities were, and to a lesser degree still are, angry. Their anger is not simply about loss, helplessness, lack of control, or the media. They are angry with all of that and more. Their anger is not inappropriate. Reacting to 9/11 with raging anger is natural, normal, and shared by survivors, the bereaved, first responders, families, mental health workers, political leaders, and the public. The challenges and dangers lie in how they and we respond to anger. The power and potential of anger need not be destructive, but it too easily can be, and that only leads to more anger and rage to fuel other terrible events. Postevent interventions hold promise for reducing the destructive aspects of the anger that naturally follows, and for enhancing the positive, self-protective, and growth-enabling possibilities that comprise recovery from events like 9/11.

It may be important as a community of disaster responders to ask ourselves how the concept of *posttraumatic growth* impacts on us. Do we as an emerging field of practice grow as a result of the experiences we have responding to each of the tragedies we are called to? Will we take the opportunities we are handed in the aftermath of disaster and choose to push ourselves to learn all we can about what is helpful, to whom, and at what interval postincident? How can we best engage the funding community as our partner in long-term studies that can teach us more about the process of recovery from trauma and grief, while keeping services available?

In writing this book about one community and the experience of different subsets within it, we are reporting on our activities, impressions, and some very preliminary data. We felt it was important to write about this experience now in the hopes it might assist others in thinking about a potential response in their community. Simultaneously, we recognize the importance of continuing to study and learn about the impact of this event on our population and the effectiveness, or not, of our response.

Postscript

RECENTLY SOME of us had the opportunity to apply some of the principles expressed in this book to a natural disaster situation in the aftermath of hurricane Katrina and the devastation of the gulf coast region. While the differences between this event and 9/11 are clear, the issues of trauma and loss for firefighters and emergency service personnel were equally profound and clearly underscored the need to provide for the long-term mental health needs of first responders and their families as a distinct and separate population. To this end, the work of establishing an appropriate peer and mental health network, sensitive to the culture of the particular departments and communities, who can begin to work collaboratively to ensure the long-term needs of the community was of paramount importance, even as the crisis was still underway. Unlike New York in 2001, there was no apparent pre-existing model to build on, making the work in many ways more difficult. This lends support to our belief that developing collaborative relationships between first responders and mental health providers in your community *now* can make the path less difficult should your community face a disaster of such magnitude that large-scale mental health efforts would be needed.

References

9/11 Commission Report. (n.d.). Retrieved from http://www.9-11commission.gov/report/911Report.pdf

Achenbach, T. M., & Edelbrock, C. S. (1983). *Manual for the child behavior checklist and revised child behavior profile*. Burlington, VT: Thomas M. Achenbach.

Akabas, S. H., & Kurzman, P. A. (2005). *Work and the workplace: A resource for innovative policy and practice*. New York: Columbia University Press.

Allen, J., Whittlesey, S., & Pfefferbaum, B. (1999). Community and coping of mothers and grandmothers of children killed in a human-caused disaster. *Psychiatric Annals, 29*(2), 85–91.

American Group Psychotherapy Association (AGPA) Protocol. (2005).

American Psychiatric Association. (1994). *Diagnostic and statistical manual of mental disorders* (4th ed.). Washington, DC: Author.

Baker, J., Sedney, M., & Gross, E. (1992). Psychological tasks for bereaved children. *American Journal of Orthopsychiatry, 62*(1), 105–116.

Banauch, G., McLaughlin, M., Corrigan, M., Kelly, K., & Prezant, D. (2002). Injuries and illnesses among New York City Fire Department rescue workers after responding to the World Trade Center attacks. *Journal of the American Medical Association, 288*(13), 1581–1584.

Bauer, P. A., & Okun, M. A. (1983). Stability of life satisfaction in late life. *The Gerontologist, 23*(3), 261–265.

Benedict, R. (1934). Anthropology and the abnormal. *Journal of General Psychology, 10*, 59–92.

Bifulco, A., Brown, G., & Harris, T. (1987). Childhood loss of a parent, lack of adequate parental care and adult depression: A replication. *Social Psychology, 16*, 187–197.

Bifulco, A., Harris, T., & Brown, G. (1992). Mourning or inadequate care? Reexamining the relationship of maternal loss in childhood with adult depression and anxiety. *Development and Psychopathology, 4*, 433–449.

Bodley, J. (2000). *Cultural anthropology: Tribes, states and the global system* (3rd ed.). Mountain View, CA: Mayfield Publishing.

Bonanno, G. A., Moskowitz, J. T., Papa, A., Folkman, S. (2005). Resilience to loss in bereaved spouses, bereaved parents, and bereaved gay men. *Journal of Personality and Social Psychology, 88*(5), 827–843.

Boss, P. (1999). *Ambiguous loss*. Cambridge, MA: Harvard University Press.

Breier, A., Kelsoe, J., Kirwin, P., Wolkowitz, O., & Pickar, D. (1988). Early parental loss and development of adult psychopathology. *Archives of General Psychiatry, 45,* 987–993.

Brown, E., & Goodman, R. (2005). Childhood traumatic grief: An exploration of the construct in children bereaved on September 11. *Journal of Child Clinical & Adolescent Psychology, 34*(2), 248–259.

Brown, G., Harris, T., & Bifulco, A. (1986). Long term effects of early loss of parent. In M. Rutter, C. Izard, & P. Read (Eds.), *Depression in childhood: Developmental perspectives* (pp. 251–297). New York: Guilford Press.

Buchele, B. J., & Spitz, H. I. (Eds). (2000). *Group interventions for treatment of psychological trauma*. American Group Psychological Association.

Bureau of National Affairs, Inc. (1987). *Employee assistance programs: Benefits, problems, and prospects*. Washington, DC: BNA Response Center.

Burkeman, O. (2002, November 16). Ground Zero heroes agree rise after bitter two-year battle. The Guardian, New York.

Caplan, G. (1964). *Principles of preventive psychiatry*. New York: Basic Books.

Cardwell, D. (2001, November 11). City to drop charges against 17 of 18 firefighters arrested in protest. *The New York Times*, p. 41.

Christ, G. (2000). *Healing children's grief: Surviving a parent's death from cancer*. New York: Oxford University Press.

Christ, G., Raveis, V., Siegel, K., Karus, D., & Christ, A. (2005). Evaluation of a bereavement intervention. *Social Work in End-of-life and Palliative Care, 1*(3), 57–81.

Christ, G., Siegel, K., Mesagno, F., & Langosch, D. (1991). A preventive intervention program for bereaved children: Problems of implementation. *American Journal of Orthopsychiatry, 61,* 168–178.

Clark, S. (1988). The violated victim: Prehospital psychological care for the crime victim. *Journal of Emergency Medical Services*, March, 48–51.

Cohen, J. (2004). Early mental health interventions for trauma and traumatic loss in children and adolescents. In Brett T. Litz (Ed.), Early intervention for trauma and traumatic loss (pp. 468–478). New York: Guilford Press.

Coopersmith, S. (1984). *SEI: Self-esteem inventories*. Palo Alto, CA: Consulting Psychologist Press.

Corry, J. (2002). New York, New York: America's hero. In W. Pleszczynski (Ed.), *Our brave new world: Essays on the impact of September 11* (pp. 119–136). Stanford, CA: Hoover Institution Press.

Council of the City of New York, Office of Communications. (2003, March 7). *Speaker Miller and council members unveil alternatives to firehouse closings*. Retrieved April 26, 2003, from http://www.council.nyc.ny.us/pdf_files/newswire/firehouse4pointplan.pdf

Cowman, S. E., Ferrari, J. E., & Liao-Troth, M. (2004). Mediating effects of social support on firefighters' sense of community and perceptions of care. *Journal of Community Psychology, 32*(2), 121–126.

Crook, T., & Eliot, J. (1980). Parental death during childhood and adult depression: A critical review of the literature. *Psychological Bulletin, 87*(2), 252–259.

Everly, G., Phillips, S., Kane, D., & Feldman, D. (2005). *Principles and practice of acute group psychological first aid after disasters*. Johns Hopkins Center for Public Health Preparedness.

Fairbrother, G., Stuber, J., Galea, S., Pfefferbaum, B., & Fleischman, A. R. (2004). Unmet need for counseling services by children in New York City after the September 11th attacks on the World Trade Center: Implications for pediatricians. *Pediatrics, 113*(5), 1367.

Farrell, B. (2002, November 13). FDNY can't ignite Black's interest. *The Daily News* (p. 9).

Federal Emergency Management Administration (FEMA) press release. (January 7, 2004).

Figley, C. (1995). *Compassion fatigue: Coping with secondary traumatic stress disorder in those who treat the traumatized.* New York: Brunner/Mazel.

Fire Department of New York City History and Heritage of Fire Service. (n.d.). (2005). Retrieved from the New York Fire Department Web site http://www.nyc.gov/html/fdny/html/history/index.shtml

Floyd, F. J., Haynes, S. N., Droll, E. R., Winmiller, D., Lemsky, C., Murphy, C., et al. (1992). Assessing retirement satisfaction and perceptions of retirement experience. *Psychology and Aging, 7*(4), 609–621.

Fullerton, C. S., McCarroll, J. E., Ursano, R. J., & Wright, K. M. (1992). Psychological responses of rescue workers: Firefighters and trauma. *American Journal of Orthopsychology, 62,* 371–378.

Geertz, C. (1973). *The interpretation of cultures: Selected essays.* New York: Basic Books.

Golway, T. (2002). *So others might live: A history of New York's bravest; The FDNY from 1700 to the present.* New York: Basic Books.

Greenberg, L. (1975). Therapeutic work with children. *Social Casework, 56,* 396–403.

Greenson, Ralph R. (1967). *The technique and practice of psychoanalysis* (Vol. I, pp. 151–152). CT: International Universities Press.

Halberstam, D. (2002). *Firehouse.* New York: Hyperion.

Harris, T., Brown, G., & Bifulco, A. (1986). Loss of parent in childhood and adult psychiatric disorder: The role of lack of adequate parental care. *Psychological Medicine, 16,* 641–659.

Harris, T., Brown, G., & Bifulco, A. (1987). Loss of parent in childhood and adult psychiatric disorder: The role of social class position and premarital pregnancy. *Psychological Medicine, 17,* 163–183.

Herman, J. (1997). *Trauma and recovery* (Rev. ed.). New York: Basic Books.

Institute of Medicine. (2003). *Preparing for the psychological consequences of terrorism.* Washington, DC: National Academy Press.

James, R. K., & Gilliland, B. E. (2005). *Crisis intervention strategies.* Belmont, CA: Thomson Brooks/Cole.

Johnson, S. M. (2002). *Emotionally focused couples therapy with trauma survivors: Strengthening attachment bonds.* New York: Guilford Press.

Jones, R. (2003). Keynote speech retrieved from http://www.wfsi.org/NYSconf.html

Jordan, J. R., & Neimeyer, R. A. (2003). Does grief counseling work? *Death Studies 27*(9), 765–786.

Kleinman, A. (1988). *The illness narratives: Suffering, healing and the human condition.* New York: Basic Books.

Kluckhohn, C. (1949). *Mirror for man: The relation of anthropology to modern life.* New York: McGraw-Hill.

Kovacs, M. (1992). *Children's depression inventory: CDI manual.* North Tonawanda, NY: Multi-Health Systems.

Kwok, O., Haine, R. A., Sandler, I. N., Ayers, T. S., Wolchik, S. A., & Tein, J. (2005). Positive parenting as a mediator of the relations between parental psychological distress and mental health problems of parentally bereaved children. *Journal of Clinical Child & Adolescent Psychology, 34*(2).

Lifton, R. J. (1968). *Death in life: Survivors of Hiroshima.* New York: Random House.

Limpus, L. M. (1940). *History of the New York Fire Department.* New York: E. P. Dutton.

Lindemann, E. (1944). Symptomatology and management of acute grief. *American Journal of Psychiatry, 101,* 141–148.

Lindy, J. (1985). The trauma membrane and other clinical concepts. *Psychiatric Annals, 15*(3), 153–160.

Lindy, J., Grace, M., & Green, B. (1981). Survivors: Outreach to a reluctant population. *American Journal of Orthopsychiatry, 51*(3), 468–478.

Linkh, D. (2005). *From a cloudless sky.* Unpublished doctoral dissertation, Columbia University School of Social Work.

Luchins, A. S. (1948). The role of the social field in psychotherapy. *Journal of Consulting Psychology, 12,* 417–425.

Malkinson, R., Rubin, S., & Witzman, E. (2005). Terror, trauma, and bereavement: Implications for theory and therapy. *Journal of Aggression, Maltreatment & Trauma, 10*(1–2), 467–477.

McCann, I., & Pearlman, L. (1990). Vicarious traumatization: A framework for understanding the psychological effects of working with victims. *Journal of Traumatic Stress, 3*(1), 131–149.

Mead, M. (1966). *New Lives for old: Cultural transformation manus, 1928–1953.* New York: William Morrow and Company.

Miller, L. (2002). Psychological interventions for terroristic trauma: Symptoms, syndromes, and treatment. *Psychotherapy: Theory, Research, Practice, Training, 39*(4), 283–296.

Miller, L., & Schlesinger, L. B. (2000). Survivors, families, and co-victims of serial offenders. In L. B. Schlesinger (Ed.), *Serial offenders: Current thought, recent findings, unusual syndromes* (pp. 309–334). Boca Raton, FL: CRC Press.

National Fallen Firefighters Foundation and Bureau of Justice Assistance. (n.d.) *Taking care of our own: A resource guide.*

North, C. S., Tivis, L., McMillen, J. C., Pfefferbaum, B., Cox, J., Sptiznagel, E., et al. (2002). Coping, functioning, and adjustment of rescue workers after the Oklahoma City bombing. *Journal of Traumatic Stress, 15*(3), 171.

Northern, H., & Kurland, R. (2001). *Social work with groups* (3rd ed.). New York: Columbia University Press.

New York State Association of Fire Chaplains. (2003, April 20). Retrieved from http://www.nysafc.org

Pearlman, L. (1999). Self-care for trauma therapists: Ameliorating vicarious traumatization. In B. Stamm (Ed.), *Secondary traumatic stress: Self-care issues for clinicians, researchers, and educators* (pp. 51–64). Towson, MD: Sidran Press.

Phillips, S. & Thomas, N. (in press). Protocol for disaster intervention with uniformed service personnel. In R. H. Klein & S. Phillips (Eds.), *Public Mental Health Service Delivery Protocols: Group Interventions for Disaster Preparedness and Response.* New York: American Group Psychotherapy Association.

Phillips, S. B. (2005). Countertransference: Effects on the group therapist working with trauma. In B. J. Buchele & H. I. Spitz (Eds.), *Group interventions for treatment of psychological trauma*. New York City: AGPA.

Pfefferbaum, B., Flynn, B., Brandt, E., & Lensgraf, S. (1999). Organizing the mental health response to human-caused community disasters with reference to the Oklahoma City Bombing. *Psychiatric Annals, 29*(2), 109–112.

Prezant, D. J. (2002). Cough and bronchial responsiveness in firefighters at the World Trade Center. *New England Journal of Medicine, 347*(11), 806–815.

Quick, H. E., & Moon, P. (1998). Gender, employment, and retirement quality: A life course approach to the differential experiences of men and women. *Journal of Occupational Health Psychology, 3*(1), 44–64.

Rando, T. (1999). Introduction. In E. S. Zinner and M. B. Williams (Eds.), *When a community weeps: Case studies in group survivorship*. New York: Brunner/Mazel.

Raveis, V., Siegel, K., & Karus, D. (1999). Children's psychological distress following the death of a parent. *Journal of Youth and Adolescence, 28*(2), 165–180.

Rosenthal, P. (1980). Short term family therapy and pathological grief resolution with children and adolescents. *Family Process, 19*, 151–159.

Saler, L., & Skolnick, N. (1992). Childhood parental death and depression in adulthood: Roles of surviving parent and family environment. *American Journal of Orthopsychiatry, 62*, 504–516.

Samson, A. Y., & Opp, R. E. (1989). Taxonomy of guilt for combat veterans. *Professional Psychology: Research and Practice, 20*(3), 159–165.

Sandler, L., West, S., Baca, L., Pillow, D., Gersten, J., Rogosch, F., et al. (1992). Linking empirically based theory and evaluation: The family bereavement program. *American Journal of Community Psychology, 20*, 491–521.

Schouten, R., Callahan, M. V., & Bryant, S. (2004). Community response to disaster: The role of the workplace. *Harvard Review of Psychiatry, 12*(4), 229–237.

Shear, K., Frank, E., Houck, P., & Reynolds, C. F. (2005). Treatment of complicated grief: A randomized controlled trial. *Journal of the American Medical Association, 293*(21), 2601.

Siegel, K., Karus, D., & Raveis, V. (1996). Adjustment of children facing the death of a parent due to cancer. *Journal of the American Academy of Child/Adolescent Psychiatry, 35*, 442–450.

Siegel, K., Mesagno, R., & Christ, G. (1990). A preventive program for bereaved children. *American Journal of Orthopsychiatry, 60*, 168–175.

Siegel, K., Raveis, V., & Karus, D. (1996). Patterns of communication with children when a parent has cancer. In C. Cooper, L. Baider, & A. DeNous (Eds.), *Cancer and the family* (pp. 109–128). New York: Wiley.

Spielberger, C., Edwards, C., Lushene, R., Montuori, J., & Paltzek, D. (1973). *STAIC: Preliminary manual*. Palo Alto, CA: Consulting Psychologist Press.

Spielberger, C., Lushene, R., Vagg, P., & Jacobs, G. (1983). *Manual for the state-trait anxiety inventory (Form Y)*. Palo Alto, CA: Consulting Psychologists Press.

Stroebe, M., & Schut, H. (1999). The dual process model of coping with bereavement: Rationale and description. *Death Studies, 23*, 1–28, 197–224.

Stroebe, M., & Schut, H. (2001). Models of coping with bereavement: A review. In M. Stroebe, R. Hansson, W. Stroebe, & H. Schut (Eds.), *Handbook of bereavement research: Consequences, coping, and care* (pp. 375–403). Washington, DC: American Psychological Association.

Stroebe, M., Schut, H., & Stroebe, W. (2005). Attachment in coping with bereavement: A theoretical integration. *Review of General Psychology, 9*(1), 48–66.

Stroebe, W., & Stroebe M. (1993). Determinants of adjustment to bereavement in younger widows and widowers. In M. Stroebe, W. Stroebe, & R. Hansson (Eds.), *Handbook of bereavement: Theory, research, and intervention* (pp. 208–226). Cambridge UK: Cambridge University Press.

Tedeschi, R. G., Park, C., & Calhoun, L. (1998). *Posttraumatic growth positive changes in the aftermath of crisis.* Mahwah, NJ: Erlbaum.

Tennant, C. (1988). Parental loss in childhood: Its effect in adult life. *Archives of General Psychiatry, 45,* 1045–1049.

Thorne, F. T. (1952). Psychological first aid. *Journal of Clinical Psychology, 8*(2), 210–211.

Tremblay, G. C., & Israel, A. C. (1998). Children's adjustment to parental death. *Clinical Psychology: Science and Practice, 5*(4), 424–438.

van der Kolk, B. A., Perry, J. C., & Herman, J. L. (1991). Childhood origins of self destructive behavior. *American Journal of Psychiatry, 148,* 1665–1671.

van Eederwegh, M., Bieri, M., Parilla, R., & Clayton, P. (1982). The bereaved child. *British Journal of Psychiatry, 140,* 23–29.

Verdery, K. (1999). *The political lives of dead bodies: Reburial and postsocialist change.* New York: Columbia University Press.

Walker, J. W., Kimmel, D. C., & Price, K. F. (1980–81). Retirement style and retirement satisfaction: Retirees aren't all alike. *International Journal of Aging and Human Development, 12*(4), 267–281.

Weissenstein, M., Williams, T. (2002, November 13). NYC firefighter wages boosted in contract accord. The Associated Press, New York.

Weller, R., Weller, E., Fristad, M., & Bowes, J. (1991). Depression in recently bereaved prepubertal children. *American Journal of Psychiatry, 148,* 1536–1540.

Whittlesey, S. W., Allen, J., Bell, B., Liliana, F., Lucan, A., Ware, M., et al. (2000). Avoidance in trauma: Conscious and unconscious defenses. *Psychiatry: Interpersonal & Biological Processes.*

Williams, R. (1958). Moving from high culture to ordinary culture. In N. McKenzie (Ed.), *Convictions.* London: Mac Gibbon & Kee.

Worden, W. (1982). *Grief counseling and grief therapy: A handbook for the mental health practitioner.* New York: Springer Publishing.

Worden, W. (1996). *Children and grief: When a parent dies.* New York: Guilford Press.

Worden, W. (2001). *Grief counseling and grief therapy: A handbook for the mental health practitioner* (2nd ed.). New York: Springer Publishing.

Wrich, J. T. (1982). *Guidelines for developing an employees' assistance program.* New York: American Management Associations Publications Division.

Yalom, I. (1970). *The theory and practice of group psychotherapy.* New York: Basic Books.

Yule, W., & Williams, R. (1990). Post-traumatic stress reactions in children. *Journal of Traumatic Stress, 3*(2), 279–295.

Zinner, E. S., & Williams, M. B. (1999). *When a community weeps: Case studies in group survivorship.* Philadelphia: Brunner/Mazel.

Index